FORD CAPRI 2000 AND 3000

by J H Haynes

Associate member of the Guild of Motoring Writers

and

J R S Hall

Models covered

1996 cc (V4)	(Saloon and GT) L, XL, XLR	January 1969 on
2994 cc (V6)	(GT and E) L, XL, XLR	October 1969 on

SBN 90055 035 X

Ⓒ J.H.HAYNES & CO.LTD. 1972

24 Lower Odcombe Yeovil Somerset
Telephone West Coker 2406

Price £1.80 (UK only)

D1341323

Acknowledgements

Thanks are due to the Ford Motor Company Ltd., for their assistance with regard to the use of technical material and illustrations; to Castrol Ltd., for lubrication chart information; and to Champion Ltd., for the sparking plug photographs.

Thanks are especially due to D.H.Stead, R.T.Grainger and L.Tooze for their assistance when working on the engine and gearbox, and to Tim Parker for advice on the text.

Whilst every care is taken to ensure that the information in this manual is correct bearing in mind the changes in design and specification which are a continuous process, even within a model range, no liability can be accepted by the authors and publishers for any loss, damage or injury caused by any errors or omissions in the information given.

Photographic captions and cross references

The book is divided into twelve chapters. Each chapter is divided into numbered sections which are headed in **bold** type between horizontal lines. Each section consists of serially numbered photographs.

There are two types of illustration. (1) Figures which are numbered according to Chapter and sequence of occurrence in that chapter and having an individual caption to each figure. (2) Paragraphs which have a reference number in the bottom left-hand corner. All photographs apply to the chapter in which they occur so that the reference figures pinpoint the pertinent section and paragraph numbers.

Procedures, once described in the text, are not normally repeated. If it is necessary to refer to another chapter the reference will be given in chapter number and section number thus:— Chapter 1/6.

If it is considered necessary to refer to a particular paragraph in another chapter the reference is 'Chapter 1/6:5'. Cross references given without use of the word 'Chapter' apply to sections and/or paragraphs in the same chapter, e.g. 'see Section 8' means also 'in this chapter'.

When the left or right-hand side of a car is mentioned it is as if one was looking in the forward direction of travel.

Introduction

This manual is intended for those who wish to find out more about the Capri 2000 GT and 3000 GT and E, which they may own, and to show them also how to carry out the maintenance and repairs necessary to keep it performing safely and economically.

The older a car gets the more attention it will need as normal wear and tear takes its toll. Thus the buyer of a cheaper, older model is faced with the need for more attention to his vehicle in order to enable it to run safely and pass the tests required by law every 12 months. As the purchase of a cheaper car is usually due to economic necessity it follows that garage bills are equally to be avoided.

This manual is the only one written which is based on the author's personal experiences. The hands in most of the photographs are those of the person who has written the book. Manufacturers' own official workshop manuals are all very well for those whose knowledge on certain basic terminology and methods is assumed. For the rest, this manual provides clear illustrations and descriptions of the order and method for the jobs to be done, step by step.

It must be assumed that a range of tools is available to the do-it-yourself owner. The accumulation of good tools is normally done over a period of time and this is the one expense that the do-it-yourself man must be prepared for. Never buy cheap tools. Be discreet in borrowing tools and do not be annoyed if someone refuses to lend them. Appreciate how much they cost if lost or damaged.

Certain jobs required specialised tools and where these are essential this manual will say so. Otherwise alternative means are given. Much of the work involved in looking after a car and carrying out repairs depends on accurate diagnosis in the first place. Where possible therefore, a methodical and progressive way of diagnosis is presented. The time that can be wasted in hopping from one possible source of trouble to another suggested at random quite often by self styled 'experts' must have been experienced by many people. It is best to say at the start therefore, 'this could be one of several things - let's get the book out'.

Contents

Routine maintenance

Maintenance should be regarded as essential for ensuring safety and desirable for the purpose of obtaining economy and performance from the car. By far the largest element of the maintenance routine is visual examination. Each chapter of the manual gives details of the routine maintenance requirements. In the summary given here the safety items are shown in **bold** type. These must be attended to regularly in the interests of preventing accidents and possible loss of life.

Neglect of other items results in unreliability, overall increased running costs and more rapid depreciation of the value of the car.

500 miles

EVERY 500 MILES (or weekly)

ENGINE
Check the oil level in the sump and top up as required.
Check the radiator coolant level and top up as required.
Check the battery electrolyte level and top up as required.

STEERING
Check the tyre pressures.
Examine tyres for wear or damage.
Is the steering still smooth and accurate?

BRAKES
Check the hydraulic fluid reservoir level. If a significant drop is apparent examine the system for leaks immediately.
Is there any reduction in braking efficiency?
Try an emergency stop. Is adjustment necessary?

LIGHTS
Do all bulbs work at the front and rear?
Are the headlight beams correctly aligned?

Replacing oil filter

6,000 miles

EVERY 6,000 MILES (or every six months if 6,000 miles are not exceeded) or if indications are that safety items in particular are not performing correctly.

ENGINE
Drain the sump of oil when hot, renew the oil filter element and refill the sump with fresh oil.
Check the valve clearances and adjust as necessary.
Check the distributor contact breaker points and adjust as necessary.
Check the tension of the fan belt.
Clean the fuel pump filter.
Check the sparking plug electrode gaps.
Lubricate the distributor.
Lubricate the generator rear end bush.

CLUTCH
Check the clutch cable adjustment and adjust as required.

STEERING
Is there free play between the steering wheel and road wheels?
Examine all steering linkage rods, joints and bushes for signs of wear or damage.
Check the front wheel hub bearings and adjust if necessary.
Check the oil level in the steering box and top up as required.

BRAKES
Examine the disc pads and drum shoes to determine the amount of friction material remaining. Renew as necessary.
Examine all hydraulic pipes, cylinders and unions for signs of chafing, corrosion, dents or any other form of deterioration or leaks.

SUSPENSION
Examine all bolts and shackles securing the suspension units and springs and tighten as necessary.
Check for play in the rubber bushes.

Checking fan belt tension

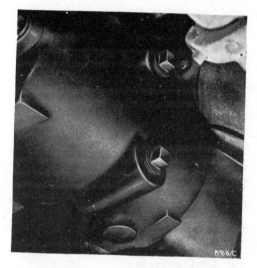
Capri 3000 GT & E gearbox filler and drain plugs

12,000 miles

EVERY 12,000 MILES (or annually if 12,000 miles are not exceeded) or if indications are that safety items in particular are not performing correctly.

ENGINE
Fit new distributor contact breaker points
Fit new sparking plugs.
Fit a new carburetter air cleaner element.
Flush out the cooling system.

GEARBOX
Check the oil level and top up as required.

REAR AXLE
Check the oil level and top up as required.

STEERING
Remove front wheel hub bearings, flush, inspect and repack with grease.

BODYFRAME
Examine for rust where suspension is attached.

Air filter element

24,000 miles

EVERY 24,000 MILES (or bi-annually if 24,000 miles are not exceeded) or if indications are that safety items in particular are not performing correctly.

FRONT WHEEL BEARINGS
Repack the bearings with grease and adjust.

36,000 miles

GEARBOX
Drain and replenish the oil.

REAR AXLE
Drain and replenish the oil.

Capri 2000 GT gearbox filler and drain plugs

Additionally the following items should be attended to as time can be spared:—

CLEANING
Examination of components requires that they be cleaned. The same applies to the body of the car, inside and out, in order that deterioration due to rust or unknown damage may be detected. Certain parts of the bodyframe, if rusted badly, can result in the vehicle being declared unsafe and it will not pass the annual test for roadworthiness.

EXHAUST SYSTEM
An exhaust system must be leakproof, and the noise level below a certain minimum. Excessive leaks may cause carbon monoxide fumes to enter the passenger compartment. Excessive noise constitutes a public nuisance. Both these faults may cause the vehicle to be kept off the road. Repair or replace defective sections when symptoms are apparent.

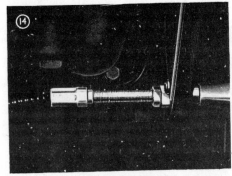

Clutch cable adjustment

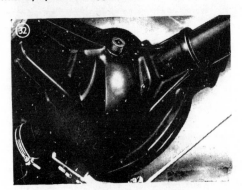

Rear axle filler plug

Ordering spare parts

Buy genuine Fo Mo Co spare parts from a Ford dealer direct, or through a local garage. If you go to an authorised dealer the correctly fitting genuine parts can usually be supplied from stock which, of course, is a greatly added convenience.

Always have details of the car's serial number available when obtaining parts. If you can take along the part to be renewed as well it is helpful. Modifications are a continuing and unpublicised process in car manufacture, apart from all the variations of model types. If a storeman says he cannot guarantee that the part he supplies is correct, because the engine number is not known, he is perfectly justified. Variations can occur from month to month.

The vehicle identification plate is mounted on the right hand mudguard apron inside the engine compartment. It is not a bad idea to write down the details in your diary or pocket book.

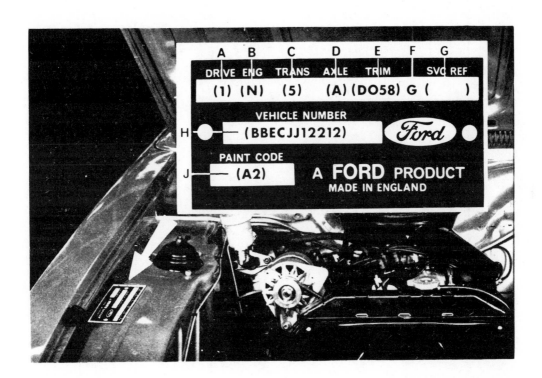

| A:– | DRIVE | 1. Right-hand drive | 2. Left-hand drive |

A:– DRIVE — 1. Right-hand drive — 2. Left-hand drive

B:– ENGINE — N–2000 cc / H–3000 cc

C:– TRANSMISSION — 5–Manual / 7–Automatic

D:– REAR AXLE — 2.0 litre S–3.44 to 1 / 3.0 litre R–3.22 to 1

E:– TRIM — This code consists of a letter and three numbers (D058) and indicates the colour and type of material used within the car.

F:– BODY — 'G' denotes the model is G.T.

G:– S.V.C. — This denotes the date of manufacture of the car if the vehicle is shipped unassembled from one factory to another for assembly.

H:– VEHICLE NUMBER — A code, which is explained at the front of every parts list denoting country and plant of manufacture, body style, year and month of manufacture and serial number.

PAINT CODE — Indicates the colour and type of original paint.

COMPONENT	TYPE OF LUBRICANT OR FLUID	CASTROL PRODUCT
ENGINE	Multigrade engine oil	Castrol GTX
GEARBOX	S.A.E. 80 E.P	Castrol Hypoy Light
REAR AXLE	S.A.E. 90 E.P	Castrol Hypoy
STEERING BOX	S.A.E. 90 E.P	Castrol Hypoy
FRONT WHEEL BEARINGS	Medium grade multi-purpose grease	Castrol L.M. Grease
DISTRIBUTOR, STARTER & GENERATOR BUSHES ...	Engine or light oil...	Castrol GTX
DISTRIBUTOR CONTACT BREAKER CAM & BATTERY	Petroleum jelly...	'Castrollo'
UPPER CYLINDER LUBRICANT...	... ...	Castrol Rubber Grease
HYDRAULIC PISTONS	Rubber grease	Castrol Rubber Grease
BRAKE MASTER CYLINDER FLUID RESERVOIR... ...	Hydraulic fluid	Castrol Girling Brake Fluid
BORG WARNER TYPE 35 AUTOMATIC GEARBOX... ...	Automatic transmission fluid	Castrol TQF

Additionally Castrol 'Everyman' oil can be used to lubricate door, boot and bonnet hinges, locks and pivots etc.

LUBRICATION CHART

CASTROL GTX
An ultra high performance motor oil approved for use in the engine in summer and winter.

CASTROL HYPOY LIGHT GEAR OIL
A powerful, extreme pressure lubricant recommended for the transmission and steering gear.

CASTROL HYPOY GEAR OIL
A powerful, extreme-pressure gear oil essential for the lubrication of the hypoid rear axle.

CASTROL LM GREASE
Recommended for the wheel bearings. May also be used for chassis lubrication.

WEEKLY

ENGINE
Check oil level, and if necessary refill to correct level with **Castrol GTX.**

EVERY 24,000 MILES

FRONT WHEEL BEARINGS.
After the first 27,000, thereafter every 24,000 miles, repack and adjust the front wheel bearings. Use **Castrol LM Grease.**

EVERY 6,000 MILES

REAR AXLE
At the first 3,000 miles, thereafter every 6,000 miles, check the oil level and top up if necessary to the correct level with **Castrol Hypoy Gear Oil.**
Capacity: 2 pints
V.4. models only:
Rear axle capacity: 1.9 pints.

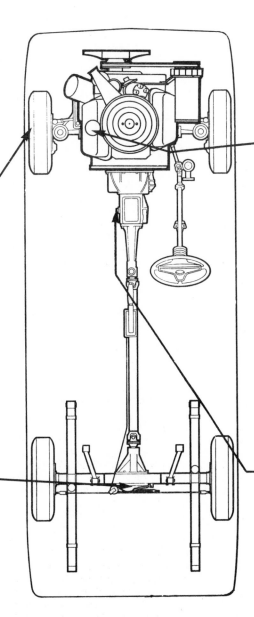

EVERY 6,000 MILES Including Weekly service

ENGINE
After the first 3,000 miles, and thereafter every 6,000 miles, drain off the old oil while warm, clean and replace drain plug, change complete filter unit. Refill with fresh **Castrol GTX.**

NOTE:—Owners are advised that more frequent sump-draining periods are desirable if the operation of the car involves:—
(1) *Frequent stop/start driving.
(2) *Operation during cold weather, especially when appreciable engine idling is involved.
(3) *When much driving is done under dusty conditions.
*When such conditions are experienced, consult your authorised dealer regarding **Ford Midway Service.**
SUMP CAPACITY:

V4 — 8.4 pints
V6 — 9.5 pints

GEARBOX.
At the first 3,000 miles, drain the gearbox while warm and refill with **Castrol Hypoy Light Gear Oil.** No further draining of this unit is required and it is only necessary to check and top up the level if required every 6,000 miles. Use **Castrol Hypoy Light Gear Oil.**
Capacity— V4 — 1.97 pints
V6 — 3.55 pints

Chapter 1 Engine

Contents

Specifications - Engine Specifications & Data — 1996 cc V4

Engine - General

Type...	4 cylinder 60° V pushrod operated OHV
Bore	3.6878 in. (93.67 mm)
Stroke	2.851 in. (72.42 mm)
Cubic capacity...	1996 cc (121.8 cu.in.)
Compression ratio...	9.0 to 1
Compression pressure..	160 lb/sq.in. (11.25 kg/cm^2) at 300 r.p.m.
Maximum BHP	105 (net) at 5,700 r.p.m.
Maximum torque	122.5 lbs/ft. (16.86 kg.m) gross at 4,000 r.p.m.
Location of No.1 cylinder	Right-hand bank next to radiator
Idling speed..	680 to 720 r.p.m
Firing order..	1(R), 3(L), 4(L), 2(R)
Engine mountings...	3, one on each side of engine and one beneath the gearbox extension

Camshaft and Camshaft Bearings

Camshaft drive		Fibre gearwheel from crankshaft
Camshaft bearings		3, steel back babbit
Bearing oversize available		.020 in. (0.51 mm) oversize on O.D standard I.D
Camshaft journal diameter	- front	1.8737 to 1.8745 in. (47.59 to 47.67 mm)
	- intermediate..	1.8137 to 1.8145 in. (46.07 to 46.15 mm)
	- rear	1.7537 to 1.7545 in. (44.54 to 44.56 mm)
Camshaft bearing I.D	- front	1.8753 to 1.8763 in. (47.63 to 47.66 mm)
	- intermediate..	1.8153 to 1.8163 in. (46.36 to 46.39 mm)
	- rear	1.7553 to 1.7563 in. (44.58 to 44.60 mm)

Diametrical bearing clearance	0.0008 to 0.0026 in. (0.023 to 0.066 mm)
Endfloat	0.003 to 0.007. in. (0.076 to 0.178 mm)
Thrust plate thickness	0.180 to 0.182 in. (4.572 to 4.623 mm)
Maximum cam lift - Inlet	0.283676 in. (7.2061 mm)
Exhaust	0.289676 in. (7.3586 mm)
Backlash - crankshaft to camshaft gear	0.002 to 0.004 in. (0.05 to 0.10 mm)

Balance Shaft and Balance Shaft Bearings

Balance shaft drive	Steel gear from crankshaft
Balance shaft bearings	2 steel back, white metal bushes
Endfloat..	0.005 to 0.010 in. (.127 to .254 mm)

Connecting Rods & Big & Small End Bearings

Connecting rod type	'H' section steel forging
Length between centres	5.641 to 5.643 in. (14.328 to 14.332 cm)
Big end bearings - material and type	Steel back copper/lead
Big end diameter	2.521 to 2.5215 in. (64.003 to 64.047 mm)
Undersize bearing available	0.002, 0.010, 0.020, 0.030, 0.040 in.) I.D. 0.051, 0.254, 0.508, 0.760, 1.02 mm)
Crankpin endfloat	0.004 to 0.010 in. (.102 to .254 mm)

Crankshaft and Main Bearings

Number of bearings	3
Main bearing journal diameter	2.5006 to 2.5014 in. (63.52 to 63.54 mm)
Main journal length - front...	0.95 to 1.00 in. (2.41 to 2.54 mm)
- centre	1.059 to 1.061 in. (2.69 to 2.695 mm)
- rear	1.06 to 1.09 in. (2.69 to 2.77 mm)
Main bearing material	Steel back copper/lead
Undersize bearings available	0.010, 0.020, 0.030, 0.040 in.) I.D. 0.254, 0.508, 0.760, 1.02 mm.)
Oversize bearings available	0.015 in. (.381 mm) O/S on O.D with standard I.D or undersizes as above
Bearing bore in cylinder block	2.6654 to 2.6662 in. (67.701 to 67.72 mm)
Crankpin journal diameter	2.3761 to 2.3769 in. (60.35 to 60.37 mm)
Crankpin journal length	0.838 to 0.842 in. (2.128 to 2.139 mm)
Crankshaft endfloat	0.003 to 0.011 in. (0.076 to 0.279 mm)
Thrust washers	On centre main bearing
Thrust washer thickness	0.091 to 0.093 in. (2.31 to 2.36 mm)
Oversize thrust washers available	0.0025, 0.005, 0.0075, 0.010 in. (0.064, 0.130, 0.191, 0.250 mm)

Cylinder Block

Type	Cylinder cast integral with top of crankcase
Water jackets	Full length
Vee angle	60º
Cylinder bore diameters	Graded
Grade 1	3.6869 to 3.6872 in. (93.647 to 93.655 mm)
Grade 2	3.6872 to 3.6875 in. (93.655 to 93.663 mm)
Grade 3	3.6875 to 3.6878 in. (93.663 to 93.670 mm)
Grade 4	3.6878 to 3.6881 in. (93.670 to 93.678 mm)
Grade 5	3.6881 to 3.6884 in. (93.678 to 93.686 mm)
Grade 6	3.6884 to 3.6887 in. (93.686 to 93.693 mm)
Grading point	1.875 in. (47.63 mm) from block face on thrust plane
Cylinder liners available	Std. and .020 (.51 mm) O/S on O.D
Bore for cylinder liners	3.8315 to 3.8325 in. (97.320 to 97.345 mm)

Cylinder Heads

Type	Cast iron with vertical valves
Port arrangement	Inlet and exhaust ports separate on opposite sides
Number of ports	4 inlet, 4 exhaust
Valve seat angle - head	44º 30' to 45º
- valve	45º to 45º 15'
Valve seat width - Inlet	0.055 in. (1.40 mm)
- Exhaust	0.076 in. (1.93 mm)

Gudgeon Pin

Type	Semi-floating, interference fit into connecting rod
Material	Machined seamless steel tubing
Length	2.925 to 2.955 in. (74.30 to 75.06 mm)
Outside diameter	0.9370 to 0.9373 in. (2.3798 to 2.3806 mm)
Fit in piston	0.0003 to 0.0005 in. (.0076 to .0127 mm) selective

Lubrication System

Type	Wet sump - pressure and splash
Oil filter	Full flow with replaceable cartridge
Oil filter capacity	1.416 pints (1.8 U.S pints, 0.85 litres)
Sump capacity (less filter..	6.544 pints (7.8 U.S pints, 3.72 litres)
Service fill	8.4 pints (10.0 U.S pints, 4.77 litres)
Oil pump type...	Eccentric bi-rotor
Oil pressure	47 to 57 lb/sq.in. (3.30 to 4.00 kg/cm^2)
Eccentric bi-rotor oil pump	
Capacity...	9 galls (10.8 U.S galls, 40.88 litres) per minute at 2,500 r.p.m
Body bore diameter	0.50 to 0.501 in. (12.7 to 12.725 mm)
Drive shaft diameter	0.498 to 0.4985 in. (12.649 to 12.662 mm)
Shaft to body clearance	0.0015 to 0.003 in. (0.038 to 0.076 mm)
Inner and outer rotor clearance..	0.006 in. (0.152 mm) max.
Outer rotor and housing clearance...	0.010 in. (0.254 mm) max.
Inner and outer rotor endfloat	0.005 in. (0.127 mm) max.

Pistons

Type	Cutaway skirt with combustion chamber in crown
Material...	Aluminium alloy, tin plated
Clearance in cylinder...	0.0023 to 0.0029 in. (0.051 to 0.066 mm)
Number of rings	3, two compression, one oil control
Width of ring grooves:—	
Compression rings...	0.080 to 0.081 in. (2.032 to 2.057 mm)
Oil control ring	0.1875 to 0.1885 in. (4.762 to 4.787 mm)
Gudgeon pin bore...	Graded
Grade - Red	0.9374 to 0.9375 in. (23.810 to 23.813 mm)
- Yellow	0.9375 to 0.9376 in. (23.813 to 23.815 mm)
- Blue	0.9376 to 0.9377 in. (23.815 to 23.818 mm)
Gudgeon pin bore offset...	0.06 in. (1.5 mm) towards thrust face
Piston oversizes available..	0.0025, 0.005, 0.015, 0.030, 0.045, 0.060 in. (0.0635, 0.127, 0.381, 0.762, 1.14, 1.52 mm)

Piston Rings

Upper compression ring:

Material...	Cast iron, chrome plated
Type	Barrel face
Radial thickness	0.157 to 0.167 in. (3.98 to 4.24 mm)
Width	0.077 to 0.078 in. (1.956 to 1.981 mm)
Ring to groove clearance	0.002 to 0.004 in. (0.0508 to 0.1016 mm)
Ring gap	0.010 to 0.020 in. (0.254 to 0.508 mm)

Lower compression ring:

Material...	Cast iron, molybdenum coated
Type	Parallel faced, externally stepped
Radial thickness	0.163 to 0.184 in. (4.14 to 4.67 mm)
Width	0.077 to 0.078 in. (1.956 to 1.981 mm)
Ring to groove clearance	0.002 to 0.004 in. (0.0508 to .1016 mm)
Ring gap	0.010 to 0.020 in. (0.254 to 0.508 mm)

Oil control ring:

Material...	Cast iron
Type	'Micro-land' slotted scraper
Radial thickness	0.150 to 0.160 in. (3.81 to 4.06 mm)
Width	0.1855 to 0.1865 in. (4.711 to 4.74 mm)
Ring to groove clearance	0.001 to 0.003 in. (0.0254 to 0.0762 mm)
Ring gap	0.010 to 0.015 in. (0.254 to 0.381 mm)
Oversize rings available	0.0025, 0.005, 0.015, 0.030, 0.045, 0.060 in. (0.0635, 0.127, 0.381, 0.762, 1.14, 1.52 mm)

Tappets

Type	Cylindrical flat based
Diameter	0.8740 to 0.8745 in. (22.2 to 22.21 mm)
Length	2.00 in. (50.8 mm)

Valves

Head diameter	- Inlet...	1.617 in. (41.0 mm)
	- Exhaust...	1.453 in. (37.0 mm)
Valve lift	- Inlet...	0.373 in. (9.476 mm)
	- Exhaust...	0.375 in. (9.525 mm)

Valve stem to rocker arm clearance:
Hot - Inlet	0.013 in. (0.330 mm)
- Exhaust	0.020 in. (0.508 mm)
Cold - Inlet..	0.013 in. (0.330 mm)
- Exhaust..	0.020 in. (0.508 mm)

Valve Guides
Type	Machined in cylinder head, insert bushes available
Valve timing - Inlet opens...	29° B.T.D.C.
- Inlet closes...	67° A.D.D.C.
- Exhaust opens...	71° B.B.D.C.
- Exhaust closes...	25° A.T.D.C.
Timing marks	Dimples on crankshaft, camshaft and balance shaft gear wheels

Valve Springs
Type	Single coil spring
Free length...	1.888 in. (47.96 mm)
Outside diameter ... ..., ...	1.276 to 1.284 in. (32.41 to 32.61 mm)
Total number of coils	6.5
Wire diameter	167 to .169 in. (4.24 to 4.29 mm)

Torque Wrench Settings
Big end bolts	38 to 43 lbs/ft (3.25 to 5.49 kg/m)
Camshaft gear bolt	40 to 45 lbs/ft (5.53 to 6.22 kg/m)
Crankshaft pulley bolt	40 to 45 lbs/ft (5.53 to 6.22 kg/m)
Cylinder head bolts	65 to 70 lbs/ft (8.98 to 9.67 kg/m)
Flywheel to crankshaft bolts	50 to 55 lbs/ft (6.91 to 7.60 kg/m)
Main bearing bolts..	55 to 60 lbs/ft (7.60 to 8.29 kg/m)
Inlet manifold bolts	13 to 16 lbs/ft (1.80 to 2.21 kg/m)
Oil pump to block..	12 to 15 lbs/ft (1.66 to 2.07 kg/m)
Rear oil seal retainer bolts	11 to 13 lbs/ft (1.52 to 1.80 kg/m)
Rocker cover	2.5 to 3.5 lbs/ft (.35 to .42 kg/m)
Sump..	6 to 8 lbs/ft (.83 to 1.11 kg/m)
Sump drain plug	20 to 25 lbs/ft (2.76 to 3.46 kg/m)
Balance shaft gear bolt	40 to 45 lbs/ft (5.53 to 6.22 kg/m)
Carburetter attaching nuts	15 to 18 lbs/ft (2.07 to 2.49 kg/m)

Engine Specifications & Data — 2994 cc V6

The engine specification is identical to the 1996 c c engine except for the differences listed below:

Engine - General
Type	6 cylinder 60° V Pushrod operated O.H.V.
Cubic capacity...	2994 cc (182.7 cu.in.)
Compression ratio	8.9 to 1
Maximum B.H.P	Up to Oct 1971 128 (net) at 4,750 r.p.m.
	from Oct 1971 138 (net)
Maximum torque	192.5 lb/ft (26.6 kg.m) at 4,000 r.p.m.
Firing order	1(R), 4(L), 2(R), 5(L), 3(R), 6(L)

Camshaft and Camshaft Bearings
Bearings		4, steel back babbit
Camshaft journal diameter	- Front...	1.8737 to 1.8745 in. (47.59 to 47.67 mm)
	- No.2	1.8137 to 1.8145 in. (46.07 to 46.15 mm)
	- No.3	1.7537 to 1.7545 in. (44.54 to 44.56 mm)
	- Rear	1.7387 to 1.7395 in. (44.16 to 44.18 mm)
Camshaft bearing I.D.	- Front...	1.8753 to 1.8763 in. (47.63 to 47.66 mm)
	- No.2	1.8153 to 1.8163 in. (46.11 to 46.13 mm)
	- No.3	1.7553 to 1.7563 in. (44.58 to 44.60 mm)
	- Rear	1.7403 to 1.7413 in. (44.22 to 44.24 mm)

No balance shaft fitted to V6 engine

Crankshaft and Main Bearings
Number of bearings		4
Main journal length	- Front...	0.95 to 1.00 in. (24.13 to 25.40 mm)
	- 2nd	1.059 to 1.061 in. (26.90 to 26.95 mm)
	- 3rd	1.05 to 1.07 in. (26.67 to 27.18 mm)
	- Rear	1.06 to 1.09 in. (26.90 to 27.70 mm)

Lubrication System

    Service fill including filter ... ...   9.5 pints (11.5 U.S pints, 5.4 litres)

    Oil pressure   ... ...   57 to 67 lb/sq.in. (4.00 to 4.71 kg/cm^2)

Pistons

    Clearance in cylinder... ... ...   .0014 to .002 in. (.035 to .050 mm)

Valves

    Valve lift - Inlet   ... ...   .337 in. (8.560 mm)

           - Exhaust   ... ...   .337 in. (8.560 mm)

Valve Timing

    Inlet open ... ...   20° B.T.D.C.

    Inlet closes ... ...   64° A.B.D.C.

    Exhaust opens... ... ...   70° B.B.D.C.

    Exhaust closes... ... ...   14° B.T.D.C.

    Timing marks ... ...   Dimples on crankshaft and camshaft gear wheels

1 General Description

The engine fitted to the Capri 2000 GT is a 4 cylinder unit, and that fitted in the 3000 GT and E, a 6 cylinder unit. Both engines have the cylinders arranged in a 60° Vee formation. The V4 engine has a capacity of 1996 cc and the V6 a capacity of 2994 cc.

The bores are machined directly into the block which has full length water jacketing. The V4 has three main bearings and the V6 four main bearings each of which have removable caps. The cast iron crankshaft runs in the bearings mentioned above which have renewable shell liners of steel backed copper/lead. Endfloat on the V4 engine is controlled by thrust washers on each side of the centre bearing. On the V6 engine the thrust washers are on the first intermediate bearing. The rear oil seal runs on the crankshaft flange, whereas the front crankshaft oil seal is mounted in the front cover and bears on the crankshaft pulley hub.

The camshaft is mounted centrally in the vee above the crankshaft and is driven at half engine speed by a large fibre helical gear in direct mesh with the crankshaft gear. The V4 camshaft runs in three, and the V6 in four white metal steel backed bushes.

A skew gear is machined into the camshaft just behind the front bearing and this drives the distributor which is mounted centrally above the camshaft in the vee.

This, indirectly, also drives the oil pump which is connected by a long, hexagonal-section shaft which fits into a recess in the bottom of the distributor drive shaft. The camshaft thrust is taken by a plate bolted to the front block face.

The valves are mounted overhead and are pushrod operated from the camshaft via rockers. The rockers are each mounted on a stud and pivot on a hemispherical fulcrum seat which is located on the stud.

The height of this seat is adjusted by a self-locking nut and this provides the means of adjusting the valve to rocker clearances.

The pistons are made of aluminium alloy, tin plated, and have the combustion chambers machined in the crown. The skirts are cut away.

The gudgeon pins are semi-floating, being a shrink fit in the connecting rods. The connecting rods are made of forged steel and are of 'H' section with detachable big end caps located by hollow dowel pins. The bearing liners are renewable shells of steel backed copper/lead.

Each piston has two compression rings and an oil control ring. The top compression ring is barrel faced and chromium plated on its cylinder wall surface. The lower compression ring is internally chamfered on the top face and molybdenum coated on its cylinder wall face.

As both engines of a 60° Vee configuration on the rotating and reciprocating parts are inherently out of balance. To compensate for this imbalance the crankshaft pulley, crankshaft and flywheel all have counterbalances built in.

On the V4 engine only a separate counterbalance shaft is installed, driven at engine speed by the crankshaft gear.

The oil pump is of the bi-rotor type of exceptionally high capacity. Oil pressure is maintained at 47 to 57 lb/sq.in. to the main, big end, camshaft, and balance shaft bearings and also to the tappets where oil flow is controlled to run up the inside of the hollow pushrods to lubricate the rocker gear. Cylinder bores are lubricated by a small jet of oil once every revolution from a fine hole in the connecting rod web. Gudgeon pins are lubricated by oil mist in the crankcase, and oil scraped from the cylinder walls which passes through the scraper ring groove. Oil circulates at 9 gallons per minute at an engine speed of 2,500 r.p.m.

The procedures shown in the following sections for dismantling, examination and repair etc, were carried out on a Capri 2000 GT

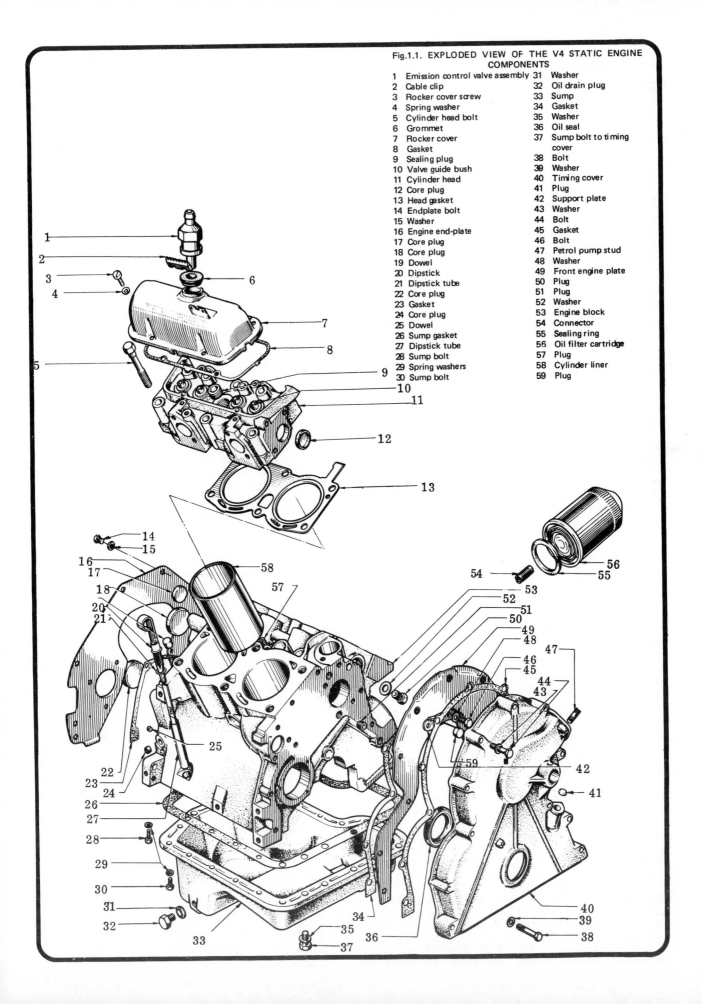

Fig.1.1. EXPLODED VIEW OF THE V4 STATIC ENGINE COMPONENTS

1 Emission control valve assembly
2 Cable clip
3 Rocker cover screw
4 Spring washer
5 Cylinder head bolt
6 Grommet
7 Rocker cover
8 Gasket
9 Sealing plug
10 Valve guide bush
11 Cylinder head
12 Core plug
13 Head gasket
14 Endplate bolt
15 Washer
16 Engine end-plate
17 Core plug
18 Core plug
19 Dowel
20 Dipstick
21 Dipstick tube
22 Core plug
23 Gasket
24 Core plug
25 Dowel
26 Sump gasket
27 Dipstick tube
28 Sump bolt
29 Spring washers
30 Sump bolt
31 Washer
32 Oil drain plug
33 Sump
34 Gasket
35 Washer
36 Oil seal
37 Sump bolt to timing cover
38 Bolt
39 Washer
40 Timing cover
41 Plug
42 Support plate
43 Washer
44 Bolt
45 Gasket
46 Bolt
47 Petrol pump stud
48 Washer
49 Front engine plate
50 Plug
51 Plug
52 Washer
53 Engine block
54 Connector
55 Sealing ring
56 Oil filter cartridge
57 Plug
58 Cylinder liner
59 Plug

GT V4 engine. The procedures for the V6 engine are virtually identical, but differences where they occur can be found listed in Section 53, and it would be wise to refer to this section before carrying out any task on the V6 engine.

2. Routine Maintenance

1. At weekly intervals (or every 300 miles) check the oil level in the sump by removing the dipstick, wiping it clean, replacing it and noting the level on withdrawing it again. The 'fill' mark is the absolute minimum to which the level must be allowed to fall and to regain the 'full' mark 1½ pints of oil will be required. If oil consumption exceeds 1 pint per 300 miles then there is either a leak or the cylinder bores or rings are very worn. Do not overfill with oil as it is simply a waste.
2. At intervals of 5,000 miles (8,000 kms.) the engine oil should be changed. Run the engine until it is hot, place a container of 10 pints capacity under the drain plug in the sump and undo the drain plug. Let the oil drain for at least 10 minutes.
3. At the same time unscrew the filter unit from the left side of the block and fit a new one.
4. Clean the sump drain plug and washer and replace and tighten them. Refill the engine with 7½ pints for the V4 engine or 9½ pints for the V6 engine of the recommended oil, run the engine, and check that the level is correct.
5. At 5,000 miles the valve rocker clearances should be checked and adjusted if necessary, as described in Section 48.2.
6. Check also and clean the oil filler cap and crankcase emission valve in the left and right rocker covers respectively. (See Section 27 for details).

3. Major Operations with Engine in Place

The following major operations may be carried out without taking the engine from the car:—

1. Removal and replacement of the cylinder heads.
2. Removal and replacement of the timing gear.
3. Removal and replacement of the front engine mountings.
4. Removal and replacement of the engine—gearbox rear mounting.

4. Major Operations with the Engine Removed

Although it would be possible to carry out some of the following operations with the engine in the car if the gearbox and clutch were removed, it is deemed inadvisable.

1. Removal and replacement of the flywheel.
2. Removal and replacement of the rear main bearing oil seal.
3. Removal and replacement of the sump.
4. Removal and replacement of the big end bearings.
5. Removal and replacement of the pistons and connecting rods.
6. Removal and replacement of the oil pump.
7. Removal and replacement of the crankshaft and crankshaft main bearings
8. Removal and replacement of the camshaft and camshaft bushes.

5. Method of Engine Removal

The engine may be lifted out together with the gearbox or separated from the gearbox and lifted out by itself. If the gearbox is left attached the disadvantage is that the engine has to be tilted to a steep angle to get it out.

6. Engine Removal Without Gearbox

1. A do-it-yourself owner should be able to remove the engine from the car in about 3 hours. It is essential to have a good hoist. If an inspection pit is not available, two support stands will also be required. In the later stages, when the engine is being separated from the gearbox and lifted, the assistance of another person is most useful to help guide the engine and prevent it from swaying about and possibly causing damage.
2. Undo and remove the two nuts and bolts on either side holding the bonnet to the hinge assembly then lift off the bonnet (photo).
3. Disconnect the battery by removing the negative earth lead (photo).
4. Undo the bolt securing the battery clamp (photo) remove the clamp, disconnect the positive lead and remove the battery from the car.
5. Obtain two suitable receptacles to collect the engine oil and cooling water. Rather than use the washing up bowls from the kitchen, it is better to find an empty gallon oil can and cut one side out to use as a container for the oil. Two cans will be needed for the V6 engine. If the coolant is to be kept because of anti-freeze a 2 gallon container will be required.
6. Drain the cooling system and remove the radiator as described in Chapter 2.7.
7. Undo and remove the nuts and washers from the top of the air cleaner (photo).
8. Lift off the cover (photo) then remove the filter and the tubular spacers over the long bolts.
9. The next step is to remove the air cleaner base from the top of the carburetter. Knock back the tabs on the locking plates on the carburetter (photo) undo the nuts and remove the washers and rubber spacers (photo).
10 For safe keeping, leave the washers, nuts, etc in the air cleaner body then undo and remove the bolt from the air cleaner support stay (photo) then lift off the air cleaner (photo).
11 Take the servo vacuum pipe off the inlet manifold by springing the clip with a pair of pliers (photo).
12 Disconnect both heater hoses at the bulkhead by undoing the clips (photo) and pulling them off. The following two paragraphs do not apply to models fitted with an automatic choke.
13 Release the choke outer cable by loosening the clamp bolt on the rear of the carburetter (photo).
14 By undoing the small screw on the side of the choke linkage (photo) release the choke inner cable.
15 Disconnect the accelerator cable from the linkage at its very end by sliding the small cylindrical spring clip off the ball and socket housing (photo).
16 Then remove the outer cable from the bracket by releasing the spring clip just above the rubber bellows (photo). Tuck the accelerator cable and the choke cable out of harms way.
17 Pull the connectors off the rear of the alternator (photo) then pull the L.T. lead off the coil (photo).
18 From just forward of the carburetter in the centre of the V pull off the lead from the water temperature sender unit (photo).
19 Separate the oil pressure gauge supply pipe on the left-hand side of the engine just under the oil filler cap (photo) and tuck the rear end out of the way.
20 Disconnect the engine earth strap from the front left-hand side of the engine just adjacent to the oil filter by undoing the bolt (photo) which secures it to the block.
21 Spring the clip on the fuel pump inlet pipe with a pair of pliers (photo) then pull off the pipe.
22 As it is possible for the fuel level in the tank to be higher than the inlet pipe, block it with a suitably sized bolt or similar object (photo).
23 Disconnect the starter motor lead by undoing the single retaining nut (photo) and remove the washers.
24 As it will now be necessary to work under the car, raise the front on a jack and place chassis stands under the front crossmember.

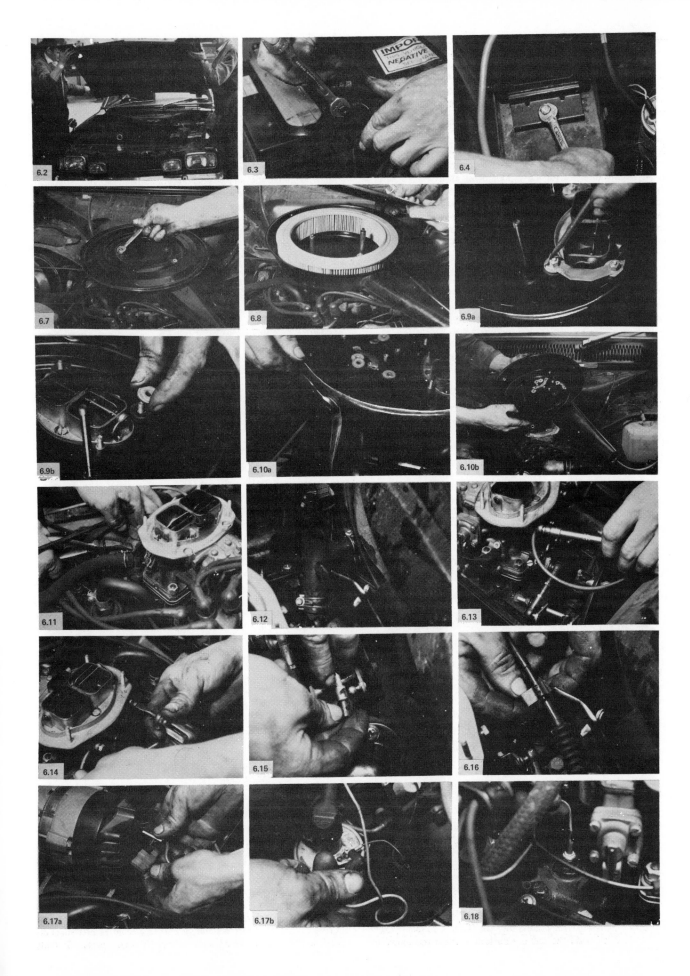

25 Undo the clamps on the two exhaust manifold extensions to exhaust manifolds (photo).

26 Now remove the exhaust manifolds by removing the four bolts on either side of the engine (photo). Lift the manifolds and gaskets from the car.

27 Working under the car, pull the rubber boot off the bellhousing where the clutch mechanism enters the bellhousing on the right-hand side.

28 Undo the locknut on the clutch cable (photo) and slacken off the sleeved adjusting nut until the pedal in the car is about one inch from the floor.

29 Now pull the cable towards the rear of the car and slide the ball end of the cable out of its slot in the clutch release mechanism (photo).

30 Moving to the other side of the car remove the three bolts which hold the starter motor to the bellhousing and carefully lift out the starter motor. If a pre-engaged type of starter motor is fitted there will only be two retaining bolts.

31 Undo and remove the lower bellhousing bolts and remove the cover plate. On some models this plate is also retained by small pressed in expanding studs, these can easily be levered out (photo A). Photo B shows the stud and its expanding sleeve.

32 Place a jack under the bellhousing and support it under the front edge with a piece of wooden packing between the jack and the bellhousing.

33 Undo and remove the remaining bellhousing bolts.

34 Undo the lower retaining nut from each front engine mounting point (photo). The engine is now resting on its mountings at the front, and is supported at the rear by the gearbox input shaft in the clutch, so is now ready to be removed from the car.

35 Two methods can be used to lift the engine from the car; ideally a chain should be used as shown in photo 6.40, but should a chain not be available a good quality strong rope will do just as well.

36 Using a rope make a looped sling so that the rope passes right under the engine to the rear of the front mounting brackets.

37 Tie the loop above the engine as close to the block as possible using a knot that will not slip or jam.

38 Hook in the lifting gear either cantilever beam or hoist and then take some strain and see that the sling will not bend or damage anything when completely tight with the full weight of the engine on it.

39 Whether using a chain or rope take some more strain on the lifting gear until the front of the car starts to rise, which indicates that the full weight of the engine is now held by the lifting gear. The engine must now be lifted clear of the two front mounting studs.

40 The engine must now be pulled forward to disengage it from the splined end of the gearbox input shaft. This may call for two people and a certain amount of sideways rocking to disengage it completely. It will be free when the gap between the engine and the bellhousing is about 3 inches (75 mm). Care must be taken at this point as the rear of the engine will tend to drop down (photo) when it comes clear of the gearbox. It is helpful if two people are available, one to steady the engine and one to operate the lifting gear.

41 It is unwise to hurry this final stage of engine removal as damage and accidents can occur unless the engine is watched carefully all the way out.

7. Engine Removal with Gearbox

1. Proceed exactly as outlined in Section 6 up to and including paragraph 29.

2. Unscrew the gearbox drain plug (photo) and allow the oil to drain away for at least five minutes. Replace the drain plug.

3. From inside the car remove completely the gear change lever remote control assembly as described in Chapter 6/3.

4. Support the gearbox with a jack in the area of the drain plug.

5. Remove the centre bolt which locates the gearbox extension into the support member. Then making sure the gearbox support jack is firmly in position undo the four bolts attaching the crossmember to the body frame (photo A). Then remove the crossmember (photo A).

6. With the crossmember removed it is now an easy task to disconnect the speedometer cable from the gearbox by removing the circlip and withdrawing the cable (photo).

7. Disconnect the reversing light wire at its snap connector (photo).

8. Remove the front engine mounting bolts as described in Section 6, paragraph 34.

9. With the jack under the gearbox still in position start lifting and at the same time, once the front mountings have been cleaned, move the engine forwards until the propeller shaft is nearly ready to come out of the gearbox extension. Do not let the propeller shaft drop on the ground but support it until clear and then lower it and rest it on a suitable block.

10 Due to the fact that the gearbox is attached, the engine will have to be lifted out at a much steeper angle than for removing the engine on its own (photo). As the weight is more towards the rear, it will be fairly easy to achieve this angle.

11 Continue to raise the engine and move it forwards at the necessary angle. At this stage the forward edge of the bellhousing is likely to catch against the front crossmember and the tail of the gearbox will need raising until the whole unit is forward and clear of it.

12 Finally the whole unit will rise clear and if the maximum height of the lifting tackle has been reached, it will be necessary to swing the unit so that the tail can be lifted clear whilst the hoist is moved away or the car lowered from its axle stands and pushed from under the unit.

13 The whole unit should be lowered to the ground (or bench) as soon as possible and the gearbox may then be separated from the engine.

8. Engine Dismantling - General

1. Ideally, the engine is mounted on a proper stand for overhaul but it is anticipated that most owners will have a strong bench on which to place it. If a sufficiently large strong bench is not available then the work can be done at ground level. It is essential, however, that some form of substantial wooden surface is available. Timber should be at least ¾ inch thick, otherwise the weight of the engine will cause projections to punch holes straight through it.

2. It will save a great deal of time later if the engine is thoroughly cleaned down on the exterior before any dismantling begins. This can be done by using paraffin and a stiff brush or more easily, by the use of a proprietary solvent such as 'Gunk' which can be brushed on and then the dirt swilled off with a water jet. This will dispose of all the heavy muck and grit once and for all so that later cleaning of individual components will be a relatively clean process and the paraffin bath will not become contaminated with abrasive material.

3. As the engine is stripped down, clean each part as it comes off. Try to avoid immersing parts with oilways in paraffin as pockets of liquid could remain and cause oil dilution in the critical first few revolutions after reassembly. Clean oilways with pipe cleaners, or, preferably, an air jet.

4. Where possible avoid damaging gaskets on removal, especially if new ones have not been obtained. They can be used as patterns if new ones have to be specially cut.

5. It is helpful to obtain a few blocks of wood to support the engine whilst it is in the process of dismantling. Start dismantling at the top of the engine and then turn the block over and deal with the sump and crankshaft etc., afterwards.

6. Nuts and bolts should be replaced in their locations where possible to avoid confusion later. As an alternative keep each group of nuts and bolts (all the timing gear cover bolts for example) together in a jar or tin.

7. Many items dismantled must be replaced in the same position, if they are not being renewed. These include valves, rocker arms, tappets, pistons, pushrods, bearings and connecting rods. Some of these are marked on assembly to avoid any possibility of mixing them up during overhaul. Others are not, and it is a great help if adequate preparation is made in advance to classify these parts. Suitably

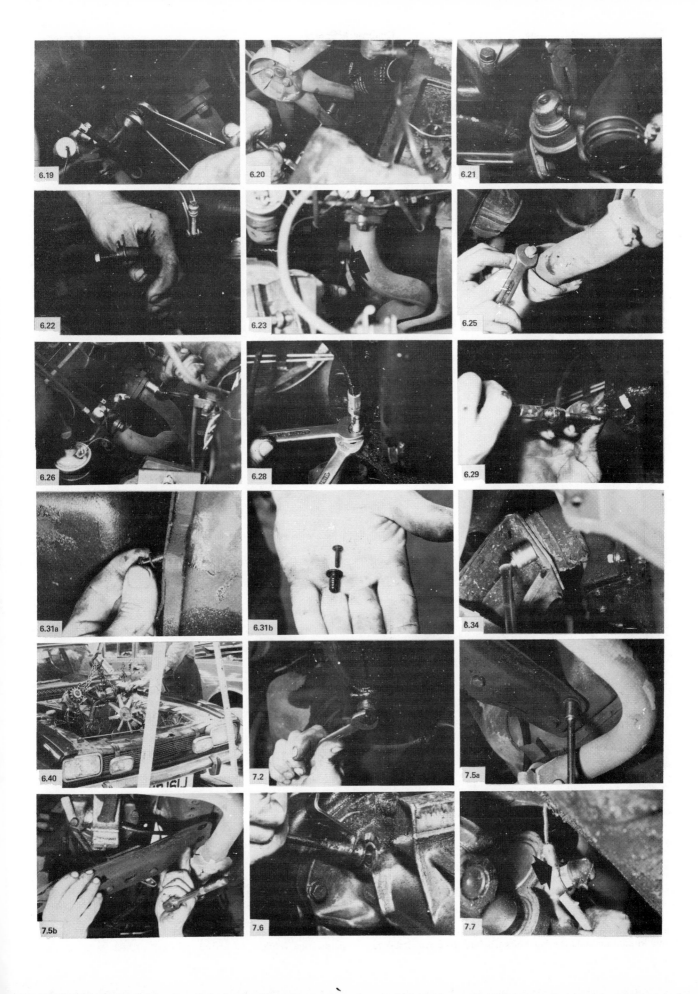

labelled tins or jars and, for small items, egg trays, tobacco tins and so on, can be used. The time spent in this preparation will be amply repaid later.

9. Engine Ancillaries - Removal

1. Before beginning a complete overhaul or if the engine is being exchanged for a works reconditioned unit the following items should be removed:—

Fuel system components:
   Carburetter
   Inlet and Exhaust manifolds
   Fuel pump
   Fuel lines

Ignition system components:
   Sparking plugs
   Distributor
   Coil

Electrical system components:
   Generator and mounting brackets
   Starter motor

Cooling system components:
   Fan and Fan pulley
   Water pump, Thermostat housing and thermostat
   Water temperature sender unit

Engine:
   Crankcase ventilation tube
   Oil filter element
   Oil pressure sender unit
   Oil level dipstick
   Oil filler cap
   Engine mounting brackets

Clutch:
   Clutch pressure plate and total assembly
   Clutch friction plate and total assembly

Some of these items have to be removed for individual servicing or renewal periodically and details can be found under the appropriate Chapter.

10. Cylinder Heads - Removal with Engine Out

1. Remove the two valve rocker covers by undoing the four screws holding each one to its respective cylinder head.
2. Remove the distributor (Chapter 4.6) and plug leads.
3. Remove the carburetter (Chapter 3.12).
4. Remove the inlet manifold by slackening first the two bolts holding the centre section and then the other four at the corners. The manifold casting may stick to the heads at the joint in which case tap it on the ends in the centre with a soft mallet to dislodge it. Then lift it off (photo).
5. Taking each cylinder head in turn, remove the six holding down bolts. As the bolts are slackened off the pressure of the springs on any open valves should force the head away from the block.
6. When the head is sufficiently clear remove the four pushrods and note which valve they came from and which way up. Keep them in order and the right way up by pushing them through a piece of stiff paper or cardboard with the valve numbers marked and the top and bottom ends identified.
7. On occasions the heads stick to the block in which case they should be struck smartly with a block of wood and hammer or soft mallet in order to break the joint. However, the exhaust manifold should provide sufficient grip to provide the necessary lifting force required. Do not try and prise them off with a blade of any description or damage will be caused to the faces of the head or block, or both.
8. Lift the heads off carefully. Note which side each head comes

from as they are identical and it is essential to replace them on the same bank of cylinders. Place them where they cannot be damaged. Undo the bolts holding the exhaust manifold to each head if not previously removed.

11. Cylinder Heads - Removal with Engine in Car

1. The procedure described in Section 10 should be followed exactly except that the following should be done first:—
a) Disconnect the battery leads (Chapter 10.2).
b) Drain the cooling system (Chapter 2.3).
c) Remove the top hose from the thermostat housing and the heater hose connection from the inlet manifold. Remove also the by-pass hose connection at the thermostat (Chapter 2).
d) Remove the fan belt and generator or alternator if fitted (Chapter 10). The generator brackets may also be removed but this is not essential.
e) Disconnect the exhaust manifolds from the exhaust pipes by removing the clamping rings (Section 6/25).
f) Disconnect the water temperature sender unit lead (Section 6/18).
g) Remove the coil from the front of the left-hand head by undoing the securing bolt.
h) Remove the accelerator linkage cross-shaft.

12. Cylinder Heads - Dismantling of Rocker Gear, Valves & Springs

1. With the cylinder head on the bench undo the nut from each rocker stud in the centre of the rocker arm. Lift out the hemispherical rocker pivot and then lift off the rocker arm.
2. Lay the cylinder head on its side and using a proper valve spring compressor tool place the 'U' shaped end cover, the valve collar (photo), and the screw on the valve head and compress the spring. Sometimes the valve collar sticks, in which case the end of the compressor over the spring should be tapped with a hammer to release the collar from the valve.
3. As the spring is pressed down the valve stem two tapered split collars (collets) will be revealed and these should be taken from the recess in the valve stem.
4. When the compressor is released the spring may be removed from the valve. Pull off the seal cap from the valve stem and then push the valve out of the head.
5. It is essential that the valves, springs, rocker arms and nuts are all kept in order so that they may be replaced in their original positions.

13. Tappet - Removal

1. The tappets may now be removed from the cylinder block by pushing them up from the camshaft (which can be revolved if necessary to raise the tappets) and lifting them out.
2. If necessary the pushrod bearing caps in each tappet can be taken out by first extracting the retaining circlip.
3. Make sure that all the tappets are kept in order so that they may be replaced in the location they came from.

14. Crankshaft Pulley Wheel - Removal

1. Remove the bolt and washer locating the pulley to the front of the crankshaft. The pulley is keyed to the crankshaft and must be drawn off with a proper sprocket puller. Attempts to lever it off with long bladed articles such as screwdrivers or tyre levers are not suitable in this case because the timing cover behind the pulley is a light and relatively fragile casting. Any pressure against it could certainly crack it and possibly break a hole in it.
2. The pulley may be removed with the engine in the car but it may be necessary to remove the radiator, depending on the type of pulley extractor used and the clearance it allows.

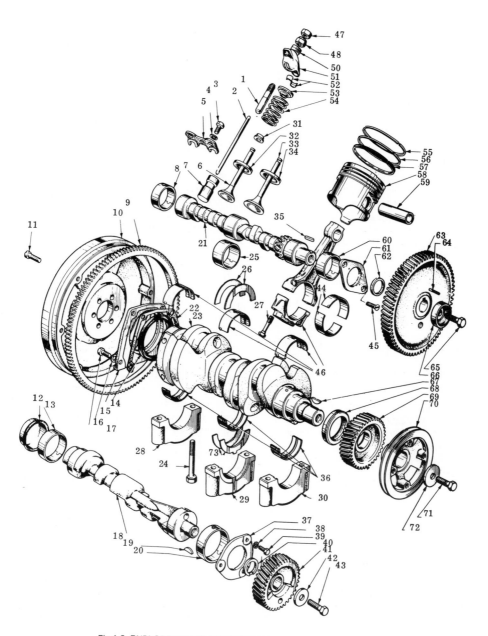

Fig.1.2. EXPLODED VIEW OF THE V4 MOVING ENGINE COMPONENTS

1 Rocker stud	19 Woodruff key	37 Balance shaft thrust plate	56 Lower compression ring
2 Pushrod	20 Balance shaft bearing-front	38 Stem washer	57 Oil control ring
3 Bolt	21 Camshaft	39 Bolt	58 Piston
4 Washer	22 Gasket	40 Spacer	59 Gudgeon pin
5 Pushrod guide	23 Crankshaft	41 Gear	60 Camshaft bearing-front
6 Exhaust valve	24 Bolt, main bearing	42 Washer	61 Camshaft thrust plate
7 Tappet	25 Camshaft bearing-centre	43 Bolt	62 Spacer
8 Camshaft bearing-rear	26 Crankshaft thrust washers	44 Big end bearing shells	63 Camshaft fibre gear
9 Starter ring	27 Bolt, big end	45 Camshaft thrust plate screw	64 Key
10 Flywheel	28 Main bearing cap - rear	46 Main bearing shells-upper	65 Bolt
11 Bolt	29 Main bearing cap - centre	47 Lock nut (if fitted)	66 Fuel pump drive cam
12 Plug	30 Main bearing cap - front	48 Self locking nut	67 Woodruff key
13 Balance shaft bearing-rear	31 Seal	50 Pivot ball	68 Oil seal
14 Crankshaft oil seal	32 Valve seat insert-exhaust	51 Rocker arm	69 Crankshaft gear
15 Oil seal retainer	33 Valve - inlet	52 Collets	70 Pulley wheel
16 Washer	34 Valve seat insert-inlet	53 Valve collar	71 Bolt
17 Bolt	35 Key	54 Spring	72 Washer
18 Balance shaft	36 Main bearing shells-lower	55 Upper compression ring	73 Crankshaft thrust washers

15. Flywheel - Removal

1. Remove the clutch assembly as described in Chapter 5.4.
2. The flywheel is held in position to the crankshaft by six bolts. One of these bolts is spaced unevenly so that the flywheel will only fit in one position.
3. Remove the six bolts, taking care to support the weight of the flywheel as they are slackened off in case it slips off the flange. Secure it carefully, taking care not to damage the mating surfaces on the crankshaft and flywheel (photo).

16. Sump Removal

1. With the engine out of the car, first invert the engine and then remove the bolts which hold the sump in place.
2. The sump may be stuck quite firmly to the engine if sealing compound has been used on the gasket. It is in order to lever it off in this case. The gasket should be removed and discarded in any case.

17. Timing Gear & Cover - Removal

1. With the engine out of the car, remove the sump and the crankshaft pulley wheel.
2. Take out the fixing bolts and lift off the cover complete with the fan.
3. If the engine is still in the car it will be necessary to remove the front six sump bolts which run through the timing cover and also the fan belt and fuel pump.
4. The camshaft timing drive mechanism consists of a helical gear on the crankshaft and a large fibre gear on the camshaft. There is also another gear in mesh with the crankshaft which drives the balance shaft. (V4 engines only).
5. Remove the camshaft and balance shaft gears by removing the bolts and washers and drawing them off. They should not require the services of a puller to come off. Be careful with the large fibre gear as this can be damaged very easily if mishandled. The crankshaft gear should be left in position as this is not normally detached. On the front of the fibre gear there is an eccentric boss held also by the locating bolt and this operates the fuel pump actuating lever.

18. Camshaft - Removal

1. The camshaft cannot be conveniently removed with the engine in the car as the tappets will jam it in position and therefore the valve rocker gear, pushrods and tappets all need to be removed in addition to the radiator, timing cover and gear.
2. With the timing cover and gear removed, undo the bolts holding the front cover backplate. Note the pressure plate underneath the three bolts.
3. The camshaft thrust plate is held to the block by two countersunk cross-head screws and these will need removing with an impact screwdriver.
4. The camshaft may then be withdrawn. Take great care to avoid hitting the three bearing bushes with the cam lobes as this could damage them. If the tappets have not been removed the camshaft may also need rotating to avoid them.

19. Oil Pump - Removal

1. Remove the sump.
2. Undo the two mounting bolts holding the pump to the crankcase and lift it out (photo). Note that the long hexagonal section driveshaft will come out with the pump. This is driven in turn from the distributor shaft.

20. Pistons, Connecting Rods & Big End Bearings - Removal

1. Pistons and connecting rods may be removed with the engine in the car, provided the sump and cylinder heads are first removed. The bearing shells may be removed with the heads on.
2. Slacken the two bolts holding each bearing cap to the connecting rod. Use a good quality socket spanner for this work. A ring spanner may be used for removal only - not replacement which calls for a special torque spanner. Having slackened the bolts two or three turns tap the bolt heads to dislodge the caps from the connecting rods. Hollow dowel pegs locate the caps in position. When the caps are free of the pegs they can be easily lifted off after the bolts are completely removed.
3. Each bearing cap normally has the cylinder number etched on one end as does the connecting rod. However, this must be verified and if in doubt the cap should be marked with a dab of paint or punch mark to ensure that its relationship with the connecting rod is not altered.
4. The piston and connecting rod may then be pushed out of the top of each cylinder (photo).
5. The big end bearing shells can be removed from the connecting rod and cap by sliding them round in the direction of the notch at the end of the shell and lifting them out. If they are not being renewed it is vital that they are not interchanged - either between pistons or between cap and connecting rod.

21. Piston Rings - Removal

1. Remove the pistons from the engine.
2. The rings come off over the top of the piston. Starting with the top one, lift one end of the ring out of the groove and gradually ease it out all the way round. With the second and third rings an old feeler blade is useful for sliding them over the other grooves. However, as rings are only normally removed if they are going to be renewed it should not matter if breakages occur.

22. Gudgeon Pins - Removal

1. The gudgeon pins need removing if the pistons are being renewed. New pistons are supplied with new pins for fitting to the existing connecting rods. The gudgeon pin is semi-floating - that is it is a tight shrink fit with the connecting rod and a moving fit in the piston. To press it out requires considerable force and under usual circumstances a proper press and special tools are essential. Otherwise piston damage will occur. If damage to the pistons does not matter, then the pins may be pressed out using suitable diameter pieces of rod and tube between the jaws of a vice. However, this is not recommended as the connecting rod might be damaged also. It is recommended that gudgeon pins and pistons are removed from, and refitted to, connecting rods by Ford dealers with the necessary facilities.

23. Crankshaft Rear Oil Seal - Removal

1. The rear oil seal comprises a spring inset type flexible ring fitted in a separate carrier plate. This plate is bolted to the crankcase and the seal bears directly onto the crankshaft flange.
2. The engine rear plate may first be removed by undoing the bolts (photo A) and lifting it away (photo B). Although this is not essential it is a simple operation and prevents the plate from becoming bent when the engine is being moved about.
3. Undo the four bolts holding the oil seal retainer plate to the engine and lift the plate away.

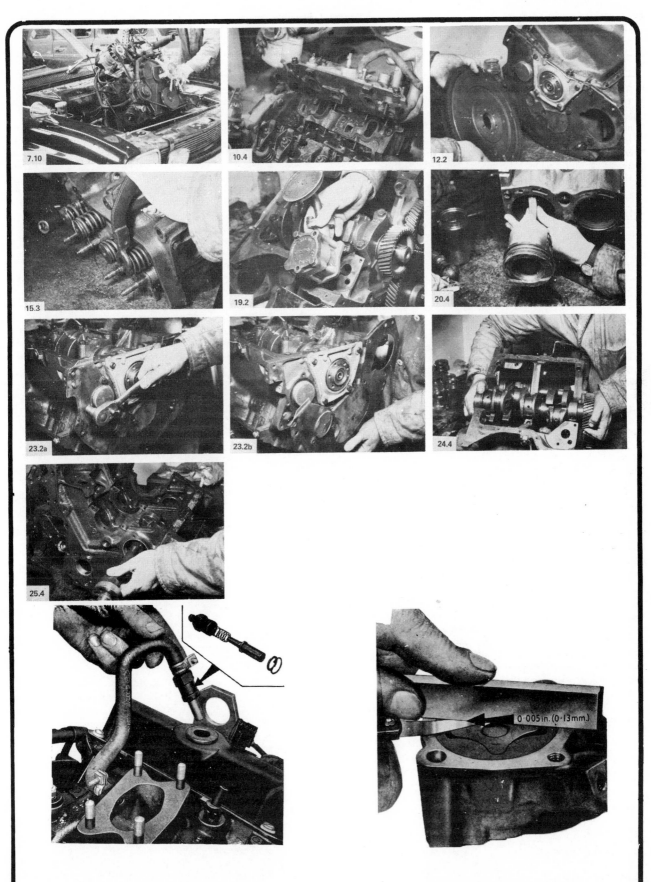

7.10 10.4 12.2 15.3 19.2 20.4 23.2a 23.2b 24.4 25.4

Fig.1.3. (left) VIEW OF THE EMISSION CONTROL VALVE (See Section 27.2)

0·005in. (0·13mm.)

Fig.1.4. (above) CHECKING OIL PUMP END FLOAT CLEARANCE (Section 28)

24. Main Bearings & Crankshaft - Removal

1. The engine should be taken from the car and the sump, cylinder heads, timing gears and pistons removed.
2. With a good quality socket spanner undo the six bolts holding the three main bearing caps in position (V4 engines) or the eight bolts holding the four main bearing caps on V6 engines.
3. When all the bolts are removed lift out the caps. If they should be tight, tap the sides gently with a piece of wood or soft mallet to dislodge them.
4. Lift out the crankshaft (photo).
5. Slide out the bearing shells from the caps and also from the crankcase seats. Also take away the thrust washers on each side of the centre main bearing. The half which is on each side of the centre bearing cap is fitted with a tang to prevent rotation.

25. Balance Shaft - Removal - 2000 GT Only

1. If it is wished to remove the balance shaft the engine need not be out of the car but the timing cover, radiator and grille should first be removed.
2. Remove the balance shaft gear as described in Section 17/5. The key and spacer collar may be left in position on the shaft.
3. Undo the three bolts holding the thrust plate to the face of the block.
4. Withdraw the balance shaft carefully so as not to damage the bearing bushes in which it runs (photo).

26. Lubrication & Crankcase Ventilation System - Description

1. A general description of the oil circulation system is given in Section 1 of this Chapter.
2. The oil pump is of the eccentric bi-rotor type.
3. The oil is drawn through a gauze screen and tube which is below the oil level in the well of the sump. It is then pumped via the full flow oil filter to the system of oil galleries in the block as previously described. The oil filter cartridge is mounted externally on the left-hand side of the block.
4. The crankcase is positively ventilated. Air enters through the oil filler cap in the left-hand rocker cover which is fitted with a washable gauze filter. Air enters directly under the rim of the cap or as in the closed system, the cap is connected to the carburetter air filter by a pipe so that filtration of the air is by the existing air filter.
5. Air passes through the pushrod and oil drain channels in the tappet chamber and up the right-hand bank of the block to the right-hand rocker cover. The right-hand rocker cover is fitted with an outlet connected by a pipe to the engine intake manifold. A tapered valve in the rocker cover outlet controls the outlet of fumes so that when manifold depression is high the valve closes partially, thus reducing the flow proportionately.

27. Crankcase Ventilation System - Routine Maintenance

1. Every 5,000 miles, or when changing the oil, remove the oil filler cap (if fitted with the gauze filter) and wash the whole unit thoroughly in petrol. Blow dry and apply a little clean engine oil to the gauze filter.
2. Clean the emission control valve. First remove the hose and then pull the valve out of the grommet in the right-hand rocker cover. Dismantle the valve by removing the circlip and taking out the valve seal, valve and spring. Wash thoroughly in petrol, reassemble and replace.
3. Do not try and run the engine with any part of the emission valve or pipe disconnected as this will completely upset the fuel mixture due to the inlet manifold being opened to atmospheric pressure. It should also be borne in mind that malfunctioning of the emission control valve may affect the fuel mixture to the engine.

28. Oil Pump - Overhaul

1. The oil pump maintains a pressure of around 45 lbs.in.^{2}. An oil pressure gauge is fitted to give earlier warning of falling oil pressures due either to overheating, pump or bearing wear.
2. At a major engine overhaul it is as well to check the pump and exchange it for a reconditioned unit if necessary. The efficient operation of the oil pump depends on the finely machined tolerances between the moving parts of the rotor and the body and re-conditioning of these is generally not within the competence of the non-specialist owner.
3. To dismantle the pump first remove it from the engine as described in Section 19.
4. Remove the two bolts holding the end cover to the body and remove the cover and relief valve parts which will be released.
5. The necessary clearances may now be checked using a machined straight edge (a good steel rule) and a feeler gauge.
6. On bi-rotor type pumps the critical clearances are between the lobes of the centre rotor and convex faces of the outer rotor, between the outer rotor and the pump body, and between both rotors and the end cover plate.
7. The rotor lobe clearances may be checked as shown in Fig.1.6. The clearances should not exceed .006 in. (.152 mm). The clearance between the outer rotor and pump body should not exceed .010 inch (.254 mm) as shown in Fig.1.7.
8. The endfloat clearance can be measured by placing a steel straight edge across the end of the pump and measuring the gap between the rotors and the straight edge as shown in Fig.1.4. The gap on either rotor should not exceed .005 inch (.127 mm).
9. If the only excessive clearances are endfloat it is possible to reduce them by removing the rotors from the pump body and lapping away the face of the body on a flat bed until the necessary clearances are obtained. It must be emphasised, however, that the face of the body must remain prefectly flat and square to the axis of the rotor spindle otherwise the clearances will not be equal and the end cover will not be a pressure tight fit to the body. It is worth trying, of course, if the pump is in need of renewal any way but unless done properly it could seriously jeopardise the rest of an overhaul. Any variations in the other clearances should be overcome with an exchange unit.
10 When reassembling the pump and refitting the end cover make sure that the interior is scrupulously clean and that the pressure relief valve parts are assembled in the correct positions as indicated in the exploded drawings.

29. Oil Filter - Removal & Replacement

The oil filter is a complete throwaway cartridge screwed into the left-hand side of the engine block (photo). Simply unscrew the old unit, clean the seating on the block, and screw the new one in, taking care not to cross the thread. Continue until the sealing ring just touches the block face. Then tighten one half turn. Always run the engine and check for signs of leaks after installation.

30. Engine Components - Examination for Wear

When the engine has been stripped down and all parts properly cleaned decisions have to be made as to what needs renewal and the following sections tell the examiner what to look for. In any border line case it is always best to decide in favour of a new part. Even if a part may still be serviceable its life will have been reduced by wear and the degree of trouble needed to replace it in the future must be taken into consideration. However, these things are relative and it depends on whether a quick 'survival' job is being done or whether the car as a whole is being regarded as having many thousands of miles of useful and economical life remaining.

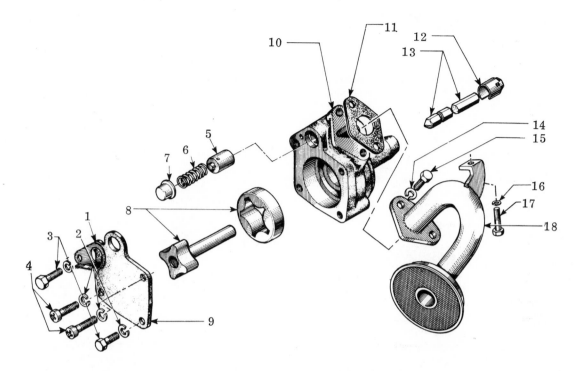

Fig.1.5. EXPLODED VIEW OF THE OIL PUMP ASSEMBLY

1	Baffle plate	6	Spring	11	Gasket	16 Washer
2	Spring washers	7	Spring seat	12	Clip	17 Bolt
3	Mounting bolts	8	Rotor assembly	13	Drive shaft	18 Strainer
4	Set screws	9	End plate	14	Washer	
5	Relief valve plunger	10	Body	15	Bolt	

Fig.1.6. CHECKING THE OIL PUMP INNER ROTOR TO OUTER ROTOR CLEARANCE (Section 28)

Fig.1.7. CHECKING THE OIL PUMP OUTER ROTOR TO BODY CLEARANCE (Section 28)

31. Crankshaft - Examination & Renovation

1. Look at the three main bearing journals and the four crankpins and if there are any scratches or score marks then the shaft will need regrinding. Such conditions will nearly always be accompanied by similar deterioration in the matching bearing shells.
2. Each bearing journal should also be round and can be checked with a micrometer or calliper gauge around the periphery at several points. If there is more than .001 inch of ovality regrinding is necessary.
3. A main Ford agent or motor engineering specialist will be able to decide to what extent regrinding is necessary and also supply the special under-size shell bearings to match whatever may need grinding off the journals.
4. Before taking the crankshaft for regrinding check also the cylinder bores and pistons as it may be more convenient to have the engineering operations performed at the same time by the same engineer.

32. Crankshaft (Main) Bearings & Big End (Connecting Rod) Bearings- Examination & Renovation

1. With careful servicing and regular oil and filter changes bearings will last for a very long time but they can still fail for unforseen reaons. With big end bearings the indications are regular rhythmic loud knocking from the crankcase, the frequency depending on engine speed. It is particularly noticeable when the engine is under load. This symptom is accompanied by a fall in oil pressure although this is not normally noticeable unless an oil pressure gauge is fitted. Main bearing failure is usually indicated by serious vibration, particularly at higher engine revolutions, accompanied by a more significant drop in oil pressure and a 'rumbling' noise.
2. Bearing shells in good condition have bearing surfaces with a smooth, even, matt silver/grey colour all over. Worn bearings will show patches of a different colour where the bearing metal has worn away and exposed the underlay. Damaged bearings will be pitted or scored. It is nearly always well worthwhile fitting new shells as their cost is relatively low. If the crankshaft is in good condition it is merely a question of obtaining another set of standard size. A reground crankshaft will need new bearing shells as a matter of course.

33. Cylinder Bores - Examination & Renovation

1. A new cylinder is perfectly round and the walls parallel throughout its length. The action of the piston tends to wear the walls at right angles to the gudgeon pin due to side thrust. This wear takes place principally on that section of the cylinder swept by the piston rings.
2. It is possible to get an indication of bore wear by removing the cylinder heads with the engine still in the car. With the piston down in the bore first signs of wear can be seen and felt just below the top of the bore where the top piston ring reaches and there will be a noticeable lip. If there is no lip it is fairly reasonable to expect that bore wear is low and any lack of compression or excessive oil consumption is due to worn or broken piston rings or pistons (see next section).
3. If it is possible to obtain a bore measuring micrometer measure the bore in the thrust plane below the lip and again at the bottom of the cylinder in the same plane. If the difference is more than .003 in. then a rebore is necessary. Similarly, a difference of .003 inch or more across the bore diameter is a sign of ovality calling for a rebore.
4. Any bore which is significantly scratched or scored will need reboring. This symptom usually indicates that the piston or rings are damaged also in that cylinder. In the event of only one cylinder being in need of reboring it will still be necessary for all four to be

bored and fitted with new oversize pistons and rings. Your Ford agent or local motor engineering specialist will be able to rebore and obtain the necessary matched pistons. If the crankshaft is undergoing regrinding also it is a good idea to let the same firm renovate and reassemble the crankshaft and pistons to the block. A reputable firm normally gives a guarantee for such work. In cases where engines have been rebored already to their maximum new cylinder liners are available which may be fitted. In such cases the same reboring processes have to be followed and the services of a specialist engineering firm are required.

34. Pistons and Piston Rings - Examination & Renovation

1. Worn pistons and rings can usually be diagnosed when the symptoms of excessive oil consumption and low compression occur and are sometimes, though not always, associated with worn cylinder bores. Compression testers that fit into the sparking plug holes are available and these can indicate where low compression is occuring. Wear usually accelerates the more it is left so when the symptoms occur early action can possibly save the expense of a rebore.
2. Another symptom of piston wear is piston slap - a knocking noise from the crankcase not to be confused with big end bearing failure. It can be heard clearly at low engine speed when there is no load (idling for example) and the engine is cold, and is much less audible when the engine speed increases. Piston wear usually occurs in the skirt or lower end of the piston and is indicated by vertical streaks in the worn area which is always on the thrust side. It can also be seen where the skirt thickness is different.
3. Piston ring wear can be checked by first removing the rings from the pistons as described in Section 21. Then place the rings in the cylinder bores from the top, pushing them down about 1½ inches with the head of a piston (from which the rings have been removed) so that they rest square in the cylinder. Then measure the gap at the ends of the ring with a feeler gauge. If it exceeds .020 inch for the two top compression rings, or .015 inch for the oil control ring then they need renewal.
4. The grooves in which the rings locate in the piston can also become enlarged in use. The clearance between ring and piston, in the groove, should not exceed .004 inch for the top two compression rings and .003 inch for the lower oil control ring.
5. However, it is rare that a piston is only worn in the ring grooves and the need to replace them for this fault alone is hardly ever encountered. Wherever pistons are renewed the weight of the four piston/connecting rod assemblies should be kept within the limit variation of 8 gms. to maintain engine balance.

35. Connecting Rods & Gudgeon Pins - Examination & Renovation

1. Gudgeon pins are a shrink fit into the connecting rods. Neither of these would normally need replacement unless the pistons were being changed, in which case the new pistons would automatically be supplied with new gudgeon pins.
2. Connecting rods are not subject to wear but in extreme circumstances such as engine seizure they could be distorted. Such conditions may be visually apparent but where doubt exists they should be changed. The bearing caps should also be examined for indications of filing down which may have been attempted in the mistaken idea that bearing slackness could be remedied in this way. If there are such signs then the connecting rods should be replaced.

36. Camshaft & Camshaft Bearings - Examination & Renovation

1. The camshaft bearing bushes should be examined for signs of scoring and pitting. If they need renewal they will have to be dealt

Fig.1.9. CHECKING THE RING TO GROOVE CLEARANCE
(Section 34)

Fig.1.8. CHECKING A COMPRESSION RING GAP (Section 34)

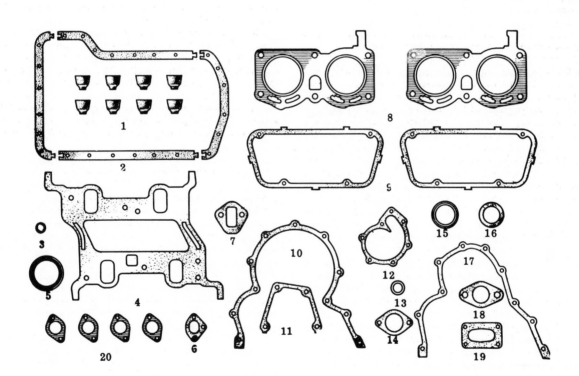

Fig 1:10 COMPLETE ENGINE GASKET SET

1 Valve stem seals	6 Water pump to block	11 Crankshaft oil seal retainer	16 Crankshaft front bearing
2 Sump	7 Fuel pump to front cover	12 Water pump body	17 Front plate to block
3 Dipstick	8 Cylinder heads	13 Sump drain plug	18 Oil pump to inlet tube
4 Inlet manifold	9 Rocker covers	14 Thermostat elbow	19 Carburettor to manifold
5 Crankshaft rear oil seal	10 Front cover to engine	15 Balance shaft rear bearing	20 Exhaust manifolds

with professionally as although it may be relatively easy to remove the old bushes, the correct fitting of new ones requires special tools. If they are not fitted evenly and square from the very start they can be distorted thus causing localised wear in a very short time. See your Ford dealer or local engineering specialist for this work.

2. The camshaft itself may show signs of wear on the bearing journals, cam lobes or the skew gear. The main decision to take is what degree of wear justifies replacement, which is costly: Any signs or scoring or damage to the bearing journals must be rectified and as undersize bearing bushes are not supplied the journals cannot be reground. Renewal of the whole camshaft is the only solution. Similarly, excessive wear on the skew gear which can be seen where the distributor driveshaft teeth mesh will mean renewal of the whole camshaft.

3. The cam lobes themselves may show signs of ridging or pitting on the high points. If the ridging is light then it may be possible to smooth it out with fine emery. The cam lobes, however, are surface hardened and once this is penetrated wear will be very rapid thereafter. The cams are also offset and tapered to cause the tappets to rotate - thus ensuring that wear is even - so do not mistake this condition for wear.

37. Tappets - Examination & Renovation

1. The faces of the tappets which bear on the camshaft should show no signs of pitting, scoring or other forms of wear. They should also not be a loose fit in their housing. Wear is only normally encountered at very high mileages or in cases of neglected engine lubrication. Renew if necessary.

38. Valves & Valve Seats - Examination & Renovation

1. With the valves removed from the cylinder heads examine the heads for signs of cracking, burning away and pitting of the edge where it seats in the port. The seats of the valves in the cylinder head should also be examined for the same signs. Usually it is the valve that deteriorates first but if a bad valve is not rectified the seat will suffer and this is more difficult to repair.

2. The inlet valve heads are coated with diffused aluminium to increase their resistance to oxidisation and to give a hard wear resistant surface on the valve seat area. These valves should in no circumstances be ground as this will remove the aluminium coating: If the valves are worn or pitted they should be replaced with a new set. The inlet valve seats can however, be lapped with an old or dummy valve in the usual way as described below.

3. As far as the exhaust valves are concerned; provided there are no obvious signs of serious pitting the valve should be ground with its seat. This may be done by placing a smear of carborundum paste on the edge of the valve and using a suction type valve holder grinding the valve in situ. This is done with a semi-rotary action, twisting the handle of the valve holder between the hands and lifting it occasionally to redistribute the paste. Use a coarse paste to start with and finish with a fine paste. As soon as a matt grey unbroken line appears on both the valve and the seat the valve is 'ground in'. All traces of carbon should also be cleaned from the head and the neck of the valve stem. A wire brush mounted in a power drill is a quick and effective way of doing this.

4. If an exhaust valve requires renewal it should be ground into the seat in the same way as an old valve.

5. Another form of valve wear can occur on the stem where it runs in the guide in the cylinder head. This can be detected by trying to rock the valve from side to side. If there is any movement at all it is an indication that the valve stem or guide is worn. Check the stem first with a micrometer at points all along and around its length and if they are not within the specified size new valves will probably solve the problem. If the guides are worn, however, they will need reboring for oversize valves or for fitting fuide inserts. The valve seats will also need recutting to ensure they are concentric

with the stems. This work should be given to your Ford dealer or local engineering works.

6. When valve seats are badly burnt or pitted, requiring replacement, inserts may be fitted - or replaced if already fitted once before - and once again this is a specialist task to be carried out by a suitable engineering firm.

7. When all valve grinding is completed it is essential that every trace of grinding paste is removed from the valves and ports in the cylinder head. This should be done with thorough washing in petrol or paraffin and blowing out with a jet of air. If particles of carborundum should work their way into the engine they would cause havoc with bearings or cylinder walls.

39. Timing Gears - Examination & Renovation

1. Any wear which takes place in the timing mechanism will be on the teeth of the fibre gear which is driven from the crankshaft gear. The backlash, which can be measured with a feeler gauge between the gear teeth, should not exceed .004 inch. On V4 engines the balance shaft gear backlash should be the same but this is not so critical. If the crankshaft gear to camshaft gear backlash is excessive the fibre gear wheel should be renewed.

40. Flywheel Ring Gear - Examination & Renovation

1. If the ring gear is badly worn or has missing teeth it should be renewed. The old ring can be removed from the flywheel by cutting a notch between two teeth with a hacksaw and then splitting it with a cold chisel.

2. To fit a new ring gear requires heating the ring to 400°F (204°C). This can be done by polishing four equally spaced sections of the gear, laying it on a suitable heat resistant surface (such as fire bricks) and heating it evenly with a blow lamp or torch until the polished areas turn a light yellow tint. Do not overheat or the hard wearing properties will be lost. The gear has a chamfered inner edge which should go against the shoulder when put on the flywheel. When hot enough place the gear in position quickly, tapping it home if necessary and let it cool naturally without quenching in any way.

41. Cylinder Heads & Piston Crowns - Decarbonisation

1. When cylinder heads are removed either in the course of an overhaul or for inspection of bores or valve condition when the engine is in the car it is normal to remove all carbon deposits from the piston crowns and heads.

2. This is best done with a cup shaped wire brush and an electric drill and is fairly straightforward when the engine is dismantled and the pistons removed. Sometimes hard spots of carbon are not easily removed except by a scraper. When cleaning the pistons with a scraper take care not to damage the surface of the piston in any way.

3. When the engine is in the car certain precautions must be taken when decarbonising the piston crowns in order to prevent dislodged pieces of carbon falling into the interior of the engine which could cause damage to cylinder bores, pistons and rings - or if allowed into the water passages - damage to the water pump. Turn the engine, therefore, so that the piston being worked on is at the top of its stroke and then mask off the adjacent cylinder bore and all surrounding water jacket orifices with paper and adhesive tape. Press grease into the gap all round the piston to keep carbon particles out and then scrape all carbon away by hand carefully. Do not use a power drill and wire brush when the engine is in the car as it will be virtually impossible to keep all the carbon dust clear of the engine. When completed carefully clear out the grease round the rim of the piston with a matchstick or something similar - bringing any carbon particles with it. Repeat the process on the other three piston crowns. It is not recommended that a ring of carbon is left

Fig.1.11. Correct alignment on the timing marks on the balance shaft, camshaft and crankshaft gear wheel (Section 45.21)

Fig.1.12. Correct sequence for tightening the V4 cylinder head bolts (Section 47.12)

Fig.1.13. Correct sequence for tightening the V4 inlet manifold bolts (Section 47.20)

Fig.1.14. Correct sequence for tightening the V6 cylinder head bolts (Section 47.20 and 53.5)

Fig.1.15. (left) Correct sequence for tightening the V6 inlet manifold bolts (Section 47.12 and 53.5)

round the edge of the piston on the theory that it will aid oil consumption. This was valid in the earlier days of long stroke low revving engines but modern engines, fuels and lubricants cause less carbon deposits any way and any left behind tends merely to cause hot-spots.

42. Rocker Gear - Examination & Renovation

1. The studs on which the rocker arms pivot are a press fit into the head and by placing a straight edge across the top of all four it can be seen if any have worked loose. If any have it will be necessary to have the hole bored out and an oversize stud fitted. This is a specialist task. The threads on the studs should be in good condition to ensure that the self-locking unit grips sufficiently tightly to prevent it working loose and altering the valve clearance.

2. If the torque required to turn any adjusting unit is less than 3 lbs/ft. on oiled threads the units should be replaced. If the torque is still inadequate it is possible to fit a second nut on the stud to lock the adjustment.

3. The rocker arms and fulcrum seats are matched and if either should show signs of ridging or pitting on the bearing surfaces both should be renewed.

43. Engine Reassembly - General

1. All components of the engine must be cleaned of oil sludge and old gaskets and the working area should also be cleared and clean. In addition to the normal range of good quality socket spanners and general tools which are essential, the following must be available before reassembly begins:—
1) Complete set of new gaskets
2) Supply of clean rags.
3) Clean oil can full of clean engine oil.
4) Torque spanner.
5) All new spare parts as necessary.

44. Engine Reassembly - Balance Shaft (V4) Crankshaft & Oil Pump

1. Carefully replace the balance shaft into its bearing bushes, and avoid hitting the bushes with any sharp edges (photo), (V4 only).

2. Refit the balance shaft thrust plate so that the oil hole in the block comes in the centre of the slot in the plate, both of which are arrowed (photo A). Replace and tighten the bolts (photo B).

3. Replace the camshaft carefully into the block, taking care not to let any of the cam lobes damage the bearing bushes (photo).

4. Refit the camshaft thrust plate and secure it with the two cross-head sunk screws (photo). These screws must be tightened firmly with an impact screwdriver.

5. Select the halves of the three main bearing shells which have the oil hole and grooves and place them in position in the crankcase (photo). The notches on the ends of the shells should locate in the cut-outs in the housings. It is essential that the two surfaces coming together are scrupulously clean.

6. Lubricate the bearings generously with clean engine oil (photo).

7. Make sure that the crankshaft is scrupulously clean and lower it carefully into place on the bearings with the gearwheel towards the front of the engine (photo).

8. Take the two halves of the thrust washers which do not have tags on and very carefully slide them into position round the side of the centre main bearing. The grooves in the washers should face outwards from the bearing (photo).

9. The end of the top half of the thrust washer can easily be pushed finally into position with a finger (photo).

10 Fit the plain halves of the main bearing shells into the caps with the notches in the shells corresponding with the grooves in the caps (photo).

11 The centre bearing cap has machined recesses on each side to accept the lower halves of the thrust washers which have the tags on them to prevent rotation (photo).

12 Hold the thrust washers in place while fitting the centre bearing cap (photo) and check that the grooves on the washer are facing away from the cap.

13 When the crankshaft and centre bearing cap is in position the endfloat may be checked by pushing the crankshaft as far as it will go in either direction and checking the gap between the thrust wahser and the crankshaft web with a feeler gauge (photo). The gap should be between .003 and .011 inch (.08 to .28 mm).

14 The front and rear main bearing caps do not automatically line up for bolting down and it may be necessary to tap them with a hammer handle or other soft weight to enable the bolts to pick up the threads (photo).

15 Make sure that the bolts are clean, and tighten them all down evenly to a torque of 55 to 60 lbs/ft. (photo) with a torque spanner.

16 Although not absolutely necessary it is best to renew the rear crankshaft oil seal - it is provided in the gasket set anyhow. The old one can be removed from the seal carrier by carefully but firmly punching it out (photo).

17 Place the new seal squarely in position with the open lip facing away from the shoulder in the carrier bore (photo).

18 The seal can be tapped home squarely with a soft headed mallet (photo). It is important to make sure that the seal is driven in square from the very start, otherwise it will buckle; so if one side tends to go in too far to start with pull it out and start afresh until it is squarely and firmly 'started' all round.

19 Lubricate the crankshaft flange well so that the seal will not run on a dry surface to start with and heat up (photo).

20 Fit the new retainer plate gasket (photo) and replace the plate.

21 Tighten the bolts to 11—13 lbs/ft. (photo).

22 Make sure the hexagonal driveshaft is located in the oil pump and replace the pump, tightening the two mounting bolts evenly to 12—15 lbs/ft. torque (photo).

45. Engine Reassembly - Pistons, Piston Rings, Connecting Rods, Big End Bearings, End Plates, Timing Gear & Front Cover

1. The subsequent paragraphs on assembly assume that all the checks described in Section 44 have been carried out.

2. The assembly of new pistons to connecting rods should have been carried out as recommended in Sections 34 and 35. The new pistons should be supplied with rings already fitted.

3. If new rings are being fitted to existing pistons the following procedure should be followed. Having removed the old rings make sure that each ring groove in the piston is completely cleaned of carbon deposits. This is done most easily by breaking one of the old rings and using the sharp end as a scraper. Be careful not to remove any metal from the groove by mistake!

4. The new piston rings - three for each piston - must first be checked in the cylinder bores as described in Section 34:3 and 4. It is assumed that the gap at the ends of the rings will not be too great. However, it is equally important that the gaps are not too small - otherwise the ends could meet when normal operating temperatures are reached and the rings would then break.

5. The minimum gap for all three rings is .010 in. (.25 mm). If the gap is too small, one end of the ring must be filed to increase the gap. To do this the ring should be gripped in a vice between two thin pieces of soft metal in such a way that only the end to be filed is gripped and so that it only protrudes above the jaws of the vice a very small distance. This will eliminate the possibility of bending and breaking the ring while filing the end. Use a thin, fine file and proceed in easy stages - checking the gap by replacing the ring in the bore until the necessary minimum gap is obtained. This must be done with every ring - checking each one in the bore to which it will eventually be fitted. To avoid mistakes it is best to complete one set of rings at a time and replace the piston in the cylinder bore proceeding to the next.

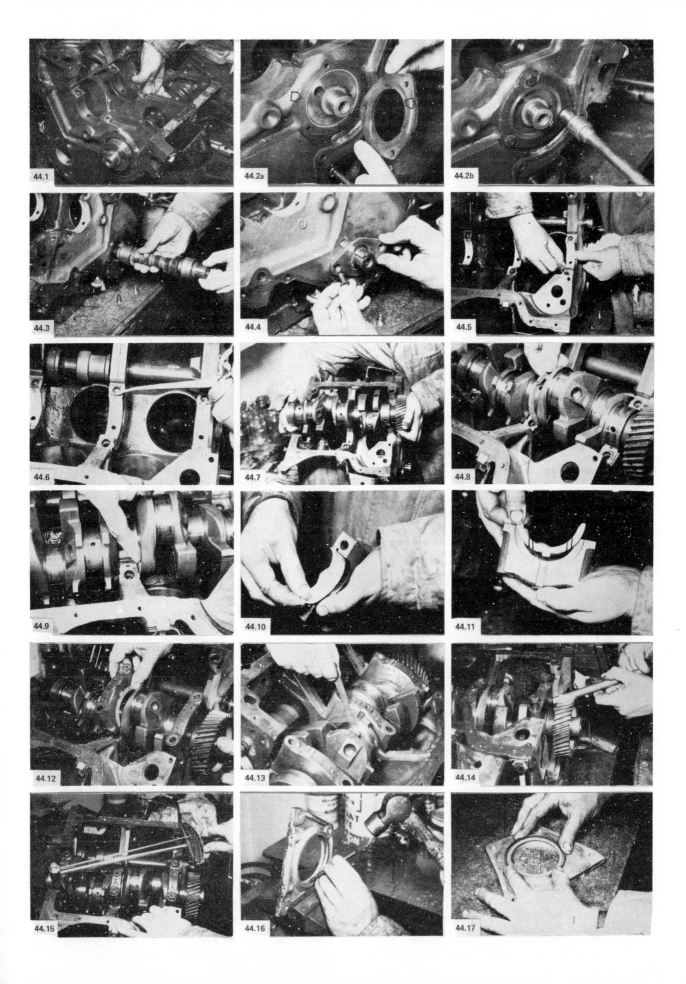

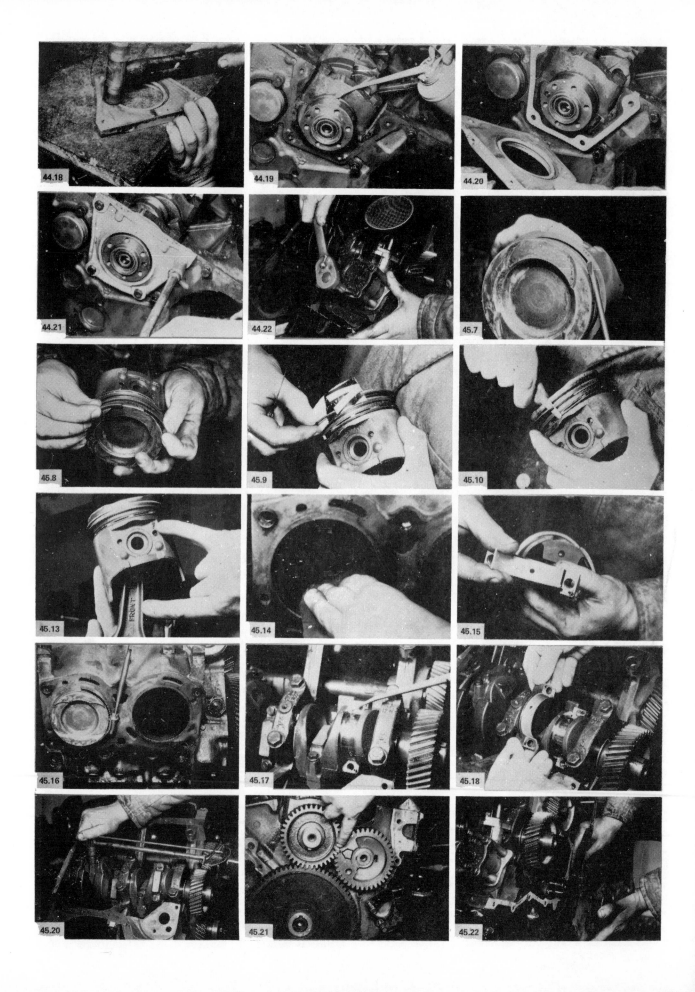

44.18

44.19

44.20

44.21

44.22

45.7

45.8

45.9

45.10

45.13

45.14

45.15

45.16

45.17

45.18

45.20

45.21

45.22

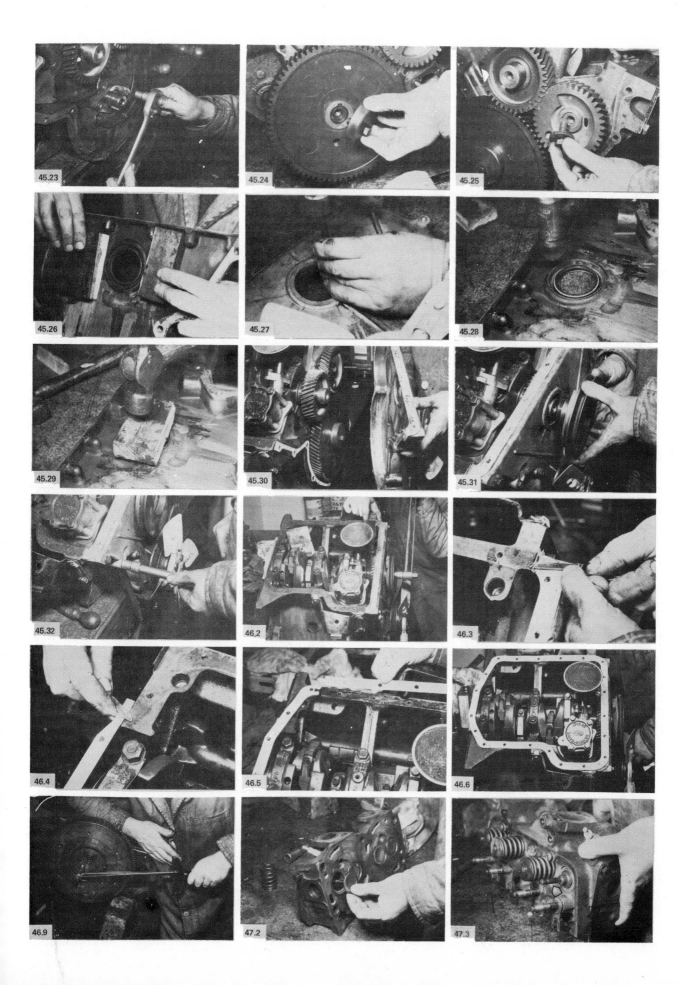

6. To replace the rings on to the pistons calls for patience and care if breakages are to be avoided. The three rings for each piston must all be fitted over the crown so obviously the first one to go on is the slotted oil control ring. Hold the ring over the top of the piston and spread the ends just enough to get it around the circumference. Then, with the fingers, ease it down, keeping it parallel to the ring grooves by 'walking' the ring ends alternately down the piston. Being wider than the compression rings no difficulty should be encountered in getting it over the first two grooves in the piston.

7. The lower compression ring, which goes on next, must only be fitted one way up. It is marked 'TOP' to indicate its upper face (photo).

8. Start fitting this ring by spreading the ends to get it located over the top of the piston (photo).

9. The lower compression ring has to be guided over the top ring groove and this can be done by using a suitably cut piece of tin which can be placed so as to cover the top groove under the ends of the ring (photo).

10 Alternatively, a feeler blade may be slid around under the ring to guide it into its groove (photo).

11 The top ring may be fitted either way up as it is barrel faced.

12 With the rings fitted the piston/connecting rod assembly is ready for replacement in the cylinder.

13 Each connecting rod and bearing cap should have been marked on removal (Section 20) but in any case the cylinder number is etched lightly on the end of the cap and connecting rod alongside. The piston and connecting rod are also marked to show which side faces the front of the engine (photo).

14 Start with No.1 cylinder and remove the existing oil 'glaze' from the bore by rubbing it down with very fine emery. This will break down the hardened skin and permit the new piston rings to bed down more quickly (photo).

15 Fit a new shell bearing half into the connecting rod of No.1 piston so that the notch in the bearing shell locates in the groove in the connecting rod (photo).

16 Place the piston in the cylinder bore the correct way round until the oil control ring abuts the face of the block. Then, using a large hose clip as a compressor (photo) contract each ring in turn and tap the piston into the cylinder. Take great care to be sure that the ring is not trapped on the top edge of the cylinder bore and when tapping the piston in do not use any force. If this is not done the rings could easily be broken.

17 When the piston has been fully located in the bore push it down so that the end of the connecting rod seats on the journal on the crankshaft. Make sure the journal is well lubricated with engine oil (photo).

18 Maintaining absolute cleanliness all the time fit the other shell bearing half into the cap, once again with the notches in the bearing and cap lined up. Lubricate it with engine oil and fit it onto the connecting rod so that the holes in the cap fit to the dowels in the connecting rod (photo).

19 Replace all pistons and connecting rods in a similar manner and do not make any mistakes locating the correct Number piston in the correct bore, Nos.1 and 2 cylinders are front and rear respectively on the right-hand bank and Nos.3 and 4 front and rear on the left-hand bank. However, due to the Vee formation of the engine the big end journals on the crankshaft starting at the front run 1,3,2,4. This is different again from the firing order so make sure you have it all clear in your mind to start with!

20 When all caps are correctly fitted tighten down the bolts to the correct torque of 38—43 lbs/ft. (photo).

21 The timing gears are easily fitted but care must be taken to ensure that the marks line up properly. Both the balance shaft (V4 only) and camshaft gears are keyed on to their respective shafts. The crankshaft gear has two countersunk dimples machined in its periphery. Both these must match up simultaneously with the single dimple in each of the other two gears. The photograph shows how this should be. An arrow points to the crankshaft/camshaft marks and the finger to the crankshaft/balance shaft marks (photo).

22 Before replacing the camshaft timing gear the front engine plate

must be fitted back. Select the new gasket and coat the clean face of the block with suitable sealing compound (Hermetite, Wellseal) and stick the gasket to it in position. Then offer up the cover plate (photo).

23 Bolt the cover plate up tight to the block, not forgetting to fit the support plate behind the three centre bolts (photo).

24 Fit the camshaft gear and balance shaft gears so that the timing marks line up. Replace the camshaft gear locking bolt together with the eccentirc boss that drives the fuel pump. Tighten the bolt to 40—45 lbs/ft. There is no special position for the boss, although it was marked by a pencil on the fibre gear in this photo before removal (photo).

25 Replace and tighten the bolt and washer (photo) holding the balance shaft gear to 40—45 lbs/ft.

26 If the crankshaft pulley wheel oil seal is being replaced in the front cover it will be necessary to take care in driving out the old one as the cover is a light alloy casting which will not stand rough treatment. As the old seal must be driven out from the front it is essential to find two pieces of wood thicker than the depth of the cover so that the immediate area near the seal ring may be supported (photo).

27 With the cover firmly supported inside, it can be laid on the bench and the old seal driven out with a punch (photo).

28 Turn the cover over and carefully tap in the new seal evenly with the inner lip facing away from the shoulder in the bore (photo).

29 Tap the seal home finally with a block of wood (photo).

30 Select the front cover gasket and using a suitable sealing compound position it on the engine front plate and offer up the cover (photo).

31 Place the front cover bolts in position and screw them up loosely. Then fit the crankshaft pulley wheel onto the keyway of the crankshaft (photo). See that the boss of the pulley is lubricated where the oil seal runs.

32 The replacement of the crankshaft pulley, before tightening the cover bolts, centralises the seal to the pulley. The bolts holding the cover may then be tightened to 11—13 lbs/ft. (photo).

46. Engine Reassembly - Rear Plate, Crankshaft Pulley Wheel, Sump & Flywheel

1. If the engine rear plate has been removed it should now be replaced. Make sure that both metal faces are quite clean before refitting. No gasket is used.

2. Replace the bolt and washer which locate the crankshaft pulley wheel, block the crankshaft with a piece of wood against the side of the crankcase and tighten the bolt to a torque of 40—45 lbs/ft. (photo).

3. Trim the projecting pieces of the front cover and backplate gaskets at the sump face of the block and front cover (photo).

4. Trim the projecting edge of the rear oil seal carrier on the sump face at the rear of the crankcase (photo).

5. Clean all traces of old gasket which may remain from the sump joint faces and cover the faces of both the crankcase and sump with sealing compound. The sump gasket is in four sections which dovetail together and these should be carefully positioned and the joints interlocked (photo).

6. The engine is then ready for the sump to be replaced (photo).

7. Clean the interior of the sump thoroughly, apply sealer to the joint edge and place it in position.

8. Replace all the sump bolts and tighten them evenly to a final torque of 6—8 lbs/ft.

9. The flywheel may now be replaced. Make sure that the mating flanges are clean and free from burrs and line up the bolt holes correctly. They are so positioned that they will only line up in one position. Do not hammer the flywheel into position if it should be difficult to get it fully onto the flange. Support it squarely and replace the bolts, tightening them evenly so as to draw the flywheel squarely onto its seat. There are no washers and the bolts should be tightened evenly and progressively to a final torque of 50—55 lbs/ft.

47. Engine Reassembly - Valve Gear, Cylinder Heads, Inlet & Exhaust Manifolds

1. When the cylinder heads have been decarbonised and the valves ground in as described in Sections 38 and 41 the cylinder heads may be reassembled. If the valves have been removed as described in Section 12 there will be no confusion as to which valve belongs in which position.

2. Make sure all traces of carbon and grinding paste have been removed, lubricate the valve stem with engine oil and place it in the appropriate guide (photo).

3. It will then protrude through the top of the cylinder head (photo).

4. Fit a new seal cup over the valve stem (photo).

5. Place the valve spring over the valve stem with the close coils of the spring nearest the cylinder head (photo).

6. Fit the circular spring collar over the spring with the protruding centre boss of the collar downwards (photo).

7. Using a proper valve spring compressor tool, compress the spring down the valve stem sufficiently far to enable the two halves of the split collar (collets) to be fitted into the groove in the valve stem (photo). If necessary the collets should be smeared with grease to keep them in position. The spring compressor may then be released. Watch to ensure that the collets stay together in position as the spring collar comes past them. If the collar is a little off centre it may force one collet out of its groove in which case the spring must be re-compressed and the collet repositioned. When the compressor is finally released tap the head of the valve stem with a soft mallet to make sure the valve assembly is securely held in position.

8. Stand the engine the right way up on the bench and replace the tappets if they have been removed from the block. If these have been kept in order on removal, as suggested, it will be a simple matter to replace them.

9. The two cylinder heads are identical so if they were marked left and right on removal they can be replaced on the same bank. If they have been muddled up no real harm will result but the pushrods will not be matched to their correct rocker arms. As these normally 'run in' together excessive wear could occur until such time as the two unfamiliar surfaces have bedded in again.

10 Select a new cylinder head gasket and place it in position on the block on one bank. These gaskets are identical and can fit either bank but they can only go on the bank one way - which is obvious from the way the bolt holes and cooling jacket holes line up (photo).

11 Locate the gasket over the protruding spigots in the block and then place the cylinder head in position (photo).

12 Make sure the cylinder head bolts are clean and lightly oiled and replace them. Nip them all down lightly and then tighten them in the sequence shown in Fig.1.12. The bolts should be tightened down to progressive torque loadings - all to 50 lbs/ft, then all to 60 lbs/ft, and finally to the specified requirement of 65—70 lbs/ft. (photo).

13 Now fit the pushrods into position, making sure that they are replaced the same way up as they came out and according to the original valve position. This will not be difficult if they have been kept in order as described in Sections 10 and 11. The pushrods are located at their upper ends in brackets bolted to the head (photo).

14 Locate the appropriate rocker arm over each stud so that the recessed end locates over the pushrod. Then place the fulcrum seat over the stud followed by the self-locking nut (photo).

15 When both heads are replaced and fully tightened down the inlet manifold may be replaced. In view of the large area to be sealed for both air and water it is a safety measure - if not essential - to use a jointing compound such as 'Wellseal' in addition to the gasket (photo) on the mating surfaces.

16 Place the inlet manifold gasket in position in the Vee so that the single square hole (arrowed) is on the left-hand cylinder head (photo). The gasket is obviously incorrect if put on any other way but this is a positive guide.

17 Apply jointing compound to the mating faces of the inlet manifold. Note the square port (arrowed) which matches the gasket hole and port in the left-hand cylinder head (photo).

18 Place the manifold in position with the thermostat housing to the front (photo).

19 Replace the six manifold securing bolts, ensuring that the gasket is lined up to permit them to pick up the threads in the cylinder heads, and screw them up lightly (photo).

20 With a torque wrench (photo) tighten the bolts down evenly in the sequence shown in Fig.1.13 to 13—16 lbs/ft. This tightening should be done in stages - all being tightened to 5 lbs/ft. then to 10 lbs/ft. before finally reaching the specified figure. Any uneven or excessive tightening may crack the manifold casting so take care.

48. Valve to Rocker Clearances - Adjustment

1. The valve stem to rocker clearance, which is in effect the mechanical free play between the camshaft and the end of the valve stem, is important to the correct operation and performance of the engine. If the clearance is too great the valve opening is reduced with consequent reduction in gas flow - and is also very noisy. If the clearance is too little the valve could open too much with the danger of it hitting the crown of the piston. The clearance is checked when the tappet is on the heel of the cam (opposite the highest point) and the valve therefore closed. This position coincides with certain other valves being fully open with their tappets on the high point of the cam. This can be seen easily when the valve spring is fully compressed.

Fig.1.16. EXPLODED VIEW OF THE V6 STATIC ENGINE COMPONENTS

1	Emssion control valve assembly	29	Gasket
2	Cable clip	30	Washer
3	Rocker cover screw	31	Bolt
4	Washer	32	Bolt
5	Cylinder head bolt	33	Washer
6	End plate bolt	34	Petrol pump stud
7	Washer	35	Front engine plate
8	End plate	36	Sypport plate
9	Core plug	37	Plug
10	Core plug	38	Plug
11	Dowel	39	Washer
12	Core plug	40	Cylinder block
13	Gasket	41	Seal
14	Dowel	42	Dipstick
15	Sump gasket	43	Stud
16	Bolt	44	Seal
17	Washers	45	Oil filter
18	Bolt	46	Gasket
19	Sump	47	Plug
20	Plug	48	Cylinder liner
21	Washer	49	Core plug
22	Sump drain plug	50	Cylinder head
23	Gasket	51	Valve guide bush
24	Oil seal	52	Sealing plug
25	Bolt	53	Gasket
26	Washer	54	Rocker cover
27	Timing cover	55	Grommet
28	Dipstick tube		

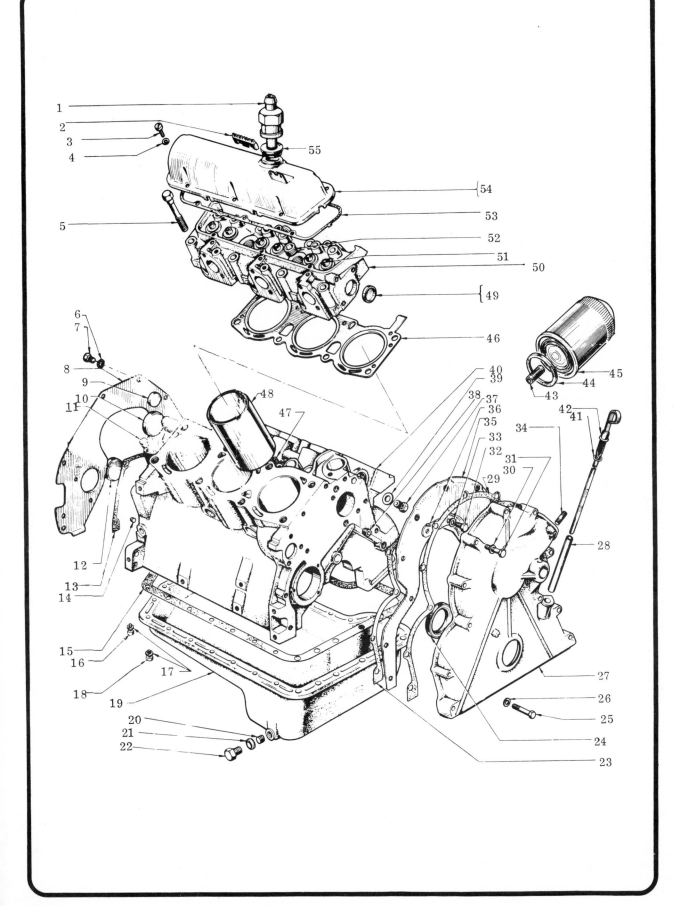

2. The table below shows the relationship between the fully open valves and the closed valves which are to be checked. The diagram shows the valve numbering - Nos. 1—4 front to rear on the right-hand bank and Nos. 5—8 to the rear on the left-hand bank.

Valves open (together)	Adjust
Nos. 1 and 4	Nos.5 (Inlet) and 8 (Exhaust)
Nos. 2 and 6	Nos.3 (Exhaust) and 7 (Inlet)
Nos. 5 and 8	Nos.1 (Exhaust) and 4 (Inlet)
Nos. 3 and 7	Nos.2 (Inlet) and 6 (Exhaust)

Front of Engine

L.H. Bank	R.H.Bank
5	1
6	2
7	3
8	4

The clearances after reassembly should be set at .013 in. (.330 mm) for the inlet valves and .020 in. (.508 mm) for the exhaust valves for both a cold and a hot engine. After the engine has been brought up to its normal running temperature the clearances should be checked to make sure they are correct.

3. The actual adjustment procedure is straightforward. With the appropriate valve ready for checking place a feeler gauge of the required thickness (for exhaust or inlet valve) between the top of the valve stem and the rocker arm (photo). If it will not go the clearance is too small so slacken off the self-locking nut on the stud until the clearance is correct. If the clearance is too large the nut should be screwed down. The correct clearance is obtained when the feeler blade can be moved readily but a firm drag is felt.

4. It is a wise precaution to check each clearance measurement after the adjusting socket spanner has been removed from the nut. This is because the socket may possibly bind against the side of the rocker arm and tilt it, thus causing a false clearance measurement.

5. After the clearance adjustments are completed replace the rocker covers, each fitted with a new gasket (photo).

6. Tighten down the screws firmly and evenly (photo). NOTE: The rocker cover with the oil filler cap goes on the left-hand bank. Rocker clearances should NOT be checked with a feeler gauge while the engine is running. In certain circumstances the valve could be forced against the crown of the piston causing serious damage. If one rocker is noisy it is possible to identify which one by removing the rocker cover and pressing a finger on each rocker in turn. The noisy one will be quiet when pressed.

49. Engine Reassembly - Final Ancillary Components

1. The exhaust manifolds are best replaced before putting the engine back into the car as they provide very useful holds if the engine has to be manhandled at all. Select the new gaskets and fit them the correct way, as they are not symmetrical.

2. Replace each manifold and tighten the bolts evenly.

3. The ancillary engine components must be replaced and the method of doing this is detailed in the appropriate Chapters. Section 9 of this Chapter gives a full list of the items involved. When this has been done the engine is ready to be put back in the car.

50. Engine Replacement - Without Gearbox

1. The engine must be positioned suitably so that the sling used to remove it can be easily refitted and the lifting tackle hooked on. Position the engine the right way round in front of the car and then raise it so that it may be brought into position over the car or the car rolled into position underneath it.

2. The gearbox should be jacked up to its approximately normal position.

3. Lower the engine steadily into the engine compartment, keeping

all ancillary wires, pipes and cables well clear of the sides. It is best to have a second person guiding the engine while it is being lowered.

4. The tricky part is finally mating the engine to the gearbox, which involves locating the gearbox input shaft into the clutch housing and flywheel. Provided that the clutch friction plate has been centred correctly as described in Chapter 5, there should be little difficulty. Grease the splines of the gearbox input shaft first. It may be necessary to rock the engine from side to side in order to get the engine fully home. Under no circumstances let any strain be imparted onto the gearbox input shaft. This could occur if the shaft was not fully located and the engine was raised or lowered more than the amount required for very slight adjustment of position.

5. As soon as the engine is fully up to the gearbox bellhousing replace the bolts holding the two together.

6. Now finally lower the engine onto its mounting brackets at the front and replace and tighten down the nuts and washers.

7. Replace all electrical connections; the fuel lines and carburetter linkages, cooling system hoses and radiator in the reverse order to that described in Section 6.

8. Reconnect the clutch cable as described in Chapter 5.8, replace the exhaust pipes and reconnect them to the manifold extensions, replace the plate covering the lower half of the bellhousing and remove the supporting jack.

9. Fill the engine with fresh oil and replace the coolant.

Fig.1.17. EXPLODED VIEW OF THE V6 MOVING ENGINE COMPONENTS

1	Rocker stud	33	Main bearing shells-upper
2	Pushrod	34	Big end bolt
3	Bolt	35	Big end cap
4	Washer	36	Screw
5	Pushrod guide	37	Big end shells
6	Exhaust valve	38	Crankshaft thrust washers
7	Tappet	39	Camshaft bearing
8	Rear camshaft bearing	40	Bolt
9	Starter ring	41	Fuel pump driving cam
10	Flywheel	42	Camshaft gear
11	Bolt	43	Key
12	Camshaft	44	Spacer
13	Camshaft bearing	45	Camshaft thrust plate
14	Crankshaft oil seal	46	Front camshaft bearing
15	Oil seal retainer	47	Connecting rod
16	Gasket	48	Key
17	Washer	49	Gudgeon pin
18	Bolt	50	Piston
19	Main bearing caps	51	Oil control ring
20	Main bearing caps	52	Lower compression ring
21	Main bearing bolt	53	Upper compression ring
22	Crankshaft thrust washers	54	Valve seat insert - inlet
23	Main bearing caps	55	Inlet valve
24	Main bearing caps	56	Valve seat insert - exhaust
25	Main bearing shells - lower	57	Seal
26	Washer	58	Valve spring
27	Bolt	59	Valve collar
28	Crankshaft pulley	60	Collets
29	Crankshaft gear	61	Rocker arm
30	Oil seal	62	Pivot ball
31	Woodruff key	63	Adjusting nut
32	Crankshaft		

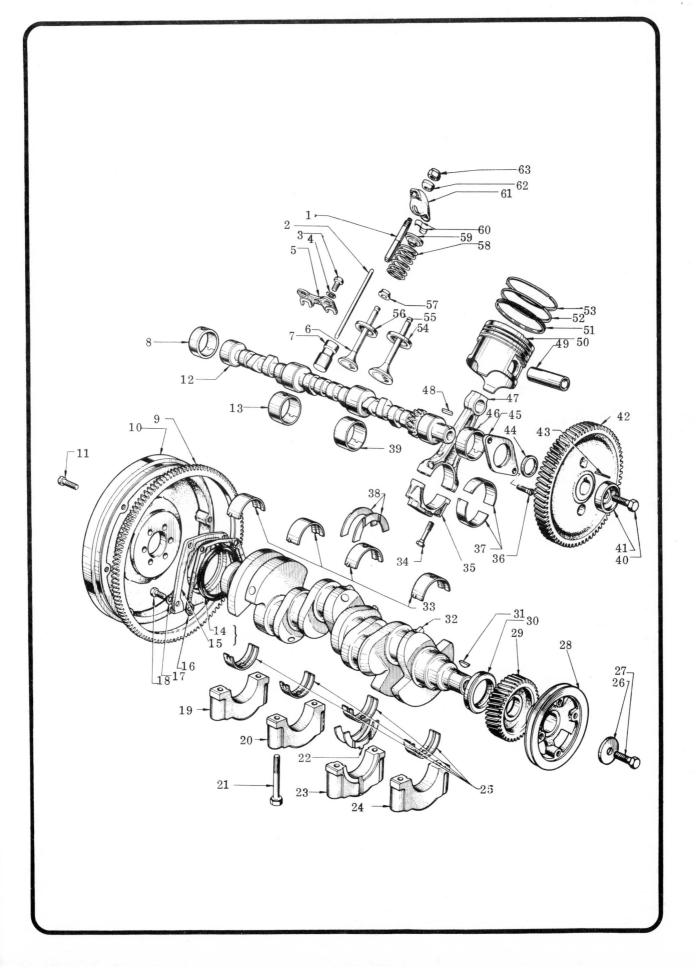

51. Engine Replacement - With Gearbox

1. The gearbox should be refitted to the engine, taking the same precautions as regards the input shaft as mentioned in Section 50.
2. The general principles of lifting the engine/gearbox assembly are the same as for the engine above but the gearbox will tilt everything to a much steeper angle as shown in the photos for Section 7. Replacement will certainly require the assistance of a second person.
3. Lift the gearbox end of the unit into the engine compartment (unless you are fortunate enough to have a hoist with a very high lift) and then lower and guide the unit down. One of the first things to be done is to reconnect the propeller shaft into the gearbox rear extension casing so someone should be ready to lift and guide the propeller shaft into position as soon as the gearbox is near enough. This cannot be done after the unit has been lowered beyond a certain position.
4. If a trolley jack is available this is the time to place it under the gearbox so that as the engine is lowered further the rear end can be supported and raised as necessary - at the same time being able to roll back as required. Without such a jack, support the rear in such a way that it can slide if possible. In any case the gearbox will have to be jacked and held up in position when the unit nears its final position.
5. Locate the front mounting brackets on the locating bolts as described in Section 50.
6. Refit the speedometer drive cable with the gearbox drive socket and refit the circlip and bolt. This MUST be done before the gearbox supporting crossmember is in place.
7. Jack up the rear of the gearbox and position the crossmember to the bodyframe. Then replace and tighten down the four retaining bolts and the centre bolt to the gearbox extension.
8. Replace the gearbox remote control change lever and housing as described in Chapter 6.
9. Reconnect the clutch cable and adjust as described in Chapter 5 and reconnect the reversing light wire. The final connections should then be made as described in Section 50 and in addition to the engine lubricant and coolant the gearbox should also be refilled with fresh oil.

52. Engine - Initial Start Up After Overhaul or Major Repair

1. Make sure that the battery is fully charged and that all lubricants, coolants and fuel are replenished.
2. If the fuel system has been dismantled it will require several revolutions of the engine on the starter motor to get the petrol up to the carburetter. An initial 'prime' of about 1/3 of a cupful of petrol poured down the choke of the carburetter will help the engine to fire quickly, thus relieving the load on the battery. Do not overdo this however, as flooding may result.
3. As soon as the engine fires and runs keep it going at a fast tickover only (no faster) and bring it up to normal working temperature.
4. As the engine warms up there will be odd smells and some smoke from parts getting hot and burning off oil deposits. The signs to look for are leaks of oil or water which will be obvious if serious. Check also the clamp connections of the exhaust pipes to the manifolds as these do not always 'find' their exact gas tight position until the warmth and vibration have acted on them and it is almost

certain that they will need tightening further. This should be done of course with the engine stopped.
5. When running temperature has been reached adjust the idling speed as described in Chapter 3.
6. Stop the engine and wait a few minutes to see if any lubricants or coolant is dripping out when the engine is stationary.
7. Road test the car to check that the timing is correct and giving the necessary smoothness and power. Do not race the engine - if new bearings and/or pistons and rings have been fitted it should be treated as a new engine and run in at reduced revolutions for 500 miles.

53. V6 Engine - Differences in Procedures

1. The detailed differences between the V4 and V6 engines are shown in the specifications at the beginning of this chapter.
2. Of particular importance are the facts that the camshaft and crankshaft run in four bearings in each case and not three as in the V4.
3. No balance shaft is fitted to the V6 engine. Referring to Section 45, paragraph 21, the dimple on the crankshaft gear must mate up with the similar dimple on the camshaft gear to obtain the correct timing.
4. Referring to Section 44, paragraphs 8 and 9, the thrust washers on the V6 crankshaft are fitted to the first intermediate main bearing looking from the front of the engine.
5. Having three cylinders per bank the tightening sequences of the cylinder head and inlet manifold bolts are different. The correct sequences are shown in Figs. 1.14 and 1.15. These figures should be referred to when carrying out the instructions given in Section 47.
6. Referring to Section 48, the V6 engine has six valves to be adjusted on each bank. The table below shows the relationship between the fully open valves and the closed valves which are to be checked. The diagram shows the valve numbering - Nos. 1—6 front to rear on the right-hand bank and Nos. 7—12 front to rear on the left-hand bank.

Valves open (together)	Adjust
Nos. 1 and 6	Nos.10 (Exhaust) and 7 (Inlet)
Nos. 8 and 11	Nos. 5 (Exhaust) and 4 (Inlet)
Nos. 2 and 3	Nos. 9 (Inlet) and 12 (Exhaust)
Nos. 7 and 10	Nos. 6 (Inlet) and 1 (Exhaust)
Nos. 4 and 5	Nos.11 (Inlet) and 8 (Exhaust)
Nos. 9 and 12	Nos. 2 (Inlet) and 3 (Exhaust)

Front of Engine	
L.H. Bank	R.H.Bank
7	1
8	2
9	3
10	4
11	5
12	6

7. The clearances after reassembly of the V6 engine should be set at .010 in. (.254 mm) for the inlet valves and .018 in. (.457 mm) for the exhaust valves for both a cold and a hot engine. After the engine has been run for a short time the clearances should be checked again.

Symptom	Reason/s	Remedy
Engine will not turn over when starter switch is operated.	Flat battery. Bad battery connections. Bad connections at solenoid switch and/or starter motor.	Check that battery is fully charged and that all connections are clean and tight.
	Starter motor jammed.	Turn the square headed end of the starter motor shaft with a spanner to free it.
	Defective solenoid.	Bridge the main terminals of the solenoid switch with a piece of heavy duty cable in order to operate the starter.
	Starter motor defective.	Remove and overhaul starter motor.
Engine turns over normally but fails to fire and run.	No spark at plugs.	Check ignition system according to procedures given in Chapter 4.
	No fuel reaching engine.	Check fuel system according to procedures given in Chapter 3.
	Too much fuel reaching the engine (flooding).	Check the fuel system as above.
Engine starts but runs unevenly and misfires.	Ignition and/or fuel system faults.	Check the ignition and fuel systems as though the engine had failed to start.
	Incorrect valve clearances.	Check and reset clearances.
	Burnt out valves. Blown cylinder head gasket.	Remove cylinder heads and examine and overhaul as necessary.
	Worn out piston rings. Worn cylinder bores.	Remove cylinder heads and examine pistons and cylinder bores. Overhaul as necessary.
Lack of power.	Ignition and/or fuel system faults.	Check the ignition and fuel systems for correct ignition timing and carburetter settings.
	Incorrect valve clearances.	Check and reset the clearances.
	Burnt out valves. Blown cylinder head gasket.	Remove cylinder heads and examine and overhaul as necessary.
	Worn out piston rings. Worn cylinder bores.	Remove cylinder heads and examine pistons and cylinder bores. Overhaul as necessary.
Excessive oil consumption	Oil leaks from crankshaft rear oil seal, timing cover gasket and oil seal, rocker cover gasket, oil filter gasket, sump gasket, sump plug washer.	Identify source of leak and renew seal as appropriate.
	Worn piston rings or cylinder bores resulting in oil being burnt by engine. Smoky exhaust is an indication.	Fit new rings or rebore cylinders and fit new pistons, depending on degree of wear.
	Worn valve guides and/or defective valve stem seals. Smoke blowing out from the rocker cover, vents is an indication.	Remove cylinder heads and recondition valve stem bores and valves and seals as necessary.
Excessive mechanical noise from engine	Wrong valve to rocker clearances.	Adjust valve clearances.
	Worn crankshaft bearings. Worn cylinders (piston slap). Worn timing gears.	Inspect and overhaul where necessary.

NOTE: When investigating starting and uneven running faults do not be tempted into snap diagnosis. Start from the beginning of the check procedure and follow it through. It will take less time in the long run. Poor performance from an engine in terms of power and economy is not normally diagnosed quickly. In any event the ignition and fuel systems must be checked first before assuming any further investigation needs to be made.

Chapter 2 Cooling system

Contents

Specifications

Type of System	Pressurised, assisted by pump and fan

Thermostat

Type	Wax
Location	Front of cylinder block between the leads
Starts to open	185° to 190°F (85° to 89°C)
Fully open	210° to 216°F (99° to 102°C)

Radiator

Type	Corrugated fin
Pressure cap opens..	13 lb/sq.in. (.91 kg/cm^2)
Core height - 2000..	14.12 in. (35.86 cm)
3000..	13.75 in. (34.92 cm)
Core width - 2000	17.25 in. (43.81 cm)
- 3000..	19.60 in. (49.78 cm)

Fan

Type - 2000	8 blade 12 in. (30.48 cm)
- 3000	6 blade 12.50 in. (31.75 cm)
Fan belt free play...	½ in. (12.7 mm)

Cooling System Capacities

2000 with heater	15 pints (18 US pints, 8.54 litres)
2000 without heater	13.6 pints (16.32 US pints, 7.74 litres)
3000 with heater	20.5 pints (24.60 US pints, 11.69 litres)
3000 without heater	19.1 pints (23.92 US pints, 10.88 litres)

Torque Wrench Settings

Water pump	5 to 7 lbs/ft. (.69 to .97 kg/m)
Thermostat housing	12 to 15 lbs/ft. (1.66 to 2.07 kg/m)
Fan blade	5 to 7 lbs/ft. (.69 to .97 kg/m)

1. General Description

The engine cooling system is of the positive circulation pressurised type, the coolant liquid being passed round the system by an impeller pump driven by a V-belt from the crankshaft pulley. The same V-belt also drives the fan which is independently mounted on the engine front cover.

Water circulates from the bottom of the radiator to the pump and from there to the right-hand bank of the cylinder block. It then passes to the left-hand bank and from both banks passes up through the cylinder heads to the jacketing of the inlet manifold. The thermostat housing is an integral part of the inlet manifold and water passes through the thermostat to the top of the radiator or by-passes back to the pump when the thermostat is shut. It then passes down through the cooling tubes, through which air is drawn by the fan, and the cycle starts over again. The thermostat restricts circulation at low coolant temperatures. Water temperature is measured by an electro-sensitive plug fitted in the inlet manifold jacketing connected to a gauge in the car.

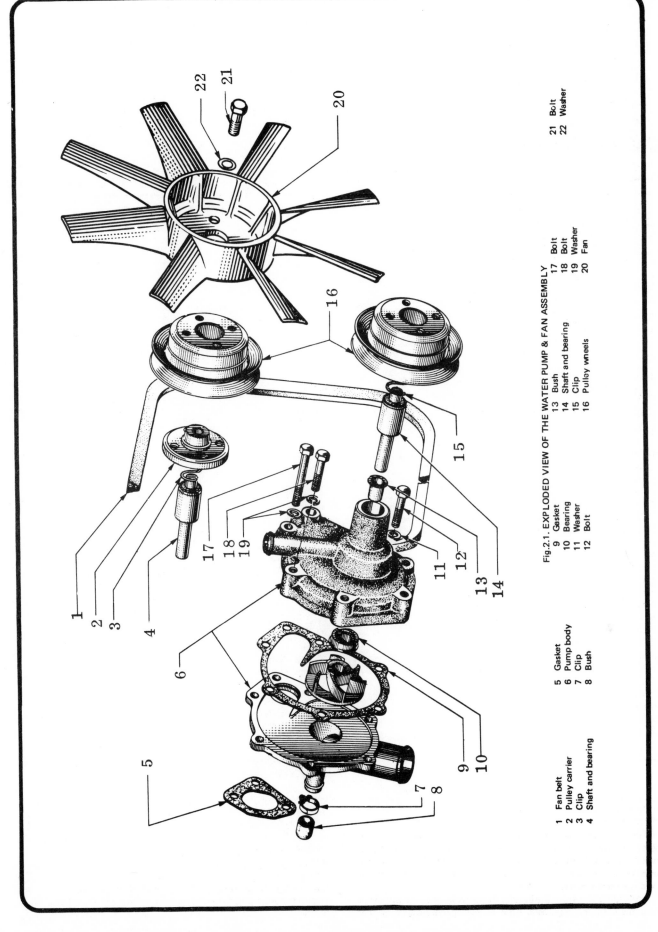

Fig.2.1. EXPLODED VIEW OF THE WATER PUMP & FAN ASSEMBLY

1	Fan belt	5	Gasket	9	Gasket	13	Bush	17	Bolt	21	Bolt
2	Pulley carrier	6	Pump body	10	Bearing	14	Shaft and bearing	18	Bolt	22	Washer
3	Clip	7	Clip	11	Washer	15	Clip	19	Washer		
4	Shaft and bearing	8	Bush	12	Bolt	16	Pulley wheels	20	Fan		

The cooling system also provides the heat for the heating system. The heater radiator is fed from a pipe connected to an outlet from the inlet manifold jacketing and the return is direct to the water pump. This ensures that the hottest water in the system goes directly to the heater under positive circulation.

2. Routine Maintenance

1. The coolant level should be checked at least weekly or more often in conditions of high mileages or exceptionally high temperatures. Coolant loss is normally negligible and any indications of excessive loss need to be investigated. Always top up with clean water, preferably soft; Rain water is perfect. When anti-freeze has been added to the system make sure that topping up is done with a mixture similar in proportion to the contents of the radiator.
2. Check the fan belt tension (details in Section 12) at least every 5,000 miles and examine all hoses and connections for signs of deterioration or leaks.

3. Cooling System - Draining

1. In the interests of cleanliness or if it is wished to retain the coolant because of anti-freeze it is necessary to remove the fibreboard deflector plate from under the radiator.
2. This is done by removing the two cross-head screws from either side and pulling the deflector off its spring clips to the bodywork; two at the front, one at the rear.
3. With the deflector plate removed a container of at least 2 gallons capacity can be placed directly under the radiator drain tap.
4. Remove the radiator cap. If the coolant is hot be careful. Cover the cap with a cloth and remove it slowly. The system is under a pressure of anything up to 13 lbs/sq.in. and unless care is taken there is a danger of being scalded when the water boils up under reduced pressure.
5. Unscrew the drain tap in the base of the radiator. It is not necessary to take it right out but if the water is very dirty it is as well to do so. The orifice can then be probed with a piece of wire to ensure that all sludge is cleared from the bottom of the radiator.
6. To ensure that all liquid leaves the block the drain tap behind the oil filter should also be opened.

4. Cooling System - Flushing

1. With time, the radiator and the jacketing waterways in the engine may become restricted or even blocked with scale and sediment deposits so reducing the efficiency of the cooling system. This is when flushing is necessary.
2. With the system drained and taps removed run water form a hose through it for several minutes to clear loose deposits. It may be necessary to probe the drain outlets while this is going on.
3. Close the drain taps and refill the system with water and a proprietary chemical radiator cleaner. Replace the filler cap and run the engine for ten to fifteen minutes. Then drain out and flush thoroughly with clean water. If the scale deposits are particularly heavy a second treatment may be necessary. Under no circumstances however, should the cleaning compound be left in the system.

5. Cooling System - Filling

1. Close both drain taps.
2. Fill the system slowly to avoid air locks and at the same time make sure the heater valve is open by moving the control lever to 'HOT'. Use soft water or rain water if possible. Use anti-freeze as prescribed in Section 6.
3. Fill within ½ inch of the neck of the filler tube cap flange and replace the cap firmly, screwing it fully clockwise up to the stops.

4. Run the engine and recheck the level.

6. Anti-Freeze Mixture

1. In climatic conditions where the ambient temperature is likely to drop below freezing point the use of anti-freeze is essential. If the coolant is permitted to freeze in the car serious damage can result.
2. Any good proprietary brand may be used of specification BS3151 or 3152. Do not use one with an alcohol base as the evaporation rate is very high.
3. The quantity of anti-freeze which should be used for various levels of protection is given in the table below, expressed as a percentage of the cooling system capacity.

Anti-freeze volume	Protection to		Spec. gravity
10%	− 8°C	(17°F)	1.017
15%	−13°C	(7°F)	1.024
20%	−19°C	(-3°F)	1.032
25%	−29°C	(-20°F)	1.040

In all cases, however, the directions on the tin should be followed as variations occur between different manufacturers products.

7. Radiator - Removal, Inspection, Cleaning & Replacement

1. Drain the cooling system as described in Section 3.
2. Undo the clip securing the top hose to the radiator (or thermostat housing), (photo).
3. Remove the clip securing the lower hose to the radiator.
4. Unscrew the cross-head self-tapping screws holding the fairing piece around the top of the radiator and take it off.
5. Remove the four bolts holding the radiator to the front panel (photo).
6. Lift out the radiator (photo).
7. If there are leaks these can usually be repaired by soldering, or with the use of one of the proprietary brands of resin based fillers such as 'Cataloy' that are generally available.
8. Make sure the honeycombe matrix is cleared of flies, etc., by hosing it with a strong water jet.
9. Flush out the radiator with clean water, inverting it to clear any deposits which may not otherwise be easy to clear from the header tank.
10 Inspect the hoses for signs of perishing and cracking, particularly near the clips and ensure that the clips are not distorted. Renew any doubtful items.
11 Examine the drain tap and tap seat for wear or damage which could cause leaking.
12 Replacement of the radiator is a reversal of the removal procedure. Always check carefully for leaks as soon as the system is refilled and has reached its normal running temperature.

8. Thermostat - Removal, Testing & Replacement

1. A faulty thermostat can cause overheating or failure of the engine to warm up quickly in cold weather. It will also affect the performance of the heater.
2. To remove it first draw off about four pints from the cooling system.
3. Undo the top radiator hose clip at the thermostat elbow (photo 7.2) and pull it off the elbow.
4. Undo the two bolts holding the elbow to the manifold (photo).
5. Lift off the elbow revealing the thermostat.
6. The thermostat is often stuck to the rim of the housing with sediment. To loosen it without damage tap it with a flat nosed punch right on the edge as if trying to rotate it in the housing. Be careful as the lip acts as a form of seal and although not critical

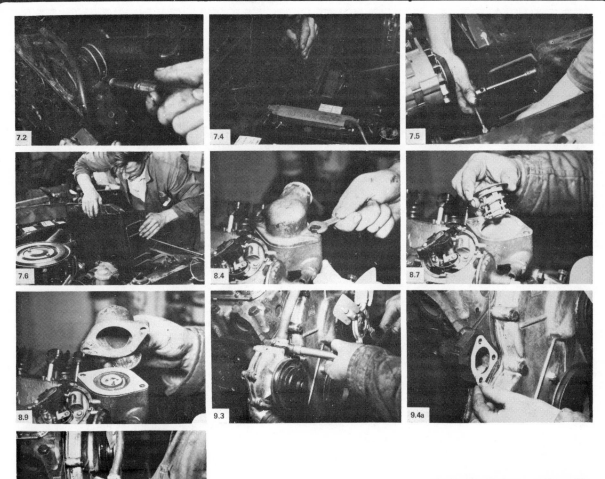

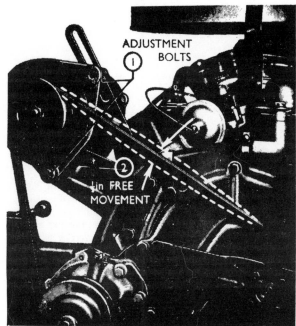

Fig.2.2. Correct tension of fan belt at arrows should be ½ inch (12 mm)

it should not be damaged.

7. The loose thermostat may then be lifted out (photo).

8. To test whether the thermostat functions as it should, suspend it in a pan of water with a piece of string. Then, with a thermometer in the water (not touching the pan) note at what temperature it starts to open (it should be 185–192°F (85°–89°C). Then note when it is fully open (.4 in. – 10.3 in.) which should be at 210–216°F (99°–102°C). Check that the thermostat closes once again at the lower temperature (after cooling naturally). Should it fail on any of these checks it must be renewed. Note that the operation of the thermostat is not instantaneous so allow sufficient time when testing it. Should the thermostat have stuck open it would have been apparent when the housing cover was removed.

9. Replacement of the thermostat is a reversal of the removal procedure. Ensure that the mating faces of the two flanges are clean and use a new gasket (photo). It is a sensible insurance to use a sealing compound also such as 'Hermetite'. If the elbow is very deeply corroded it should be renewed.

9. Water Pump - Removal & Replacement

1. Drain the cooling system as described in Section 3 and remove the fan belt as described in Section 12.

2. Slacken off the three clips and detach the three inlet hoses. It may be convenient to remove the bottom radiator hose at the radiator end and the by-pass hose at the thermostat housing in which case they can be lifted away with the pump in due course.

3. Remove the three bolts holding the pump to the face of the cylinder block (photo). (In the photo the engine is not in the car). Lift the pump away from the engine.

4. Replacement is a reversal of the removal procedure. A new gasket should be fitted (photo A) and sealed with jointing compound before replacing the pump (photo B). Do not overtighten the bolts.

10. Water Pump - Dismantling & Reassembly

1. Remove the pump from the engine. One bolt will be 'trapped' by the pulley so cannot be removed from the body of the pump.

2. Remove the four bolts attaching the rear cover to the pump housing and take it off.

3. It must be appreciated that all the component parts are held together by press fit. Obviously these press fits are tight, otherwise the pump would simply fly apart in use so before proceeding any further it is essential that for pressing operations a wide opening vice at least and an assortment of drifts and hollow tubes for use as spacers is available. The use of hammers and blocks is possible but the force required is such that the likelihood of fracturing the pump body is very high.

4. Draw off the V-belt pulley from the shaft with a hub puller.

5. Next press the shaft and bearing assembly complete with impeller, seal and slinger out of the housing. One way to do this is to support the housing with a short piece cut from a cast iron rainpipe and then placing the whole assembly in the vice jaws and pressing on the nose of the shaft. When the shaft is flush with the housing obtain a suitable piece of rod slightly smaller than the shaft in diameter and use this to press it right through.

6. No further dismantling is necessary as all the components of the shaft and bearing come together as a repair kit.

7. Using a suitable length of tube press the slinger onto the longer end of the new shaft and bearing assembly in the vice so that the slinger flange abuts the bearing.

8. Then press the shaft and bearing into the housing, short end first, so that the bearing race comes flush with the end of the housing. A suitable sleeve will be needed to go over the pulley end of the shaft and up against the housing during the final pressing operation.

9. Next press the pump seal into the housing with the carbon face away from the bearing.

10 With the flat face of the impeller supported by a piece of flat steel plate the shaft is now pressed into it. The correct distance is reached when the rear face of the housing has a 0 to .005 in. (0 to 0.13 mm) clearance from the plate supporting the impeller. Any over-pressing will dislodge the position of the bearing in the housing.

11 Replace the trapped bolt into its correct hole and re-fit the pulley to the shaft, recessed side over the housing. When pressing the pulley on care must be taken to ensure that support is so arranged that the shaft is not dislodged in the housing. The pulley is in position when the centre line of the 'V' is 2.2 to 2.25 inches. (56 to 57 mm) from the rear face of the housing.

12 Clear off the faces of the pump body and rear cover, fit a new gasket and replace the rear cover, tightening down the four bolts evenly and not too tightly, bearing in mind that the housing and cover are made from aluminium alloy.

11. Fan - Removal, Overhaul & Replacement

1. Remove the fan belt (Section 12).

2. Remove the fan blades and pulley by unscrewing the four bolts and lockwashers holding them to the hub.

3. Remove the engine front cover (see Chapter 1/17).

4. A circlip is located in a groove in the bearing and a corresponding groove in the housing. Remove this circlip and then press the shaft bearing and expansion plug together with the hub, out of the front cover. The shaft can then be pressed out of the hub.

5. The new shaft and bearing assembly is first pressed into the housing so that the circlip grooves are in alignment. The circlip is then refitted.

6. The hub is pressed in until the front face is 3.3/8 inch (85.8 mm) from the REAR face of the front cover.

7. Fit a new expansion plug to the shaft bore in the rear face of the bearing housing.

8. Replace the front cover and refit the pulley and fan blades.

9. Replace the fan belt and adjust as described in Section 12.

12. Fan Belt - Adjustment, Removal & Replacement

1. The tension of the fan belt is of considerable importance. If too tight the bearings in the water pump, generator and fan will be subjected to excessive strain - thus wearing them out, or if too slack it will slip, reducing the efficiency of the water pump and the output of the generator.

2. To adjust the tension it is necessary to move the generator or alternator, whichever may be fitted. Slacken off the three bolts which hold the generator or alternator in position. Two of these are at either end of the generator or alternator body and the third bolt which is the adjusting bolt runs in a slotted bar.

3. Pull the generator or alternator outwards to tighten the fan belt and clamp the adjustment bolt, followed by the mounting bolts.

4. The tension should be such that there is ½ inch (12 mm) of free play in the belt between the generator or alternator and the fan as shown in Fig.2.2.

5. To remove the belt entirely, simply slacken it off by moving the generator or alternator inwards enough to enable the belt to be lifted over the pulley. If the belt breaks it will immediately become apparent because the ignition warning light will come on. In order to fit a new belt slacken off the generator or alternator mounting and adjustment bolts and proceed as for adjustment after fitting the new belt over the pulleys.

6. As the V4 and V6 belts are comparatively long there is more stretch tendency so a new belt should be checked after a few hundred miles.

13. Water Temperature Gauge - Fault Finding

1. Correct operation of the water temperature gauge is important as the engine could attain a considerable degree of overheating,

unnoticed, without it.

2. To check the correct operation of the installation, first disconnect the 'Lucar' connector from the sender unit plug screwed into the top of the inlet manifold. With the ignition 'on' the gauge should be at the cold mark. Then earth the lead to the engine block when the needle should indicate hot, at the opposite end of the scale. This test shows that the gauge on the dash is functioning properly. If it is not then it will need renewal (see Chapter 10). If there is still a fault in the system with this check completed satisfactorily, there will be a fault in the sender unit or the wire leading from it to the gauge. Renew these as necessary.

3. If the fuel gauge should be showing signs of malfunctioning at the same time as the temperature gauge fault may lie in the instrument voltage regulator which should be checked as described in Chapter 10.

Fault Finding Chart - Cooling System

Symptom	Reason/s	Remedy
Loss of coolant.	Leak in system.	Examine all hoses, hose connections, drain taps and the radiator and heater for signs of leakage when the engine is cold, then when hot and under pressure. Tighten clips, renew hoses and repair radiator.
	Defective radiator pressure cap.	Examine cap for defective seal or spring and renew if necessary.
	Overheating causing rapid evaporation due to excessive pressure in system forcing vapour past radiator cap.	Check reasons for overheating.
	Blown cylinder head gasket causing excess pressure in cooling system forcing coolant past radiator cap overflow.	Remove cylinder head for examination.
	Cracked block or head due to freezing.	Strip engine and examine. Repair as required.
Overheating.	Insufficient coolant in system.	Top up.
	Water pump not turning properly due to slack fan belt.	Tighten fan belt.
	Kinked or collapsed water hoses causing restriction to circulation of coolant.	Renew hose as required.
	Faulty thermostat (not opening properly).	Fit new thermostat.
	Engine out of tune.	Check ignition setting and carburetter adjustments.
	Blocked radiator either internally or externally.	Flush out cooling system and clean out cooling fins.
	Cylinder head gaskets blown forcing coolant out of system.	Remove head and renew gasket.
	New engine not run-in.	Adjust engine speed until run-in.
Engine running too cool.	Missing or faulty thermostat.	Fit new thermostat.

Chapter 3 Fuel system and carburation

Contents

Specifications

Fuel Pump

Type	Mechanical driven from eccentric on camshaft
Delivery pressure	3½ to 5 lb/sq.in. (.25 to .35 kg/cm^2)
Inlet vacuum	8.5 in. (21.60 cm) Hg.

Fuel Tank Capacity

2000 GT	10.5 gals (12.7 US gals, 48.0 litres)
3000 GT & E	13.5 gals (16.2 US gals, 62.0 litres)

Carburetter - 2000 GT

Type ... ... Twin choke Weber

	Manual 32/36 DFV		Automatic 32/36 DFAV	
Identification number	Primary	Secondary	Primary	Secondary
Venturi diameter	26	27	26	27
Auxiliary venturi	4.5	4.5	4.5	4.5
Main jet	145	145	135	140
Air correction jet	170	180	170	180
Emulsion tube type	F6	F6	F6	F6
Slow running petrol jet	45	50	45	50
Slow running air jet (bush)	150	70	150	70
Progression holes	2 x 110	2 x 120	2 x 110	2 x 120
Slow running volume control port	180	–	180	–
Full load enrichment jet...	–	130	–	130
Full load air bleed	–	110	–	110
Full load mixture jet	–	250	–	250
Power valve jet	60		60	
Accelerator pump jet...	60		65	
Accelerator pump back bleed	40		40	
Needle valve	2.0 mm		2.0 mm	
Float level	9.5 mm		9.5 mm	
Float travel	8.0 mm		8.0 mm	
Float idle setting	1.20 mm		1.25 mm	
Choke plate pull down	5.0 mm		4.75 to 5.25 mm	
Choke plate opening	7.5 to 8.5 mm with lever backed off 10 mm		N/A	
Idling speed	680 to 720 r.p.m.		680 to 720 r.p.m.	
Fast idle speed	2,650 r.p.m.		2,000 r.p.m.	

Carburetter - 3000 GT & E

Type	Twin choke Weber
Identification number	40 DFAV
Venturi diameter	28 mm
Auxiliary venturi	4.5
Main jet	180
Idling jet	60
Idling jet air bleed...	200
Accelerator pump jet	50
Air correction jet	185
Emulsion tubes type	F2
Fast idling setting...	.75 to .80 mm
Choke plate pulldown	3.5 to 4.0 mm
Float level	5.5 to 6.0 mm
Float travel	13.5 to 14 mm
Auto choke operating temp:	
- fully closed	18° to 21°C (65° to 70°F)
- fully open	65° to 68°C (150° to 155°F)
Idling speed	580 to 620 r.p.m.
Fast idle speed	1,600 r.p.m.

Air Cleaner

Type	Replaceable paper element

Torque Wrench Settings

Fuel pump	12 to 15 lb/ft. (1.66 to 2.07 kg.m)
Air cleaner to carburetter	2.5 to 3 lb/ft. (.35 to .42 kg.m)
Air cleaner cover	12 to 15 lb/ft. (1.66 to 2.07 kg.m)

1. General Description

The fuel system consists of a fuel tank, 10½ gallons on the 2000 GT and 13½ gallons on the 3000 models, a mechanically operated fuel pump, a twin choke Weber carburetter and the necessary fuel lines between the tank and the pump, and the pump and the carburetter.

2. Air Cleaners - Removal, Replacement & Servicing

1. The paper element type air cleaner fitted to all models should be serviced at intervals of 6000 miles and the paper element itself renewed at intervals of 18,000 miles or earlier if the car is being used in dry dusty conditions.
2. To remove the cover, undo and extract the two bolts in the top dished part of the air cleaner and lift the cover away.
3. Thoroughly clean the interior of the air cleaner lid and body then gently brush out the dust from the folds of the paper element.
4. To remove the body of the air cleaner from the Weber carburetter, turn back the locking tabs and undo and remove the four nuts, tabs, plain washers and rubber washers from the bottom of the body. Remove the bolt from the support stay where it runs into the air cleaner and remove the gasket and tubular inserts.
5. To replace fit the tubular inserts over the studs and then a new gasket. Offer up and correctly position the air cleaner body on the carburetter and fit the rubber and plain washers, lock tab and nuts.
6. Before tightening down the nuts replace the bolt in the support stay and body, then tighten down the centre nuts and turn up the locking tabs.
7. Replace the paper element refit the top cover ensuring on the 2000 GT that the arrow on the cover aligns with the mark on the spout as shown in Fig.3.1. Tighten down the top cover bolts.

3. Fuel Pump - Routine Servicing

1. At intervals of 6000 miles remove the screw and washer from the top of the pump bowl and lift off the bowl together with the gauze filter.
2. Thoroughly clean the bowl inside and out, and use a paint brush and petrol to clean any sediment from the filter gauge and pump body.
3. Refit the filter to the bowl, ensure that the seal which fits in the bowl rim is in good condition, then replace the bowl on the pump and tighten down the securing screw and washer.

4. Carburetter - Routine Servicing

1. At intervals of 6000 miles, check the carburetter idling mixture and adjust as necessary as described in Section 16.

5. Fuel Pump - Description

1. The mechanically operated fuel pump is actuated through a spring loaded rocker arm. One arm of the rocker bears against an eccentric on the front of the camshaft gear and the other arm operates a diaphragm pull rod.
2. As the engine camshaft gear rotates, the eccentric moves the pivoted rocker arm outwards which in turn pulls the diaphragm pull rod and the diaphragm down against the pressure of the diaphragm spring.
3. This creates sufficient vacuum in the pump chamber to draw in fuel from the tank through the filter gauze and a non-return valve.
4. The rocker arm is held in constant contact with the eccentric by an anti-rattle spring, and as the engine camshaft gear continues to

rotate the eccentric allows the rocker arm to move inwards. The diaphragm spring is thus free to push the diaphragm upwards forcing the fuel in the pump chamber out to the carburetter through a non-return outlet valve.

5. When the float chamber in the carburetter is full, the float chamber needle valve will close so preventing further flow from the fuel pump.

6. The pressure in the delivery line will hold the diaphragm downwards against the pressure of the diaphragm spring, and will remain in this position until the needle valve in the float chamber opens to admit more fuel.

6. Fuel Pump - Removal & Replacement

1. Pull off the fuel pump outlet pipe to the carburetter and the fuel inlet pipe leading from the tank. As it is quite possible that the fuel level in the tank may be higher than the pump level, plug the inlet pipe with a suitable object. The author found that an ordinary pencil was a perfect fit.

2. Undo and remove the two bolts and spring washers which hold the pump in place on the front cover, then lift the pump together with its gasket out of the car.

3. Replacement is a reversal of the above procedure. Remember to use a new cover to fuel pump gasket. The long curved rocker arm should also be put into the hole in the front cover in such a way that the end will rest on top of the operating cam on the front of the camshaft gear. If the arm is inadvertently caught UNDER the cam it will be impossible for the pump flange to mate up properly to the front cover.

7. Fuel Pump Testing

Presuming that the fuel lines and unions are in good condition and that there are no leaks anywhere, check the performance of the fuel pump in the following manner. Disconnect the fuel pipe at the carburetter inlet union, and the high tension lead to the coil, and with a suitable container or a large rag in position to catch the ejected fuel, turn the engine over on the starter motor solenoid. A good spurt of petrol should emerge from the end of the pipe every second revolution.

8. Fuel Tank - Removal & Replacement

1. Disconnect the battery, then remove all the petrol from the tank by either syphoning or disconnecting the fuel line under the car and allowing the contents to drain into a suitable container.

2. From under the filler cap, remove the three screws which hold the filler pipe in place.

3. Remove the flexible pipe from between the filler pipe and the fuel tank by loosening off the wire clips. Lift the filler pipe from the car.

4. Undo and remove the two nuts and bolts securing the fuel tank to the rear bulkhead and withdraw the tank a few inches into the boot.

5. Disconnect the wire from the fuel gauge sender unit at its snap connector and undo the fuel pipe at its union on the floor of the boot.

6. The fuel tank can now be lifted out of the car. Replacement is a direct reversal of the above procedure.

9. Fuel Gauge Sender Unit - Removal & Replacement

1. Remove the fuel tank a few inches into the boot of the car as described in Section 8, paragraphs 1 to 4.

2. With a cold chisel carefully unscrew the sender unit retainer ring and then remove the sender unit and sealing ring from the tank.

3. Replacement is a straightforward reversal of the removal sequence. Always fit a new seal to the recess in the tank to ensure no leaks develop.

10. Fuel Tank Cleaning

1. With time it is likely that sediment will collect in the bottom of the fuel tank. Condensation, resulting in rust and other impurities, will usually be found in the fuel tank of any car more than three or four years old.

2. When the tank is removed it should be vigorously flushed out and turned upside down, and if facilities are available, steam cleaned.

3. Never weld or bring a naked light close to an empty fuel tank unless it has been steamed out for at least two hours, or washed internally with boiling water and detergent several times. If using the latter method, finally fill the tank with boiling water and detergent and allow to stand for at least three hours.

11. Weber Carburetter - 2000 GT - General Description

The 2000 GT fits either the dual barrel Weber 32/36 DFV or 32/36 DFAV carburetters; models fitted with automatic choke having the latter type. These carburetters are virtually identical, the variations in jet sizes etc, can be found in the specifications at the beginning of this chapter.

The fuel is pumped to the carburetter where a chamber holds a small reservoir of fuel at a constant level controlled by a float valve. Depression at the choke (suction at the venturi) caused by the action of the engine, draws air through the choke and fuel through small holes - jets - into the inlet manifold in proportions according to the speed of the engine and demands made upon it. For example, at idling speeds there is a jet on the manifold side of the throttle flap which is nearly closed in such conditions. Also, in conditions calling for a rich mixture, such as when starting from cold, the strangler flap restricts the inflow of air so that a great proportion of depression (suction) is applied to the fuel jets. For conditions of sudden acceleration a mechanical pump is incorporated which meters a jet of neat fuel into the choke tube when the accelerator pedal is depressed quickly.

The throttle plate in one barrel opens before that in the other barrel to ensure good performance at high revolutions as well as smooth progression when the throttle is operated at low engine speeds.

At about every 6,000 miles these carburetters should be checked for slow running, and at the same time the float level needs to be checked to ensure that the correct amount of fuel is being retained. At the same time the float bowl is cleaned of any sediment which may have collected.

12. Weber Carburetters - All Models - Removal & Replacement

1. Remove the air cleaner as described in Section 2, then pull from the carburetter the fuel inlet pipe and the vacuum advance and retard pipe.

2. Separate the accelerator linkage connecting rod from the carburetter throttle lever by removing the small spring clip at their joint and pulling the ball joint on the connecting rod from its slot in the lever.

3. On 2000 GT models fitted with a manual choke disconnect the choke outer cable by undoing the small nut holding it to the top edge of the carburetter. Disconnect the inner cable by loosening the small screw connecting it to the carburetter choke linkage.

4. On models fitted with automatic choke, drain about 4 pints from the cooling system, then undo the metal clips and pull the coolant hoses from the carburetter coolant housing.

Fig.3.1. 2000 G.T. air cleaner alignment marks (Section 2.7)

Fig.3.2. EXPLODED VIEW OF THE
FUEL PUMP
1 Screw
2 Washer
3 Filter cover
4 Fuel filter
5 Gasket
6 Pump body
7 Spring
8 Operating lever
9 Stud
10 Washer
11 Nut

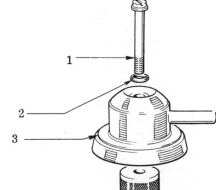

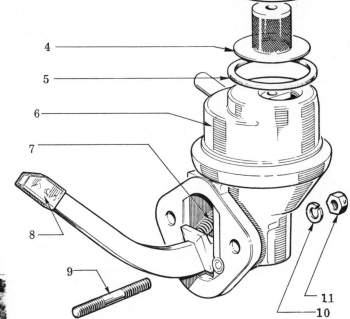

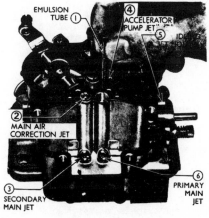

EMULSION
TUBE ①
④ ACCELERATOR
PUMP JET
⑤ IDLE
JET
② ①
MAIN AIR
CORRECTION JET
③
SECONDARY
MAIN JET
⑥
PRIMARY
MAIN JET

Fig.3.3. WEBER 32/36 DFV CARBURETTER JET LOCATIONS
(Section 11)

5. On 3000 cc models only, remove the crankcase ventilation pipe from the heat insulator spacer.

6. Now undo and remove the four carburetter retaining nuts and spring washers and lift off the carburetter and gaskets.

7. It is important to notice the correct fitting of the gaskets, spacers, etc, when removing them from the carburetter as this will be vital on refitting. The 2000 GT gaskets are marked 'upper' indicating which way they must be fitted. The 3000 cc gaskets can only be fitted one way owing to their shape. The lower gasket on the 3000 cc models has two metal 'V' notches which must locate within the inlet manifold.

8. Replacement is a direct reversal of the removal procedure, but when fitting the choke cable to the carburetter on the 2000 GT pull the choke knob out ½ inch, ensure the choke on the carburetter is fully closed and then tighten down the screw securing the inner cable.

13. Carburetters - Dismantling & Reassembly - General

1. With time the component parts of the Weber carburetter will wear and petrol consumption will increase. The diameter of drillings and jets may alter, and air and fuel leaks may develop round spindles and other moving parts. Because of the high degree of precision involved, in the authors opinion it is best to purchase an exchange rebuilt carburetter. This is one of the few instances where it is better to take the latter course rather than to rebuild the component oneself.

2. It may be necessary to partially dismantle the carburetter to clear a blocked jet or to renew the accelerator pump diaphragm. The accelerator pump itself may need attention and gaskets may need renewal. Providing care is taken there is no reason why the carburetter may not be completely reconditioned at home, but ensure a full repair kit can be obtained before you strip the carburetter down. NEVER poke out jets with wire or similar to clean them but blow them out with compressed air or air from a car tyre pump.

14. Weber Carburetter - 2000 GT - Dismantling, Inspection & Reassembly

All bracketed numbers refer to Fig.3.4.

1. Having removed the carburetter from the car as described in Section 12, disconnect the choke operating rod (68) at the lower end and separate the two halves of the carburetter by undoing the five screws (2).

2. Take out the float pivot pin (59) and remove the float (5) followed by the needle valve (60) and carrier.

3. From the upper body remove the spring loaded diaphragm assembly (62) and its gasket (63) by removing its three retaining screws.

4. Remove the accelerator pump cover (15), diaphragm (16) and spring (17) by undoing the retaining screws (14). Examine the diaphragm for signs of deterioration which may cause leakage through it, and renew it if in doubt.

5. Remove the jets from their locations using a screwdriver in good condition so as not to risk slipping and damaging the orifices. Fig. 3.3 shows the jet positions in the main body of the carburetter.

6. To remove the primary throttle spindle bend back the tab on the washer (34) and undo the nut (33) on the spindle.

7. Unhook the return spring (37) and draw off the throttle lever.

8. Disconnect the fast idle connecting rod (41) by removing the split pin (36), and then detach the bush (31), washer (29), lever (28) and washer (27) from the spindle.

9. Detach the return spring on the spindle (23) from the stop lever (44) and remove them.

10 With the two screws (13) holding the plate (12) to the spindle (11) undone, the plate can be taken out and the spindle withdrawn from the barrel.

11 Remove the secondary throttle spindle (10) by first undoing the nut (38) on the end of the spindle and taking off the washers (39,40) and the lever (44) behind it.

12 Then remove the two screws holding the plate to the spindle, remove the plate and take out the spindle.

13 Remove the screw (42) and washer (43) holding the choke operating lever (46) to the body, and then remove it, together with the return spring (47) and the toggle spring (50) from the relay lever (49).

14 Remove the split pin (61) from the rod and take off the relay lever.

15 Take the split pin from the other end of the rod, take the rod off and extract the dust seal (67).

16 The choke plate screws (71) can now be removed releasing the plates (70) and spindle (72).

17 Undo the fuel filter retaining plug (4) and remove the filter screen (3).

Fig.3.4. EXPLODED VIEW OF WEBER 32/36 DFV CARBURETTER FITTED TO 2000 G.T. WITH MANUAL CHOKE
(Section 14)

1	Stud	36	Split pin
2	Screw	37	Return spring
3	Choke operating rod	38	Nut
4	Plug	39	Spring washer
5	Float	40	Washer
6	Main metering jet	41	Fast idle connecting rod
7	Accelerator pump blanking needle	42	Screw
		43	Washer
8	Main metering jet	44	Stop lever
9	Carburetter body	45	Bolt
10	Spindle	46	Choke operating lever
11	Spindle	47	Return spring
12	Throttle plate	48	Washer
13	Screw	49	Relay lever
14	Retaining screw	50	Toggle spring
15	Accelerator pump cover	51	Split pin
16	Diaphragm	52	Idling jet holding screw
17	Spring	53	Idling jet
18	Idling jet holder	54	Gasket
19	Idling jet	55	Pump discharge nozzle
20	Volume control screw	56	Starting jet
21	Spring	57	Pump discharge valve
22	Slotted washer	58	Starting air adjusting jet
23	Return spring	59	Float pivot pin
24	Slow running adjusting screw	60	Needle valve
25	Slow running adjusting levers	61	Split pin
		62	Spring loaded diaphragm assembly
26	Adjusting screw	63	Gasket
27	Washer	64	Washer
28	Levers	65	Gasket
29	Washer	66	Carburetter top cover
30	Spring	67	Dust seal
31	Bush	68	Choke operating rod
32	Throttle control lever	69	Split pin
33	Nut	70	Choke plate
34	Tab washer	71	Choke plate screw
35	Throttle operating lever	72	Choke plate spindle

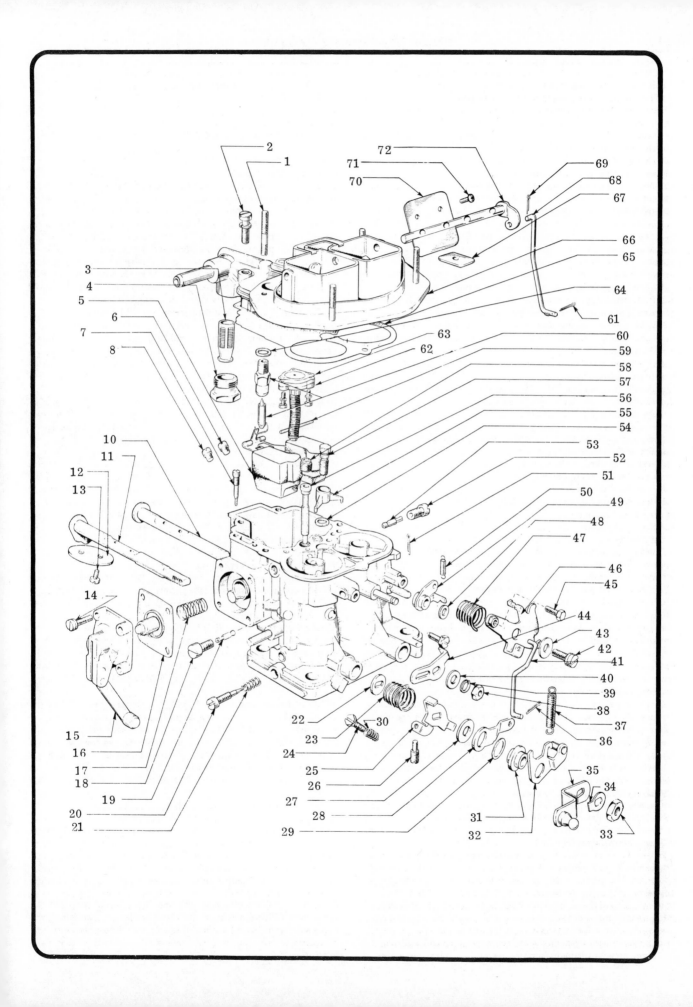

18 Before reassembly begins, wash all parts in methylated spirits which will remove any gummy petroleum deposits.

19 Jets should be blown out with compressed air and not poked with wire under any circumstances. If the carburetter is old and suspected of faulty performance the jets should be renewed, as they may have worn, or the whole carburetter replaced.

20 Reassembly is a reversal of the dismantling procedure, but the following points should be noted.

21 When fitting the choke spindle and plates make sure that the minus sign on the plates is uppermost ensuring correct fitting. The screws retaining the plates to the spindle should be staked or peened to lock them in position.

22 The throttle spindles should be located first of all with the slot parallel to the choke tube and the threaded holes inwards. The plates are fitted into the slots so that the face marked '78°' on it is below the spindle and facing outwards. This ensures that the chamfers on the plates face in the right direction.

23 Fit a new gasket beneath the accelerator pump assembly (15) and beneath the spring loaded diaphragm assembly (62).

24 When tightening the accelerator pump cover screws (14), pull the operating lever away from the cam to the limit of the travel of the diaphragm.

25 Always fit a new gasket under the needle valve housing.

26 After fitting the needle valve, float and pivot pin it will be necessary to check that the float travel is correct to maintain the required level of fuel in the float chamber.

27 As shown in Fig.3.5, hold the cover in the vertical position with the float hanging down and with the tab which is hooked to the needle valve in light contact with the ball and perpendicular.

28 The distance between the top of the float and the cover flange should be 9.5 mm. as shown in Fig.3.6. If this reading is not correct carefully adjust it by bending the arm between the pivot and the float at the float end.

29 Pull the float outwards and check that it moves another 8 mm giving a total reading of 17.5 mm. on the rule. If this is not correct adjust the position of the tab which abuts the needle valve housing until the correct travel is obtained.

30 When reassembly is complete check that all the moving parts operate freely and return correctly under their respective springs.

31 With the carburetter still detached from the engine it is necessary to check the setting of the throttle plates and choke plates.

32 The fast idle setting is checked with the choke plates in the fully closed position when the gap between the edge of the primary throttle plate and the barrel should be 1.2 mm. for manual choke models and 1.25 mm. for automatic choke models as shown in Figs.3.7 and 3.8. The gap may be adjusted by bending the connecting rod indicated by the black arrow, but this must be done with great care as the slightest alteration on the rod has a considerable effect on the throttle setting.

33 The choke plate pull-down (that is the automatic partial opening of the choke when the engine fires after starting with the choke lever in the closed position) is checked by pushing the choke plates, when closed, against the tension of the toggle spring as far as the stop. The gap between the plate and the air intake wall should be 5 mm. as shown in Fig.3.9. On manual choke models this can be adjusted if incorrect by bending the choke lever stop.

34 On models with an automatic choke adjustment is made by removing the outer water housing then moving the shaft inwards to the end of its travel whilst holding the choke plate in the closed position with light finger pressure. The travel of the shaft can now be varied by moving the adjustable stop.

35 The choke plate opening on manual choke models only can be checked by first moving the choke lever 10 mm. from the closed position. This measurement is taken at the end of the arm where the cable fits (Fig.3.10). At this position the gap between the lower edge of the plate and the air intake wall should be 7.5 to 8.5 mm. To alter this, the cam follower tag on the relay lever may be bent accordingly. Here again, great care is necessary as the slightest bending of the tag has a considerable effect on the gap being measured and adjusted.

36 Static settings of the carburetter are now complete and it should

now be replaced on the car as described in Section 12.

15. Weber Carburetter - 3000 GT & E - Dismantling, Inspection & Reassembly

All bracketed numbers refer to Fig.3.11.

1. Disconnect the choke plate operating rod (84) at its lower end by pulling out the small spring clip (83) then separate the two halves of the carburetter by removing the five screws (2).

2. From the top half of the carburetter (3) pull out the float pivot pin (85), remove the float (87) and the needle valve (6) and its carrier. Undo the fuel filter plug (94) and take out the filter (93).

3. Undo and remove the air bleed control valve from the cover.

4. Undo the three screws (68) which hold the clamping ring (63) in place then undo the single bolt (65) and washer (66) and take off the coolant housing (67) thermostatic spring and insulating spacer.

5. Disconnect the fast idle connecting rod (35) from the lever (37) on the throttle spindle (41) by removing the small spring clip (39) then undo the three retaining screws (69) and remove the automatic choke assembly from the carburetter body.

6. Remove the three screws (45) from the choke diaphragm cover (46), lift off the cover and remove the spring (54). From inside the body remove the stop and pull out the diaphragm (53).

7. Undo the screw (28) and take off the fast idle relay lever (18) and its washers (29,47), then disconnect the return spring (49). Now undo the nut (48) and take off the choke plate operating lever (56) and the return spring (52). The spindle (70) and spacer (57) can now be removed from the housing.

8. Working on the accelerator pump undo the four screws (71) and take off the cover (77). Remove the diaphragm (78) and spring (79). Examine the diaphragm for signs of deterioration which may cause leakage through it, and renew it if in doubt.

9. Undo and remove the screw to release the air bleed control valve operating rod (Fig.3.15), lever and return spring.

10 Remove the quadrant cover (31) by undoing the single retaining screw (30). This will expose the ends of the two throttle spindles.

11 Working on the left-hand spindle when viewed from this angle, knock back the tab on the lock washer (23) and remove the nut (24). Undo the quadrant adjusting screw and washers (22,21,20) and pull off the geared sector (19). Now pull off the lever (17) spacer (16) and return spring (15).

12 Undo the two screws (81) holding the throttle plate (72) to the spindle (80), take out the plate, and withdraw the spindle.

13 Moving to the right-hand spindle (41) knock back the tab on the lock washer (43) undo the nut (42) then remove the lever (44), quadrant (32) lever (37), bush (38), washer (34), lever (33) spacer (40) and return spring (25).

14 Undo the two screws (27) holding the throttle plate (72) to the spindle (41), take out the plate, and withdraw the spindle.

15 Working again on the top half of the carburetter disconnect the choke operating rod (84) from the lever, remove the two screws (91) holding each choke plate (1) on the spindle, take out the plates and withdraw the spindle.

16 Finally remove all the jets (82,8,90,86) and the emulsion tube (88).

17 Before reassembly begins, wash all parts in methylated spirits which will remove any gummy petroleum deposits.

18 Jets should be blown out with compressed air, and NOT poked with wire or hard metal under any circumstances. If the carburetter is old and suspected of faulty performance the jets should be renewed, as they may have worn, or the whole carburetter replaced.

19 Reassembly is a reversal of the dismantling procedure bearing the following points in mind.

20 When fitting the choke spindle and plates, make sure that the offset parts of the plates are to the rear and that the chamfers on the edges are parallel to the air intake when closed. The screws retaining the plates to the spindle should be staked or peened to lock them in position.

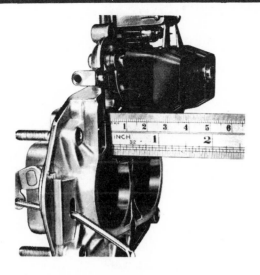

Fig.3.5. Checking the float level

Fig.3.6. Checking the float travel

1·2 mm.

Fig.3.7. Fast idle jet setting (manual choke)

1·25 mm.

Fig.3.8. Fast idle jet setting (automatic choke)

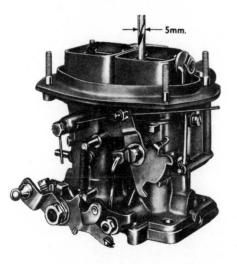

5mm.

Fig.3.10. Checking the choke plate opening

7·5 to 8·5mm.

10mm.

Fig.3.9. Checking the choke plate pull down

21 Before finally tightening down the plates on the throttle spindles, completely back off the idling stop screw and close the throttle to centralise the plates. In this position, if correctly fitted they will completely close the throttle barrel.

22 Ensure that the timing marks on the geared quadrants mate up, with the throttle fully closed before tightening down the lock screw on the left-hand quadrant or the left-hand spindle securing nut.

23 New gaskets should always be used under the needle valve housing and between the two halves of the carburetter.

24 While tightening the accelerator pump screws, pull the operating lever away from the cam to the limit of the travel of the diaphragm.

25 After fitting the needle valve, float and pivot pin it will be necessary to check that the float travel is correct to maintain the required level of fuel in the float chamber.

26 As shown in Fig.3.17, hold the cover in the vertical position with the float hanging down and with the tab which is hooked to the needle valve in light contact with the ball and perpendicular.

27 The distance between the top of the float and the cover flange should be 5.5 to 6.0 mm. In Fig.3.17, a special tool P9075 is being used for this job, but a ruler or a drill can equally well be used. If this reading is not correct carefully adjust it by bending the arm between the pivot and the float at the float end.

28 Pull the float outwards and check that it moves another 8 to 8.5 mm. to give a total reading of 14 mm maximum. If this is not correct adjust the position of the tab which abuts the needle valve housing until the correct travel is obtained.

29 When reassembly is complete check that all the moving parts operate freely and return correctly under their respective springs.

30 With the carburetter still detached from the car it is now necessary to check the setting of the choke plates and throttle plates.

31 The choke plate pull down is checked by pushing the choke plates when closed against the tension of the return spring as far as the stop. The gap between the plate and the air intake wall should be 3.5 to 4.0 mm.

32 Should the readings be incorrect, adjustment is made by removing the outer water housing then moving the shaft inwards to the end of its travel whilst holding the choke plates in the closed position with light finger pressure. The travel of the shaft can now be varied by moving the adjustable stop.

33 The fast idle setting is checked with the choke plates in the closed position when the gap between the edge of the primary throttle plate and the barrel should be 0.75 to 0.80 mm. The gap may be adjusted by bending the connecting rod, but this must be done with great care as the slightest alteration on the rod has a considerable effect on the throttle.

34 Static settings of the carburetter are now complete and it should now be replaced on the car as described in Section 12.

16. Weber Carburetters - Slow Running Adjustment

1. Ideally this job should be done with the aid of a vacuum gauge. If a gauge is available, connect it with a suitable Tee junction in the case of the 2000 GT to the rocker cover to inlet manifold ventilation tube, and in the case of the 3000 GT, to the heat insulation spacer ventilation pipe.

2. Run the engine, and adjust the throttle stop screw until the correct idling speed, as shown in the specifications, is obtained. Then adjust the volume control screws until a maximum reading possible is obtained on the vacuum gauge. It may be necessary to re-adjust the throttle stop screw to maintain the correct idling speed during this operation.

3. Should a vacuum gauge not be available, adjust the throttle stop screw until a fast idle is obtained then turn the volume control screws until the engine runs really smoothly and fires evenly. When this has been done adjust the throttle stop screw until the correct engine idling speed is obtained. (682 to 720 r.p.m. 2000 GT, 580 to 620 r.p.m. 3000 GT & E).

Fig.3.11. VIEW OF THE WEBER 40 DFAV CARBURETTER FITTED TO THE CAPRI 3000 GT & E (Section 15)

1	Choke plate	49	Return spring
2	Screws	50	Spring washer
3	Top cover	51	Washer
4	Stud	52	Spring
5	Washer	53	Diaphragm
6	Needle valve	54	Spring
7	Gasket	55	Spring
8	Idling jet holding screw	56	Choke operating plate lever
9	Idling jet	57	Spacer
10	Carburetter body	58	Housing
11	Volume control screw	59	Adjusting plate
12	Pump discharge nozzle	60	Screw
13	Gasket	61	Gasket
14	Spring	62	Thermostat
15	Return spring	63	Clamping ring
16	Spacer	64	Gasket
17	Lever	65	Bolt
18	Lever	66	Washer
19	Geared secton	67	Coolant housing
20	Washer	68	Screw
21	Shakeproof washer	69	Screw
22	Screw	70	Spindle
23	Lock washer	71	Screw
24	Nut	72	Throttle plates
25	Spring	73	Volume control screw
26	Idling adjustment screw	74	Spring
27	Screw	75	Spring
28	Screw and washer	76	Fast idle adjusting screw
29	Washer	77	Cover
30	Screw	78	Diaphragm
31	Quadrant cover	79	Spring
32	Quadrant	80	Spindle
33	Lever	81	Screw
34	Washer	82	Main jets
35	Fast idle rod	83	Spring clip
36	Washer	84	Choke operating rod
37	Lever	85	Float pivot pin
38	Bush	86	Accelerator pump blanking needle
39	Spring clip		
40	Spacer	87	Float
41	Spindle	88	Emulsion tube
42	Nut	89	Starting air adjusting jet
43	Lock washer	90	Pump discharge valve
44	Lever	91	Screw
45	Screw	92	Choke spindle
46	Choke diaphragm cover	93	Gauze filter element
47	Washer	94	Fuel filter plug
48	Nut		

NOTE: Illustrations 3.14, 3.15, 3.16 and 3.17 on page 63 refer to adjustments on the WEBER 40 DFAV carburetter

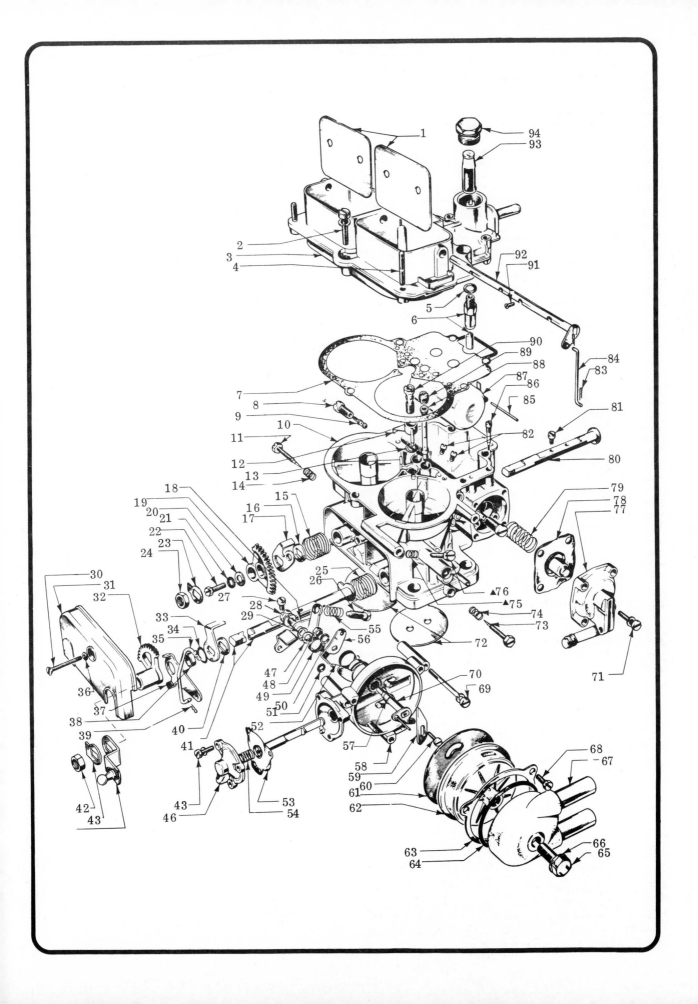

4. Do not try to set the idling speed too slow and if trouble is experienced doing this job, check the ignition timing.

17. Exhaust System - Inspection, Removal & Replacement

1. Examination of the exhaust pipes and silencers at regular intervals is worthwhile as small defects may be repairable when, if left, they will almost certainly require renewal of one of the sections of the system. Also, any leaks, apart from the noise factor, may allow poisonous exhaust gases to get inside the car which can be unpleasant, to say the least, even in mild concentrations. Prolonged inhalation could cause sickness and giddiness.

2. After the exhaust system has been on the car for some time it will prove difficult to separate sleeve connections and clamps. This task can be made easier by squirting 'plus gas' over all joints, clamps and nuts to be moved about half an hour before you actually start dismantling.

3. To remove the silencer system from the 2000 GT start by jacking up the car and supporting it on stands so as to give plenty of room to work under the car.

4. Slacken off the clamp just in front of the rear silencer assembly, unhook the rubber 'O' ring on the rear of the rear silencer then separate it from the pipe at the clamp and remove it from the car.

5. Disconnect the twin pipes from the exhaust manifolds at each side of the engine. This is done by slackening the clamps holding the two pipes and removing them together with the inserts.

6. Unhook the 'O' rings holding the front silencer assembly to the underside of the car and remove the rest of the system from the car.

7. If required the manifold extensions can now be removed from the front of the system, by undoing their respective clamps.

8. On the 3000 GT & E models after having supported the car on stands etc, slacken off the clamps just to the rear of each front silencer. Remove the 'O' rings supporting the rear silencer assembly then separate the pipes and remove the rear silencer and cross-over pipe from the car.

9. Disconnect the twin pipes from the exhaust manifold as described in paragraph 5, then unhook the 'O' rings from each front silencer assembly and remove the two front halves of the exhaust system from the car.

10 If required the cross-over pipe can be removed from the rear silencer and the manifold extensions from the front of the system by undoing their respective clamps.

11 Reassembly of both systems is the reverse of the removal sequence, but make sure that the front connections to the manifold pipes are seated correctly and that the two clamp halves are evenly spaced and the two bolts evenly tightened. It may be necessary to retighten them after a few miles of running.

18. Fuel System - Fault Finding

There are three main types of fault the fuel system is prone to, and they may be summarised as follows:—
a) Lack of fuel at engine.
b) Weak mixture.
c) Rich mixture.

19. Lack of Fuel at Engine

1. If it is not possible to start the engine, first positively check that there is fuel in the fuel tank, and then check the ignition system as detailed in Chapter 4. If the fault is not in the ignition system then disconnect the fuel inlet pipe from the carburetter and turn the engine over by the starter relay switch.

2. If petrol squirts from the end of the inlet pipe, reconnect the pipe and check that the fuel is getting to the float chamber. This is done by unscrewing the bolts from the top of the float chamber, and lifting the cover just enough to see inside.

Fig.3.12. EXPLODED VIEW OF THE CAPRI 2000 GT EXHAUST SYSTEM

1	Insert	12	Bracket
2	Clamp	13	Clamp
3	Manifold extension	14	Bolt
4	Front pipe silencer	15	Washer
5	'O' rings	16	Spacer
6	Nut	17	Nut
7	Washer	18	Bracket
8	Rear silencer	19	Nut
9	Bolt	20	Spacer
10	Extension	21	Washer
11	'O' rings	22	Bolt

Fig.3.13. EXPLODED VIEW OF THE CAPRI 3000 GT & E EXHAUST SYSTEM

1	Bolt	19	Washers
2	Washer	20	Front pipe and silencer
3	Spacer	21	Bracket
4	Bracket	22	'O' rings
5	Spacer	23	'O' rings
6	Front piece and silencer	24	Washers
7	Clamp	25	'U' clamps
8	Nut	26	Rear silencer assembly
9	Bolt	27	Extension and bolt
10	Nuts	28	'O' rings
11	Insert	29	Washer
12	Clamp	30	Bolt
13	Bolts	31	Nuts
14	Insert	32	Washer
15	Clamp	33	Bracket
16	Nuts	34	'U' clamp
17	Manifold extension	35	Cross over pipe
18	Clamp		

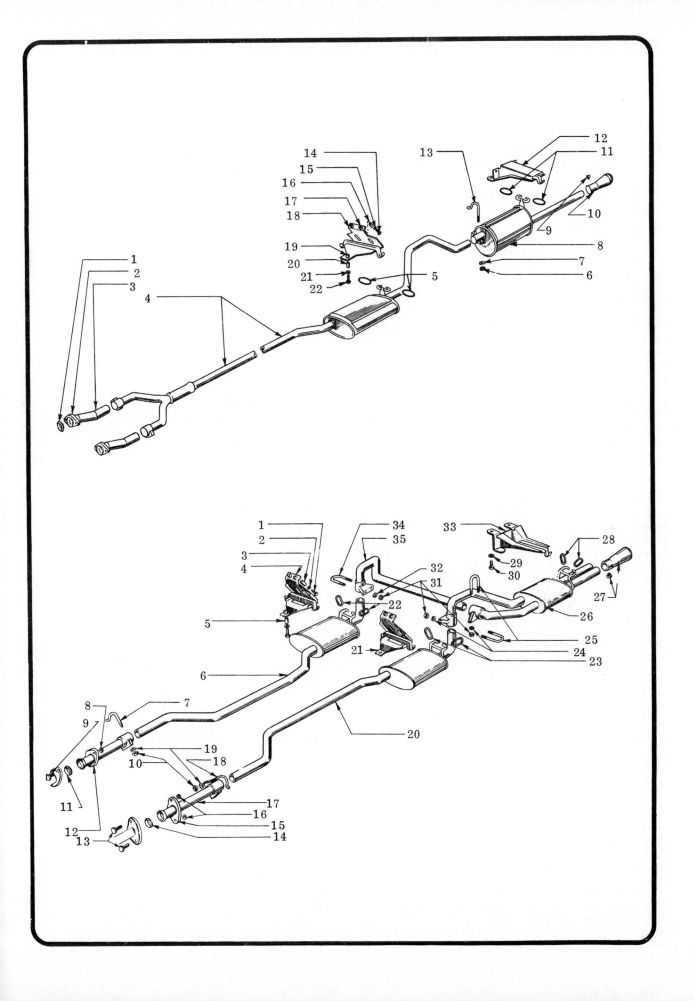

3. If fuel is there then it is likely that there is a blockage in the starting jet, which should be removed and cleaned.

4. No fuel in the float chamber, is caused either by a blockage in the pipe between the pump and float chamber or a sticking float chamber valve. Alternatively the gauze filter at the top of the float chamber may be blocked. Remove the securing nut and check that the filter is clean. Washing in petrol will clean it.

5. If it is decided that it is the float chamber valve that is sticking, remove the fuel inlet pipe, and lift the cover, complete with valve and floats, away.

6. Remove the valve spindle and valve and thoroughly wash them in petrol. Petrol gum may be present on the valve or valve spindle and this is usually the cause of a sticking valve. Replace the valve in the needle valve assembly, ensure that it is moving freely, and then reassemble the float chamber. It is important that the same washer be placed under the needle valve assembly as this determines the height of the floats and therefore the level of petrol in the chamber.

7. Reconnect the fuel pipe and refit the air cleaner.

8. If no petrol squirts from the end of the pipe leading to the carburetter then disconnect the pipe leading to the inlet side of the fuel pump. If fuel runs out of the pipe then there is a fault in the fuel pump, and the pump should be checked as has already been detailed.

9. No fuel flowing from the tank when it is known that there is fuel in the tank indicates a blocked pipe line. The line to the tank should be blown out. It is unlikely that the fuel tank vent would become blocked, but this could be a reason for the reluctance of the fuel to flow. To test for this, blow into the tank down the fill orifice. There should be no build up of pressure in the fuel tank, as the excess pressure should be carried away down the vent pipe.

20. Weak Mixture

1. If the fuel/air mixture is weak there are six main clues to this condition:—

a) The engine will be difficult to start and will need much use of the choke, stalling easily if the choke is pushed in.

b) The engine will overheat easily.

c) If the sparking plugs are examined (as detailed in the section on engine tuning), they will have a light grey/white deposit on the insulator nose.

d) The fuel consumption may be light.

e) There will be a noticeable lack of power.

f) During acceleration and on the over-run there will be a certain amount of spitting back through the carburetter.

2. As the carburetters are of the fixed jet type, these faults are invariably due to circumstances outside the carburetter. The only usual fault likely in the carburetter is that one or more of the jets may be partially blocked. If the car will not start easily but runs well at speed, then it is likely that the starting jet is blocked, whereas if the engine starts easily but will not rev, then it is likely that the main jets are blocked.

3. If the level of petrol in the float chamber is low this is usually due to a sticking valve or incorrectly set floats.

4. Air leaks either in the fuel lines, or in the induction system should also be checked for. Also check the distributor vacuum pipe connection as a leak in this is directly felt in the inlet manifold.

5. The fuel pump may be at fault as has already been detailed.

21. Rich Mixture

1. If the fuel/air mixture is rich there are also six main clues to this condition:—

a) If the sparking plugs are examined they will be found to have a black sooty deposit on the insulator nose.

b) The fuel consumption will be heavy.

c) The exhaust will give off a heavy black smoke, especially when accelerating.

d) The interior deposits on the exhaust pipe will be dry, black and sooty (if they are wet, black and sooty this indicates worn bores, and much oil being burnt).

e) There will be a noticeable lack of power.

f) There will be a certain amount of back-firing through the exhaust system.

2. The faults in this case are usually in the carburetter and the most usual is that the level of petrol in the float chamber is too high. This is due either to dirt behind the needle valve, or a leaking float which will not close the valve properly, or a sticking needle.

3. With a very high mileage (or because someone has tried to clean the jets out with wire), it may be that the jets have become enlarged.

4. If the air correction jets are restricted in any way the mixture will tend to become very rich.

5. Occasionally it is found that the choke control is sticking or has been maladjusted.

6. Again, occasionally the fuel pump pressure may be excessive so forcing the needle valve open slightly until a higher level of petrol is reached in the float chamber.

22. Fuel Gauge & Sender Unit - Fault Finding

1. If the fuel gauge fails to give a reading with the ignition on or reads 'FULL' all the time, then a check must be made to see if the fault is in the gauge, sender unit, or wire in between.

2. Turn the ignition on and disconnect the wire from the fuel tank sender unit. Check that the fuel gauge needle is on the empty mark. To check if the fuel gauge is in order now earth the fuel tank sender unit wire. This should send the needle to the full mark.

3. If the fuel gauge is in order check the wiring for shorts or loose connections. If none can be found, then the sender unit will be at fault and must be replaced.

4. Should both the fuel gauge, and the temperature gauge fail to work, or if they both give unusually high readings, then a check must be made of the instrument voltage regulator which is positioned behind the speedometer.

Fig.3.15. Air bleed control valve operating rod (Section 15.9)

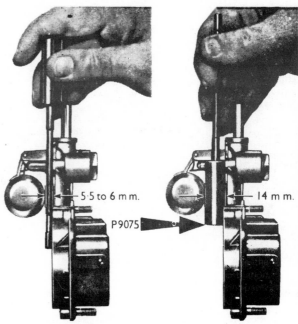

Fig.3.14. Air bleed control valve and enrichment jets (Section 15.3)

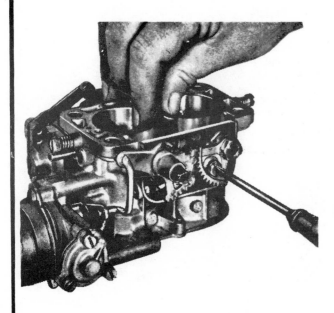

Fig.3.16. Aligning the timing marks on the quadrants and synchronising the throttle plate (Section 15.22)

Fig.3.17. Checking the float level and travel (Section 15.26)

Chapter 4 Ignition system

Contents

Specifications

Sparking Plugs

Type - 2000 GT	Autolite AG22
- 3000 GT & E	Autolite AG32
Plug gap...	.023 in. (.58 mm)

Coil

Type	Oil filled
Resistance at 20°C (68°F)	
Primary	3.1 to 3.5 ohms
Secondary..	4,750 to 5,750 ohms
Output	30 k.v.

Distributor ... ...   Ford

Contact points gap setting	.025 in. (.64 mm)
Rotation of rotor	Clockwise
Automatic advance	Mechanical and vacuum
Condenser capacity	.21 to .25 microfarad
Contact breaker spring tension...	17 to 21 oz. (482 to 595 gms)
Identification numbers:	
- 2000 GT...	C9CH—A (Black)
- 3000 GT & E	C9CH—C (Blue) or 70EB—C—A (Blue)

Initial Advance

2000 GT on 94 octane fuel	6° B.T.D.C.
2000 GT on 97 octane fuel	10° B.T.D.C.
3000 GT & E	10° B.T.D.C.
Dwell angle	30° to 40°

Firing Order

2000 GT	1, 3, 4, 2
3000 GT & E	1, 4, 2, 5, 3, 6

Torque Wrench Setting

Spark plugs	24 to 28 lb/ft. (3.32 to 3.87 kg.m)

1. General Description

In order that the engine can run correctly it is necessary for an electrical spark to ignite the fuel/air mixture in the combustion chamber at exactly the right moment in relation to engine speed and load. The ignition system is based on feeding low tension voltage from the battery to the coil where it is converted to high tension voltage. The high tension voltage is powerful enough to jump the sparking plug gap in the cylinders many times a second under high compression pressures, providing that the system is in good condition and that all adjustments are correct.

The ignition system is divided into two circuits. The low tension circuit and the high tension circuit.

The low tension (sometimes known as the primary) circuit consists of the battery, lead to the control box, lead to the ignition switch, lead from the ignition switch to the low tension or primary coil windings (terminal SW), and the lead from the low tension coil windings (coil terminal CB) to the contact breaker points and condenser in the distributor.

The high tension circuit consists of the high tension or secondary coil windings, the heavy ignition lead from the centre of the coil to

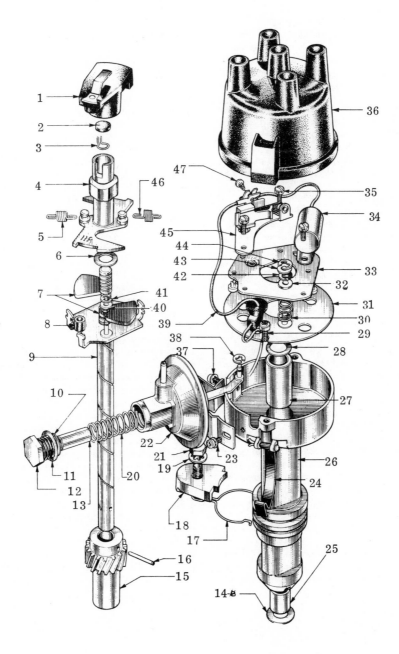

Fig.4.1. EXPLODED VIEW OF THE V4 DISTRIBUTOR

1	Rotor arm	12	Shim retaining bolt	24	Distributor cap clip	37	Screw and washer
2	Oil pad	13	Distributor to vacuum	25	Sleeve	38	Circlip
3	Spring clip		stop	26	Distributor body	39	L.T. lead
4	Mechanical advance and	14	Washer	27	Sleeve	40	Washer
	cam assembly	15	Skew gear	28	Washer	41	Circlip
5	Flyweight tension spring	16	Gear retaining pin	29	Screw	42	Washer
6	Washer	17	Clamp retainer	30	Spring	43	Washer
7	Flyweights	18	Distributor clamp	31	Lower C.B plate	44	Circlip
8	Sleeve	19	Spring	32	Washer	45	Contact breaker
9	Action plate and main	20	Shakeproof washer	33	Upper C.B plate		assembly
	shaft	21	Clamp bolt	34	Condenser	46	Flyweight tension
10	Shim	22	Vacuum unit	35	C.B retaining screw		spring
11	Washer	23	Screw and washer	36	Distributor cap	47	Screw

the centre of the distributor cap, the rotor arm, and the sparking plug leads and sparking plugs.

The system functions in the following manner. Low tension voltage is changed in the coil into high tension voltage by the opening and closing of the contact breaker points in the low tension circuit. High tension voltage is then fed via the carbon brush in the centre of the distributor cap to the rotor arm of the distributor cap, and each time it comes in line with one of the four metal segments in the cap, which are connected to the sparking plug leads, the opening and closing of the contact breaker points causes the high tension voltage to build up, jump the gap from the rotor arm to the appropriate metal segment and so via the sparking plug lead to the sparking plug, where it finally jumps the spark plug gap before going to earth.

The ignition is advanced and retarded automatically to ensure the spark occurs at just the right instant for the particular load at the prevailing engine speed.

The ignition advance is controlled both mechanically and by a vacuum operated system. The mechanical governor comprises two lead weights, which move out from the distributor shaft as the engine speed rises due to centrifugal force. As they move outwards they rotate the cam relative to the distributor shaft, and so advance the spark. The weights are held in position by two light springs and it is the tension of the springs which is largely responsible for correct spark advancement.

The vacuum control consists of a diaphragm, one side of which is connected via a small bore tube to the carburetter, and the other side to the contact breaker plate. Depression in the inlet manifold and carburetter, which varies with engine speed and throttle opening, causes the diaphragm to move, so moving the contact breaker plate, and advancing or retarding the spark. A fine degree of control is achieved by a spring in the vacuum assembly.

2. Distributor Contact Breaker Points - Adjustment

1. To adjust the contact breaker points to the correct gap, first pull off the two clips securing the distributor cap to the distributor body, and lift away the cap. Clean the cap inside and out with a dry cloth. It is unlikely that the four segments will be badly burned or scored, but if they are the cap will have to be renewed.

2. Inspect the carbon brush contact located in the top of the cap - see that it is unbroken and stands proud of the plastic surface.

3. Check the contact spring on the top of the rotor arm. It must be clean and have adequate tension to ensure good contact.

4. Gently prise the contact breaker points open to examine the condition of their faces. If they are rough, pitted, or dirty, it will be necessary to remove them for resurfacing, or for replacement points to be fitted.

5. Presuming the points are satisfactory, or that they have been cleaned and replaced, measure the gap between the points by turning the engine over until the heel of the breaker arm is on the highest point of the cam.

6. A .025 inch (.64 mm) feeler gauge should now just fit between the points, (See Fig.4.2).

7. If the gap varies from this amount, slacken the contact plate securing screw and the adjusting screw.

8. Adjust the contact gap by inserting a screwdriver in the notched hole, in the breaker plate. Turn clockwise to increase and anti-clockwise to decrease the gap. When the gap is correct, tighten the securing screws and check the gap again.

9. Make sure the rotor is in position, replace the distributor cap and clip the spring blade retainers into position.

3. Removing & Replacing Contact Breaker Points

1. If the contact breaker points are burned, pitted or badly worn, they must be removed and either replaced, or their faces must be filed smooth.

2. Lift off the rotor arm by pulling it straight up from the spindle.

3. Slacken the self-tapping screw holding the condenser and low tension leads to the contact breaker and slide out the forked ends of the leads.

4. Remove the points by taking out the two retaining screws and lifting off the points assembly.

5. Replacing the points assembly is a reversal of the removal procedure. Take care not to trap the wires between the points and the breaker plate, (Fig.4.3).

6. When the points are replaced the gap should be set as described in the previous section.

7. Finally replace the rotor arm and then the distributor cap.

NOTE: Should the contact points be badly worn, a new set should be fitted. As an emergency measure clean the faces with fine emery paper folded over a thin steel ruler. It is necessary to completely remove the built-up deposits, but not necessary to rub the pitted point right down to the stage where all the pitting has disappeared. When the surfaces are flat a feeler gauge can be used and the gap set as above.

4. Condenser Removal, Testing & Replacement

1. The purpose of the condenser, (sometimes known as a capacitor) is to ensure that when the contact breaker points open there is no sparking across them which would waste voltage and cause wear.

2. The condenser is fitted in parallel with the contact breaker points. If it develops a short circuit, it will cause ignition failure as the points will be prevented from interrupting the low tension circuit.

3. If the engine becomes very difficult to start or begins to miss after several miles running and the breaker points show signs of excessive burning, then the condition of the condenser must be suspect. A further test can be made by separating the points by hand with the ignition switched on. If this is accompanied by a flash it is indicative that the condenser has failed.

4. Without special test equipment the only sure way to diagnose condenser trouble is to replace a suspected unit with a new one and note if there is any improvement.

5. To remove the condenser from the distributor take off the distributor cap and rotor arm. Slacken the self-tapping screw holding the condenser lead and low tension lead to the points, and slide out the fork on the condenser lead. Undo the condenser retaining screw and remove the condenser from the breaker plate.

6. To refit the condenser, simply reverse the order of removal. Take care that the condenser lead is clear of the moving part of the points assembly.

5. Distributor Lubrication

1. It is important that the distributor cam is lubricated with petroleum jelly at the specified mileages, and that the breaker arm, governor weights, and cam spindle, are lubricated with engine oil once every 6,000 miles.

2. Great care should be taken not to use too much lubricant, as any excess that finds its way onto the contact breaker points could cause burning and misfiring.

3. To gain access to the cam spindle, lift away the rotor arm. Drop no more than two drops of engine oil onto the felt pad. This will run down the spindle when the engine is hot and lubricate the bearings.

4. To lubricate the automatic timing control allow a few drops of oil to pass through the hole in the contact breaker base plate through which the four sided cam emerges. Apply not more than one drop of oil to the pivot post and remove any excess.

0.025 in. (0.64 m.m.)

Fig 4:2 Adjusting the contact breaker points

Fig.4.3. Fitting a new contact breaker assembly (Section 3.5)

0·004in(0·10m.m.)

Fig.4.4. Removing the breaker plate and diaphragm assembly
(Section 7)

Fig.4.5. Setting the distributor end shaft float (section 7.14)

6. Distributor Removal

1. To remove the distributor from the engine, pull off the four leads from the sparking plugs.
2. Disconnect the high tension and low tension leads from the distributor and remove the cap. Note carefully on a piece of paper the position of the rotor arm in relation to the distributor body.
3. Pull off the rubber union holding the vacuum pipe to the distributor vacuum advance housing.
4. The distributor is held to the engine by a single bolt which goes through a clamp and retainer plate which slides into grooves in the body.
5. The bolt is down in the Vee of the inlet manifold at the base of the distributor body and is somewhat difficult to get at. First of all mark the position of the distributor body relative to the clamp plate. Ideally one would use a special socket with a flexible drive to undo the bolt. The universal connector or a conventional ½ inch square socket set is too big. However, if the socket is placed over the bolt head it is possible to undo the bolt with a broad bladed screwdriver set diagonally across the square of the socket. The tightening torque required for this bolt is not great so no difficulties should be encountered with this method. If the bolt refuses to budge then the special tool (flexible socket drive) will be required.
6. With the bolt removed, gently ease the distributor upwards. Note that as it comes up, the rotor arm will move anti-clockwise due to the skew gear drive on the end of the spindle. This movement will have to be taken into account on replacement.

7. Distributor - Dismantling, Overhaul & Reassembly

1. Remove the distributor from the car and take off the contact points as described in Sections 6 and 3.
2. Undo the screw retaining the condenser and lift it off.
3. Remove the small circlip from the post linking the upper and lower breaker plates and remove the plain and wave washers.
4. Remove the circlip from the vacuum unit connecting rod post.
5. Remove the upper breaker plate.
6. Undo the two crosshead screws securing the lower breaker plate to the distributor body and lift it out. Do not lose the small coil spring acting as an earth link between the two plates. Detach the grommet from the hole in the plate and remove the primary lead.
7. Take off the vacuum unit by removing first the two screws securing the bracket.
8. To dismantle the vacuum assembly hold the body in a vice and remove the end plug. Withdraw the shim, spring and vacuum stop.
9. Noting carefully the position of the two mechanical advance springs, which are not the same, remove them from the pivot posts on the cam and spring plate and from the grooved tabs on the action plate.
10 Lift out the felt oil wick from inside the bore of the breaker cam and then take out the circlip. The cam may then be pulled off the shaft.
11 Remove the circlips holding the governor weights in position on the action plate.
12 If the main shaft bushes are worn or the endfloat of the shaft is incorrect it will be necessary to remove the skew gear so that the shaft can be taken out of the distributor body. This can be done by driving out the tubular retaining pin with a punch, thus allowing the gear to be pulled off the shaft withdrawn.
13 New bushes may be carefully tapped into position after the old ones have been driven out with a punch or drift.
14 When replacing the shaft first refit a new washer between the action plate and distributor body and a new sealing ring and another new thrust washer at the lower end between the skew gear and body. To set the end float a piece of .004 inch shim (.1 mm) as shown in Fig.4.5 should be placed behind the washer, and the skew gear placed on the shaft so that the pinhole is at right angles to the original in the shaft. The centre line of the rotor slot should also be

in line with the top of any gear tooth.
15 Clamp the gear up to the body so that the shim is jet held. Then drill a 1/8 inch (3.18 mm) hole in the shaft and fit a new pin. Take out the shim. .
16 Reassembly of the distributor is a reversal of the dismantling procedure with particular attention to certain points.
17 Locate the governor weights correctly with the flat sides next to the shaft.
18 When refitting the cam and plate to the distributor shaft see that the advance stop on the action plate is located within the section marked '11R' (Fig.4.6).
19 Fit the primary and secondary springs correctly (Fig.4.6).
20 The original parts of the vacuum unit should be replaced if it has been dismantled. Otherwise the timing advance will be altered.

8. Distributor Replacement

1. Replacement is a reversal of the removal procedure given in Section 6.
2. Provided the engine timing has not been altered no difficulty should be encountered.
3. Align the distributor with the vacuum unit towards the front of the engine and parallel to the engine centre line.
4. Before replacing the distributor set the rotor arm in a position approximately 30° anti-clockwise on the V4 engine or 45° anti-clockwise on the V6 engine of the required installed position.
5. Push the distributor drive into mesh with the camshaft gear when the rotor will turn clockwise into the required position.
6. Provided everything has returned to the pre-marked positions, tighten down the clamp bolt when refitting will be complete.

9. Ignition Timing

1. If for any reason the timing is lost the correct setting can be found in the following manner.
2. Turn the engine so that the timing notch on the crankshaft pulley lines up with the correct position on the front cover timing lug suitable for the particular engine being worked on (see Fig.4.7) and the specifications.
3. The pulley must be set with No.1 piston (front, right-hand bank viewed from driving seat) on the compression stroke. This can be verified by removing the sparking plug and placing a finger over the hole while the engine is turned towards the timing mark. The only easy way to turn the engine is to engage top gear and move the car forwards. Removal of all the sparking plugs reduces the resistance of the engine compression when doing this.
4. With the distributor out of the car align it with the vacuum unit towards the front of the engine and parallel to the engine centre line.
5. Looking at Figs.4.8 and 4.9 according to whether you are working on a V4 or V6 engine, align the rotor arm as shown.
6. As the distributor drive is pushed into mesh with the camshaft gear the rotor arm will move clockwise into the positions shown by the dotted white lines.
7. Set the distributor body by turning it so that the contact points are just about to be opened by the cam. Remember that the rotor turns clockwise so that the 'just about to open position' of the breaker arm is on the clockwise side of the high point of the cam.
8. Finally tighten down the clamp bolts, reconnect the vacuum advance and retard mechanism, the L.T and H.T leads and road test the car.

10. Vacuum & Mechanical Advance - Adjustments

1. The distributors fitted after September 1966 are so designed that the vacuum and mechanical advance characteristics may be altered.
2. Normally no adjustment is necessary and should not be attempted.

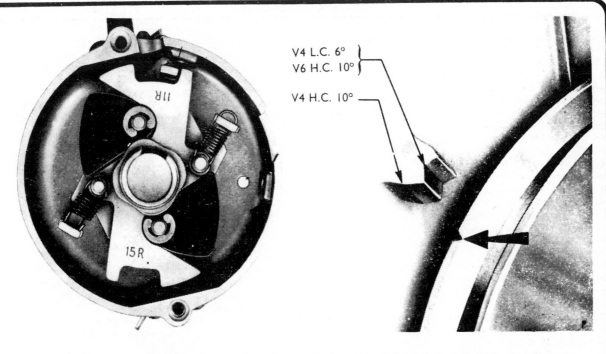

V4 L.C. 6°
V6 H.C. 10°

V4 H.C. 10°

Fig.4.6. The advance stop correctly located in the 11P section (Section 7.18, 7.19)

Fig.4.7. Ignition timing marks for V4 and V6 engines (Section 9.2)

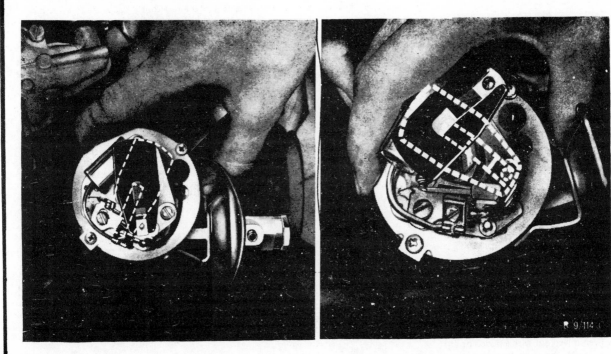

Fig.4.8. V4 engine. Correct position of rotor arm for distributor replacement (Section 9.4)

Fig.4.9. V6 engine. Correct position of rotor arm for distributor replacement (Section 9.4)

However, if a new shaft is fitted, for example, the spring anchor tabs on the action plate may be in a relatively different position and thus could alter the tension on the springs. These tabs can be altered by bending them. This, however, is quite futile without specialist test and setting equipment so should not be attempted. Similarly, the vacuum advance setting can be altered by changing the thickness of the shims behind the plug. This should not be attempted without the specialised equipment needed to check the settings.

11. Sparking Plugs & Leads

1. The correct functioning of the sparking plugs are vital for the correct running and efficiency of the engine.

2. At intervals of 6,000 miles the plugs should be removed, examined, cleaned, and if worn excessively, replaced. The condition of the sparking plugs will also tell much about the overall condition of the engine.

3. If the insulator nose of the sparking plug is clean and white, with no deposits, this is indicative of a weak mixture, or too hot a plug. (A hot plug transfers heat away from the electrode slowly - a cold plug transfers it away quickly).

4. The plugs fitted as standard are AUTOLITE as listed in specifications at the head of this chapter. If the tip and insulator nose is covered with hard black looking deposits, then this is indicative that the mixture is too rich. Should the plug be black and oily, then it is likely that the engine is fairly worn, as well as the mixture being too rich.

5. If the insulator nose is covered with light tan to greyish brown deposits, then the mixture is correct and it is likely that the engine is in good condition.

6. If there are any traces of long brown tapering stains on the outside of the white portion of the plug, then the plug will have to be renewed, as this shows that there is a faulty joint between the plug body and the insulator, and compression is being allowed to leak away.

7. Plugs should be cleaned by a sand blasting machine, which will free them from carbon more thoroughly than cleaning by hand. The machine will also test the condition of the plugs under compression. Any plug that fails to spark at the recommended pressure should be renewed.

8. The sparking plug gap is of considerable importance, as, if it is too large or too small, the size of the spark and its efficiency will be seriously impaired. The sparking plug gap should be set to the figure given in specifications at the beginning of this chapter.

9. To set it, measure the gap with a feeler gauge, and then bend open, or close, the outer plug electrode until the correct gap is achieved. The centre electrode should never be bent as this may crack the insulation and cause plug failure if nothing worse.

10 When replacing the plugs, remember to use new plug washers, and replace the leads from the distributor in the correct firing order.

11 The plug leads require no routine attention other than being kept clean and wiped over regularly.

At intervals of 6,000 miles, however, pull the leads off the plugs and distributor one at a time and make sure no water has found its way onto the connections. Remove any corrosion from the brass ends, wipe the collars on top of the distributor, and refit the leads.

12. Ignition System Fault Symptoms

There are two main symptoms indicating ignition faults. Either the engine will not start or fire, or the engine is difficult to start and misfires. If it is a regular misfire, i.e. the engine is only running on two or three cylinders the fault is almost sure to be in the secondary, or high tension circuit. If the misfiring is intermittent, the fault could be in either the high or low tension circuits. If the car stops suddenly or will not start at all, it is likely that the fault is in the low tension circuit. Loss of power and overheating, apart from faulty carburation settings, are normally due to faults in the distributor or incorrect ignition timing.

13. Fault Diagnosis - Engine Fails to Start

1. If the engine fails to start and the car was running normally when it was last used, first check there is fuel in the petrol tank. If the engine turns over normally on the starter motor and the battery is evidently well charged then the fault may be in either the high or low tension circuits. First check the H.T circuit. NOTE: If the battery is known to be fully charged; the ignition light comes on, and the starter motor fails to turn the engine CHECK THE TIGHTNESS OF THE LEADS ON THE BATTERY TERMINALS and also the secureness of the earth lead to is CONNECTION TO THE BODY. It is quite common for the leads to have worked loose, even if they look and feel secure. If one of the battery terminal posts gets very hot when trying to work the starter motor this is a sure indication of a faulty connection to that terminal.

2. One of the commonest reasons for bad starting is wet or damp sparking plug leads and distributor. Remove the distributor cap. If condensation is visible internally dry the cap with a rag and also wipe over the leads. Replace the cap.

3. If the engine still fails to start, check that current is reach g the plugs, by disconnecting each plug lead in turn at the sparking plug end, and hold the end of the cable about 3/16th inch away from the cylinder block. Spin the engine on the starter motor.

4. Sparking between the end of the cable and the block should be fairly strong with a regular blue spark. (Hold the lead with rubber to avoid electric shocks). If current is reaching the plugs, then remove them and clean and regap them to 0.025 inch. The engines should now start.

5. If there is no spark at the plug leads take off the H.T lead from the centre of the distributor cap and hold it to the block as before. Spin the engine on the starter once more. A rapid succession of blue sparks between the end of the lead and the block indicate that the coil is in order and that the distributor cap is cracked the rotor arm faulty or the carbon brush in the top of the distributor cap is not making good contact with the spring on the rotor arm. Possibly the points are in bad condition. Clean and reset them as described in this chapter, Section 2:5 to 9.

6. If there are no sparks from the end of the lead from the coil check the connections at the coil end of the lead. If it is in order start checking the low tension circuit.

7. Use a 12v voltmeter or a 12v bulb and two lengths of wire. With the ignition switch on and the points open, test between the low tension wire to the coil (it is marked S.W. or +) and earth. No reading indicates a break in the supply from the ignition switch. Check the connections at the switch to see if any are loose. Refit them and the engine should run. A reading shows a faulty coil or condenser or broken lead between the coil and the distributor

8. Take the condenser wire off the points assembly and with the points open test between the moving point and earth. If there is now a reading, then the fault is in the condenser. Fit a new one and the fault is cleared.

9. With no reading from the moving point to earth, take a reading between earth and the CB or - terminal of the coil. A reading here shows a broken wire which will need to be replaced between the coil and distributor. No reading confirms that the coil has failed and must be replaced, after which the engine will run once more. Remember to refit the condenser wire to the points assembly. For these tests it is sufficient to separate the points with a piece of dry paper while testing with the points open.

14. Fault Diagnosis - Engine Misfires

1. If the engine misfires regularly, run it at a fast idling speed. Pull off each of the plug caps in turn and listen to the note of the engine. Hold the plug cap in a dry cloth or with a rubber glove as additional

protection against a shock from the H.T. supply.

2. No difference in engine running will be noticed when the lead from the defective circuit is removed. Removing the lead from one of the good cylinders will accentuate the misfire.

3. Remove the plug lead from the end of the defective plug and hold it about 3/16th inch away from the block. Restart the engine. If the sparking is fairly strong and regular the fault must lie in the sparking plug.

4. The plug may be loose, the insulation may be cracked, or the points may have burnt away giving too wide a gap for the spark to jump. Worse still, one of the points may have broken off. Either renew the plug, or clean it, reset the gap, and then test it.

5. If there is no spark at the end of the plug lead, or if it is weak and intermittent, check the ignition lead from the distributor to the plug. If the insulation is cracked or perished, renew the lead. Check the connections at the distributor cap.

6. If there is still no spark, examine the distributor cap carefully for tracking. This can be recognised by a very thin black line running between two or more electrodes, or between an electrode and some other part of the distributor. These lines are paths which now conduct electricity across the cap thus letting it run to earth. The only answer is a new distributor cap.

7. Apart from the ignition timing being incorrect, other causes of misfiring have already been dealt with under the section dealing with the failure of the engine to start. To recap - these are that:-

a) The coil may be faulty giving an intermittent misfire.

b) There may be a damaged wire or loose connection in the low tension circuit.

c) The condenser may be short circuiting.

d) There may be a mechanical fault in the distributor (Broken driving spindle or contact breaker spring).

8. If the ignition timing is too far retarded, it should be noted that the engine will tend to overheat, and there will be a quite noticeable drop in power. If the engine is overheating and the power is down, and the ignition timing is correct, then the carburetter should be checked, as it is likely that this is where the fault lies.

Chapter 5 Clutch and actuating mechanism

Contents

Specifications

Clutch type	Single dry plate diaphragm spring
Actuation	Cable
Number of damper springs	6
Lining outside diameter:	
2000 GT	8 in. (20.32 cm)
3000 GT & E	9.5 in. (24.1 cm)
Lining inside diameter:	
2000 GT	5.75 in. (14.61 cm)
3000 GT & E	6.13 in. (15.56 cm)
Total friction area:	
2000 GT	50.8 sq.in. (328.25 sq.cm)
3000 GT & E	83 sq.in. (536 sq.cm)

Torque Wrench Setting

Clutch to flywheel bolts...	12 to 15 lb/ft. (1.66 to 2.07 kg.m)

1. General Description

1. The 2000 GT is fitted with an 8 inch (20.32 cm), and the 3000 GT & E with a 9.5 inch (24.1 cm), single dry plate diaphragm spring clutch. The unit for both models comprises a steel cover which is dowelled and bolted to the rear face of the flywheel, and contains the pressure plate, diaphragm spring and fulcrum rings.

2. The clutch disc is free to slide along the splined first motion shaft and is held in position between the flywheel and the pressure plate by the pressure of the pressure plate spring. Friction lining material is riveted to the clutch disc and it has a spring cushioned hub to absorb transmission shocks and to help ensure a smooth take-off.

3. The circular diaphragm spring is mounted on shoulder pins and held in place in the cover by two fulcrum rings. The spring is also held to the pressure plate by three spring steel clips which are riveted in position.

4. The clutch is actuated by a cable controlled by the clutch pedal. The clutch release mechanism consists of a release fork and bearing which are in permanent contact with the release fingers on the pressure plate. There should therefore never be any free play at the release fork. Wear of the friction material in the clutch is adjusted out by means of a cable adjuster at the lower end of the cable where it passes through the bellhousing.

5. Depressing the clutch pedal actuates the clutch release arm by means of the cable.

6. The release arm pushes the release bearing forwards to bear against the release fingers, so moving the centre of the diaphragm spring inwards. The spring is sandwiched between two annular rings which act as fulcrum points. As the centre of the spring is pushed in the outside of the spring is pushed out, so moving the pressure plate backwards and disengaging the pressure plate from the clutch disc.

7. When the clutch pedal is released the diaphragm spring forces the pressure plate into contact with the high friction linings on the clutch disc and at the same time pushes the clutch disc a fraction of an inch forwards on its splines so engaging the clutch disc with the flywheel. The clutch disc is now firmly sandwiched between the pressure plate and the flywheel so the drive is taken up.

2. Routine Maintenance

1. Every 6,000 miles adjust the clutch cable to compensate for wear in the linings.

2. The clutch should be adjusted until there is a clearance of 0.138 to 0.144 inch (3.5 to 3.7 mm) between the adjusting nut and its abutment on the bellhousing as indicated in Fig.5.4. When correctly adjusted there should be 0.50 to 0.75 inch (12.7 to 19.1 mm) free play at the clutch pedal.

3. To obtain the correct adjustment, slacken off the locknut (A in Fig.5.4) and get an assistant to pull the clutch pedal onto its stop, then move the adjusting nut 'B' until the correct clearance has been obtained as mentioned in paragraph 2 above.

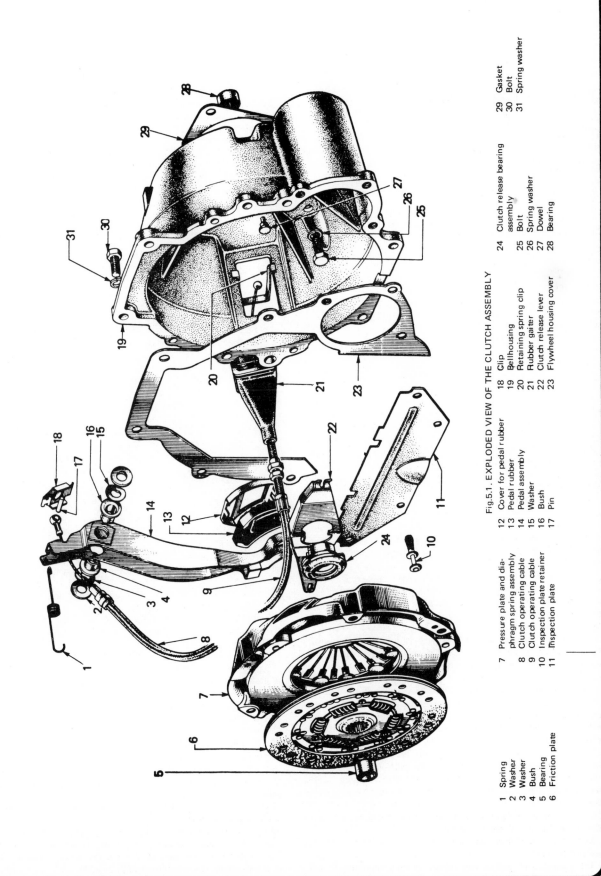

Fig.5.1. EXPLODED VIEW OF THE CLUTCH ASSEMBLY

1 Spring
2 Washer
3 Washer
4 Bush
5 Bearing
6 Friction plate

7 Pressure plate and diaphragm spring assembly
8 Clutch operating cable
9 Clutch operating cable
10 Inspection plate retainer
11 Inspection plate

12 Cover for pedal rubber
13 Pedal rubber
14 Pedal assembly
15 Washer
16 Bush
17 Pin

18 Clip
19 Bellhousing
20 Retaining spring clip
21 Rubber gaiter
22 Clutch release lever
23 Flywheel housing cover

24 Clutch release bearing
   assembly
25 Bolt
26 Spring washer
27 Dowel
28 Bearing

29 Gasket
30 Bolt
31 Spring washer

4. Hold the adjusting nut 'B' steady to prevent it moving and re-tighten the locknut 'A' then recheck the clearance and also the pedal free movement.

5. When fitting a new friction plate it will be found that the cable will need fairly extensive adjustment particularly if the old friction plate was well worn.

3. Clutch Pedal - Removal & Replacement

1. The clutch pedal is removed and replaced in exactly the same way as the brake pedal.
2. A full description of how to remove and replace the brake pedal can be found in Chapter 9/11.

4. Clutch Removal

1. Remove the gearbox as described in Chapter 6, Section 3.
2. Scribe a mating line from the clutch cover to the flywheel to ensure identical positioning on replacement and then remove the clutch assembly by unscrewing the six bolts holding the cover to the rear face of the flywheel. Unscrew the bolts diagonally half a turn at a time to prevent distortion to the cover flange.
3. With all the bolts and spring washers removed lift the clutch assembly off the locating dowels. The driven plate or clutch disc may fall out at this stage as it is not attached to either the clutch cover assembly or the flywheel.

5. Clutch Replacement

1. It is important that no oil or grease gets on the clutch disc friction linings, or the pressure plate and flywheel faces. It is advisable to replace the clutch with clean hands and to wipe down the pressure plate and flywheel faces with a clean dry rag before assembly begins.
2. Place the clutch disc against the flywheel, ensuring that it is the correct way round. The flywheel side of the clutch disc is clearly marked near the centre. If the disc is fitted the wrong way round, it will be quire impossible to operate the clutch.
3. Replace the clutch cover assembly loosely on the dowels. Replace the six bolts and spring washers and tighten them finger tight so that the clutch disc is gripped but can still be moved.
4. The clutch disc must now be centralised so that when the engine and gearbox are mated, the gearbox input shaft splines will pass through the splines in the centre of the driven plate hub.
5. Centralisation can be carried out quite easily by inserting a round bar or long screwdriver through the hole in the centre of the clutch, so that the end of the bar rests in the small hole in the end of the crankshaft containing the input shaft bearing bush. Ideally an old Ford input shaft should be used.
6. Using the input shaft bearing bush as a fulcrum, moving the bar sideways or up and down will move the clutch disc in whichever direction is necessary to achieve centralisation.
7. Centralisation is easily judged by removing the bar and viewing the driven plate hub in relation to the hole in the centre of the clutch cover plate diaphragm spring. When the hub appears exactly in the centre of the hole all is correct (photo). Alternatively the input shaft will fit the bush and centre of the clutch hub exactly obviating the need for visual alignment.
8. Tighten the clutch bolts firmly in a diagonal sequence to ensure that the cover plate is pulled down evenly and without distortion of the flange. Finally tighten the bolts down to a torque of 15 lb/ft. (photo).

6. Clutch Dismantling & Replacement

1. It is not practical to dismantle the pressure plate assembly and the term 'clutch dismantling and replacement' is the term usually used for simply fitting a new clutch friction plate.
2. If a new clutch disc is being fitted it is a false economy not to renew the release bearing at the same time. This will preclude having to replace it at a later date when wear on the clutch linings is still very small.
3. If the pressure plate assembly requires renewal (see Section 7.3 and 4) an exchange unit must be purchased. This will have been accurately set up and balanced to very fine limits.

7. Clutch Inspection

1. Examine the clutch disc friction linings for wear and loose rivets and the disc for rim distortion, cracks, broken hub springs, and worn splines. The surface of the friction linings may be highly glazed, but as long as the clutch material pattern can be clearly seen this is satisfactory. Compare the amount of lining wear with a new clutch disc at the stores in your local garage, and if the linings are more than three quarters worn replace the disc.
2. It is always best to renew the clutch driven plate as an assembly to preclude further trouble, but, if it is wished to merely renew the linings, the rivets should be drilled out and not knocked out with a punch. The manufacturers do not advise that only the linings are renewed and personal experience dictates that it is far more satis-factory to renew the driven plate complete than to try and economise by only fitting new friction linings.
3. Check the machined faces of the flywheel and the pressure plate. If either are grooved they should either be machined until smooth. or renewed.
4. If the pressure plate is cracked or split it is essential that an exchange unit is fitted, also if the pressure of the diaphragm spring is suspect.
5. Check the release bearing for smoothness of operation. There should be no harshness and no slackness in it. It should spin reasonably freely bearing in mind it has been pre-packed with grease.

8. Clutch Cable - Removal & Replacement

1. Place chocks behind the rear wheels, jack up the front of the car, and place stands under the front crossmember.
2. Loosen the locknut on the cable adjuster on the bellhousing and slacken off the adjuster.
3. Spring off the clip (A in Fig.5.2) from the top of the clutch pedal, push out the pivot pin (B) and pull the cable into the engine compartment.
4. Under the car, pull the rubber gaiter clear of the release arm and push the cable towards the gearbox and then out sideways through the slot in the outer end of the arm (See Fig.5.3).
5. Replacement is a straightforward reversal of the removal sequence. Ensure the pivot pin is lubricated.

9. Clutch Release Bearing - Removal & Replacement

1. With the gearbox and engine separated to provide access to the clutch, attention can be given to the release bearing located in the bellhousing, over the input shaft.
2. The release bearing is a relatively inexpensive but important component and unless it is nearly new it is a mistake not to replace it during an overhaul of the clutch.
3. To remove the release bearing first pull off the release arm rubber gaiter.
4. The release arm and bearing assembly can then be withdrawn from the clutch housing.
5. To free the bearing from the release arm simply unhook it, and then with the aid of two blocks of wood and a vice press off the release bearing from its hub.
6. Replacement is a straightforward reversal of these instructions.

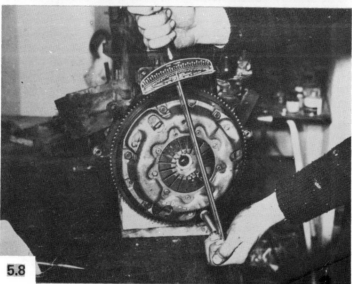

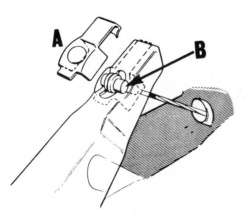

Fig.5.2. Diagram shows clutch cable attachment to the clutch pedal

Fig.5.3. Removing the clutch cable from the clutch release fork

10. Clutch Faults

There are four main faults to which the clutch and release mechanism are prone. They may occur by themselves or in conjunction with any of the other faults. They are clutch squeal, slip, spin and judder.

11. Clutch Squeal - Diagnosis & Cure

1. If on taking up the drive or when changing gear, the clutch squeals, this is a sure indication of a badly worn clutch release bearing.
2. As well as regular wear due to normal use, wear of the clutch release bearing is much accentuated if the clutch is ridden, or held down for long periods in gear, with the engine running. To minimise wear of this component the car should always be taken out of gear at traffic lights and for similar hold-ups.
3. The clutch release bearing is not an expensive item, but difficult to get at.

12. Clutch Slip - Diagnosis & Cure

1. Clutch slip is a self evident condition which occurs when the clutch friction plate is badly worn, oil or grease have got onto the flywheel or pressure plate faces, or the pressure plate itself is faulty.
2. The reason for clutch slip is that, due to one of the faults listed above, there is either insufficient pressure from the pressure plate, or insufficient friction from the friction plate to ensure solid drive.
3. If small amounts of oil get onto the clutch, they will be burnt off under the heat of clutch engagement, and in the process, gradually darkening the linings. Excessive oil on the clutch will burn off leaving a carbon deposit which can cause quite bad slip, or fierceness, spin and judder.
4. If clutch slip is suspected, and confirmation of this condition is required, there are several tests which can be made.
5. With the engine in second or third gear and pulling lightly up a moderate incline, sudden depression of the accelerator pedal may cause the engine to increase its speed without any increase in road speed. Easing off on the accelerator will then give a definite drop in engine speed without the car slowing.

6. In extreme cases of clutch slip the engine will race under normal acceleration conditions.
7. If slip is due to oil or grease on the linings a temporary cure can sometimes be effected by squirting carbon tetrachloride into the clutch. The permanent cure is, of course, to renew the clutch driven plate and trace and rectify the oil leak.

13. Clutch Spin - Diagnosis & Cure

1. Clutch spin is a condition which occurs when the release arm travel is excessive, there is an obstruction in the clutch either on the primary gear splines, or in the operating lever itself, or the oil may have partially burnt off the clutch linings and have left a resinous deposit which is causing the clutch disc to stick to the pressure plate or flywheel.
2. The reason for clutch spin is that due to any, or a combination of, the faults just listed, the clutch pressure plate is not completely freeing from the centre plate even with the clutch pedal fully depressed.
3. If the clutch spin is suspected, the condition can be confirmed by extreme difficulty in engaging first gear from rest, difficulty in changing gear, and very sudden take-up of the clutch drive at the fully depressed end of the clutch pedal travel as the clutch is released.
4. Check that the clutch cable is correctly adjusted and if in order then the fault lies internally in the clutch. It will then be necessary to remove the clutch for examination, and to check the gearbox input shaft.

14. Clutch Judder - Diagnosis & Cure

1. Clutch judder is a self evident condition which occurs when the gearbox or engine mountings are loose or too flexible, when there is oil on the faces of the clutch friction plate, or when the clutch pressure plate has been incorrectly adjusted during assembly.
2. The reason for clutch judder is that due to one of the faults just listed, the clutch pressure plate is not freeing smoothly from the friction disc, and is snatching.
3. Clutch judder normally occurs when the clutch pedal is released in first or reverse gears, and the whole car shudders as it moves backwards or forwards.

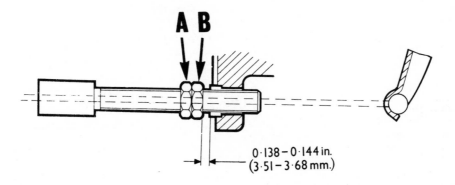

Fig.5.4. VIEW OF THE CORRECT CABLE ADJUSTMENT
CLEARANCE

A Locknut   B Adjusting nut

Chapter 6 Gearbox

Contents

Specifications

Gearbox

Number of gears	4 forward, 1 reverse
Type of gears	Helical, constant mesh
Synchromesh	All forward gears

Selective Circlips - 2000 GT Only

Mainshaft bearing to extension...	7 from .0731 in. to .0660 in. (1.857 to 1.676 mm)
Mainshaft bearing to mainshaft..	8 from .0707 in. to .0791 in. (1.796 to 2.009 mm)

Oil Capacities

Refill - 2000 GT	1.7 pints (2.1 US pints, .96 litres)
- 3000 GT & E...	3.04 pints (3.6 US pints, 1.7 litres)
Initial fill - 2000 GT	1.97 pints (2.4 US pints, 1.11 litres)
- 3000 GT & E..	3.536 pints (4.2 US pints, 1.99 litres)
Grade of oil	Castrol Hypoy Light (SAE 80 EP)

Ratios - 2000 GT

	Gearbox	Overall
1st gear	2.972	10.253
2nd gear	2.010	6.920
3rd gear...	1.397	4.811
Top gear..	1.000	3.444
Reverse gear	3.324	11.447

Ratios - 3000 GT & E

	Gearbox	Overall
1st gear	3.163	10.185
2nd gear...	2.214	7.129
3rd gear...	1.412	4.547
Top gear..	1.000	3.222
Reverse gear	3.346	10.774

Torque Wrench Settings

Bellhousing to gearbox	40 to 45 lb/ft. (5.53 to 6.22 kg.m)
Gearbox drain and filler plugs	25 to 30 lb/ft. (3.46 to 4.15 kg.m)
2000 GT - Gearbox extension to gearbox	30 to 35 lb/ft. (4.15 to 4.84 kg.m)
3000 GT - Gearbox extension to gearbox	40 to 45 lb/ft. (5.53 to 6.22 kg.m)
3000 GT - Selector housing to gearbox	12 to 15 lb/ft. (1.7 to 2.1 kg.m)
3000 GT - Mainshaft nut..	25 to 30 lb/ft. (3.46 to 4.15 kg.m)
3000 GT - Gearbox operating lever nuts	12 to 15 lb/ft. (1.7 to 2.1 kg.m)

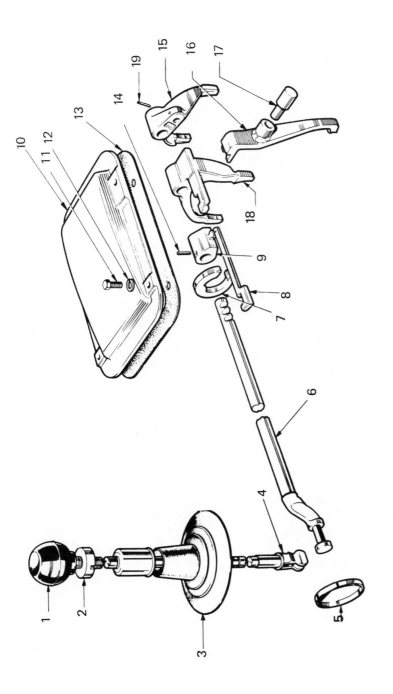

Fig 6:1 EXPLODED VIEW OF THE GEARCHANGE MECHANISM FITTED TO ALL MODELS

1 Gearlever knob
2 Knob locknut
3 Gearlever boot
4 Gearlever

5 Plug
6 Gear selector rod
7 Selector interlock plate
8 Third and fourth gearchange

gate
9 Selector arm
10 Gearbox cover
11 Bolt

12 Spring washer
13 Gasket
14 Split locking pin
15 First and second gear selec-

tor fork
16 Reverse gear selector fork
17 Fork pivot
18 Third and fourth gear selec-

tor fork
19 Pin

1. General Description - 2000 GT

The gearbox fitted to the 2000 GT contains four constant mesh helically cut forward gears and one straight cut reverse gear. Synchromesh is fitted between 1st and 2nd, 2nd and 3rd and 3rd and top. The bellhousing can be separated from the gearbox.

Attached to the rear of the gearbox casing is an aluminium alloy extension which supports the rear of the mainshaft and the gearchange shaft cum selector rod arm.

The gearbox is of á simple but clever design, using the minimum of components to facilitate speed of assembly; and the minimum of matched items to simplify fitting. Where close tolerances and limits are required, manufacturing tolerances are compensated for, and excessive endfloat or backlash eliminated by the fitting of selective circlips.

The gear selector mechanism is unusual in that the selector forks are free to slide on the one selector rod which also serves as the gearchange shaft. At the gearbox end of this rod lies the selector arm, which, depending on the position of the gearlever places the appropriate selector fork in the position necessary for the synchroniser sleeve to engage with the dog teeth on the gear selected. Another unusual feature is that some of the bolts are metric sizes. In particular this applies to the top cover bolts and some of the bellhousing bolts. The reverse idler shaft thread is also metric (a bolt is only inserted here when it is wished to remove the shaft).

It is impossible to select two gears at once because of an interlock guard plate.

2. Routine Maintenance

1. The gearbox oil will never require totally draining during use, but a drain plug is provided for use if the gearbox is to be removed.
2. Routine maintenance should be carried out every 6,000 miles. It consists of cleaning the casing in the immediate area of the filler plug. On the 2000 GT this is on the left-hand side of the casing; on the 3000 GT & E it is on the right. Undo the filler plug with a square headed key, and top up the oil until it reaches the level of the threads in the orifice with Castrol Hypoy Light.

3. Gearbox - Removal & Replacement - 2000 GT

1. The gearbox can be removed in unit with the engine through the engine compartment as described in Chapter 1/7. Alternatively the gearbox can be separated from the rear of the engine at the bellhousing and the gearbox lowered from the car. The latter method is easier and quicker than the former. First unscrew the gearlever knob (photo).
2. Remove the centre console (photo) by undoing the cross-head screws securing it in place.
3. Two of the screws are at the rear by the handbrake cover (photo).
4. Two more screws are placed either side of the consul towards the front (photo).
5. Prise out the plastic imitation wood trims to expose two screws under the handbrake (photo A) and a screw in front of the gearlever (photo B).
6. Pull the leads from the back of the electric clock.
7. At the base of the gear lever, lift off the rubber cover (photo A), knock back the locking tabs (photo B) and unscrew the plastic dome and lift off the gearlever with its washers dome and plastic ball (photo C).
8. Before jacking the car up, remove the gearbox drain plug and allow all the oil to drain into a container for about ten minutes.
9. Jack up the car and fit stands if these are available as a considerable amount of work has to be carried out under the car.
10 Undo and remove the four bolts (photo) securing the propeller shaft to the rear axle flange having first marked both flanges to ensure correct alignment on reassembly.
11 Remove the two bolts (photo) that hold the centre bearing carrier to its bracket, then slide the propeller shaft off the gearbox extension.
12 Disconnect the exhaust pipe from both manifolds by undoing the retaining nuts.
13 Slacken off the adjustment on the clutch cable, remove the rubber gaiter and take the end of the clutch cable out of its slot in the release fork (photo): Tuck the cable out of harms way.
14 Disconnect the battery by taking off the earth lead, and remove the starter motor by undoing the two or three retaining bolts depending on the type of motor fitted.
15 Undo the bolts round the bellhousing periphery, noting that some of them are longer than others.
16 Support the rear of the engine by means of a jack or blocks of wood under the sump.
17 The end of the speedometer cable proved very difficult to get at on the model worked on, and it was necessary to remove the gearbox rear crossmember completely to get at it.
18 This is done by placing a jack under the gearbox to take its weight, then undoing the two bolts found at each end of the rear crossmember and then the recessed centre bolt which attaches the crossmember to the gearbox extension (photo).
19 Now remove the circlip holding the speedometer drive in place, and slide it out of the gearbox extension. Disconnect the reversing light wire at the snap joint (photo).
20 The gearbox is heavy and on no account should it be allowed to hang on the first motion shaft when it is in the half off position. The best way to remove it is to slide it rearwards supported on a trolley jack.
21 Replacement is a direct reversal of the removal procedure, but note the following points:
22 Check that the adaptor plate is correctly in place on the rear of the engine before fitting the gearbox.
23 Do not forget that an engine earth strap may be fitted to one of the top bellhousing bolts.
24 Ensure the mating marks on the propeller shaft and rear axle flanges are in line or vibration may become apparent after reassembly.
25 Refill the gearbox with the correct amount and grade of oil as listed in the specifications at the beginning of this chapter.

4. Gearbox Dismantling - 2000 GT

1. Remove the clutch release bearing from the gearbox input shaft (photo).
2. Then lift out the clutch release lever (photo).
3. Undo and remove the four bolts holding the bellhousing to the gearbox (photo).
4. Detach the bellhousing from the gearbox (photo).
5. Slightly loosen the gearbox drain plug and mount the gearbox upright in a vice using the drain plug as a pivot. Make sure the vice is firmly gripping the drain plug so the assembly cannot tilt.
6. Referring to Fig.6.2, undo the four bolts holding the gearbox top cover (1) in place (photo A) and remove the cover (photo B).
7. Prise out the cup shaped oil seal (26) on the side of the gearbox extension (photo).
8. From under this seal pull out the speedometer gear (25) (photo). To start it, it may be necessary to tap it from the other end.
9. From where the gear lever enters the extension housing drive out the rear extension oil seal (22) (photo).
10 From the right-hand side of the gearbox casing remove the plunger screw (5) its spring (6) and the ball (7) (photo).
11 Using a small drift drive out the pin holding the selector boss to the central rod (photo).
12 Now withdraw the selector rod (photo A) at the same time holding onto the selector boss and cam (photo B) to prevent them falling into the gearbox.
13 To remove the selector forks, it is now necessary to knock the two synchro hubs towards the front of the gearbox, this can be

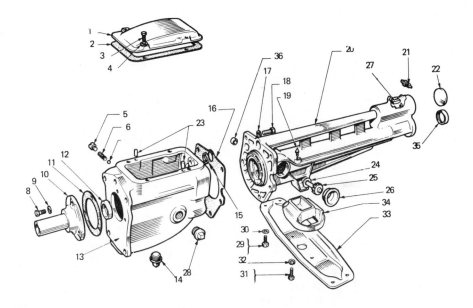

Fig 6:2 EXPLODED VIEW OF THE GEARBOX EXTERIOR

1 Gearbox cover	10 Bearing retainer	19 Breather
2 Gasket	11 Gasket	20 Gearbox extension
3 Bolt	12 Oil seal	21 Reverse light switch
4 Washer	13 Gearbox casting	22 Plug
5 Screw	14 Drain plug	23 Dowels
6 Spring	15 Selector rod seal	24 Circlip
7 Ball	16 Gasket	25 Speedometer gear
8 Bolt	17 Washer	26 Plug
9 Washer	18 Bolt	27 Gear lever orifice

28 Filler/level plug
29 Bolt
30 Washer
31 Bolt
32 Washer
33 Rear crossmember
34 Rubber mounting
35 Oil seal
36 Seal

Fig.6.3. Correct fitting of the circlip securing mainshaft bearing to the gearbox extension

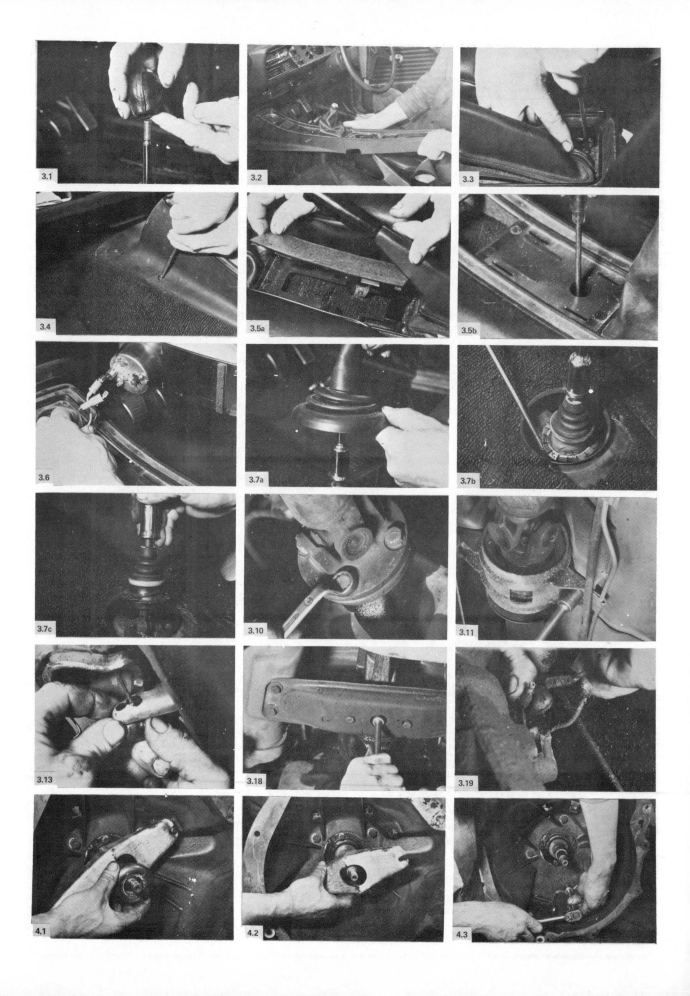

3.1

3.2

3.3

3.4

3.5a

3.5b

3.6

3.7a

3.7b

3.7c

3.10

3.11

3.13

3.18

3.19

4.1

4.2

4.3

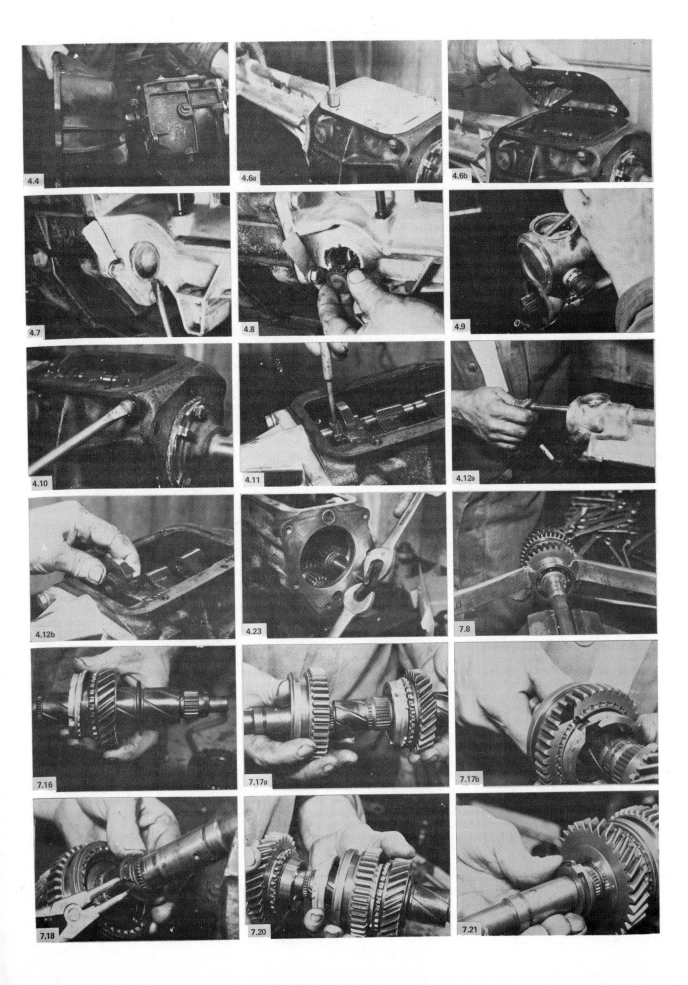

done with a small drift or a screwdriver, now lift out the selector forks.

14 Turn now to the gearbox extension (20) and remove the bolts (18) and washers (17) which hold it to the gearbox casing.

15 Knock it slightly rearwards with a soft headed hammer then rotate the whole extension until the cut-out on the extension face coincides with the rear end of the layshaft in the lower half of the gearbox casing.

16 Get hold of a metal rod to act as a dummy layshaft 6.13/16 inches long with a diameter of 5/8 inches.

17 Tap the layshaft rearwards with a drift until it is just clear of the front of the gearbox casing then insert the dummy shaft and drive the layshaft out and allow the laygear cluster to drop out of mesh with the mainshaft gears into the bottom of the box.

18 With a pair of circlip pliers release the mainshaft bearing retaining circlip and withdraw the mainshaft and extension assembly from the gearbox casing. A small roller bearing should come away on the nose of the mainshaft, but if it is not there it will be found in its recess in the input shaft and should be removed.

19 Moving to the front of the gearbox remove the bolts (8) retaining the input shaft cover (10) and take it off the shaft.

20 Remove the large circlip now exposed and then with a soft headed hammer tap the input shaft towards the rear and remove it from inside the gearbox.

21 The laygear can now be withdrawn from the rear of the gearbox together with its thrust washers (one at either end).

22 Remove the mainshaft assembly from the gearbox extension, by taking out the large circlip shown in Fig.6.3. Then tapping the rear of the shaft with a soft headed hammer.

23 The reverse idler gear can be removed by screwing a suitable bolt into the end of the shaft and then levering the shaft out with the aid of two large open ended spanners (photo).

24 The gearbox is now stripped right out and must be thoroughly cleaned. If there is any quantity of metal chips and fragments in the bottom of the gearbox casing it is obvious that several items will be found to be badly worn. The component parts of the gearbox should be examined for wear, and the laygear, input shaft and mainshaft assemblies broken down further as described in the following sections.

5. Gearbox Examination & Renovation - 2000 GT

1. Carefully clean and then examine all the component parts for general wear, distortion, slackness of fit, and damage to machined faces and threads.

2. Examine the gearwheels for excessive wear and chipping of the teeth. Renew them as necessary.

3. Examine the layshaft for signs of wear, where the laygear needle roller bearings bear. If a small ridge can be felt at either end of the shaft it will be necessary to renew it.

4. The four synchroniser rings (8,12,25,30), (Fig.6.4) are bound to be badly worn and it is false economy not to renew them. New rings will improve the smoothness and speed of the gearchange considerably.

5. The needle roller bearing and cage (2) located between the nose of the mainshaft and the annulus in the rear of the input shaft is also liable to wear, and should be renewed as a matter of course.

6. Examine the condition of the two ball bearing assemblies, one on the input shaft (7) and one on the mainshaft (19). Check them for noisy operation, looseness between the inner and outer races, and for general wear. Normally they should be renewed on a gearbox that is being rebuilt.

7. If either of the synchroniser units (37,38) are worn it will be necessary to buy a complete assembly as the parts are not sold individually.

8. Examine the ends of the selector forks where they rub against the channels in the periphery of the synchroniser units. If possible compare the selector forks with new units to help determine the wear that has occured. Renew them if worn.

9. If the bush bearing in the extension is badly worn it is best to take the extension to your local Ford garage to have the bearing pulled out and a new one fitted.

10 The rear oil seal (35 in Fig.6.2) should be renewed as a matter of course. Drive out the old seal with the aid of a drift or broad screwdriver. It will be found that the seal comes out quite easily.

11 With a piece of wood to spread the load evenly, carefully tap a new seal into place ensuring that it enters the bore in the extension squarely.

12 The only point on the mainshaft that is likely to be worn is the nose where it enters the input shaft. However examine it thoroughly for any signs of scoring, picking up, or flats and if damage is apparent renew it.

6. Input Shaft - Dismantling & Reassembly - 2000 GT

1. The only reason for dismantling the input shaft is to fit a new ball bearing assembly, or, if the input shaft is being renewed and the old bearing is in excellent condition, then the fitting of a new shaft to an old bearing.

2. With a pair of expanding circlip pliers remove the circlip (5), (Fig.6.4) from the input shaft.

3. With a soft headed hammer gently tap the bearing forward and then remove it from the shaft.

4. When fitting the new bearing ensure that the groove cut in the outer periphery faces away from the gear. If the bearing is fitted the wrong way round it will not be possible to fit the large circlip which retains the bearing in the housing.

5. Using the jaws of a vice as a support behind the bearing tap the bearing squarely into place by hitting the rear of the input shaft with a plastic or hide faced hammer.

6. Then refit the circlip (5) which holds the bearing to the input shaft.

7. Mainshaft - Dismantling & Reassembly - 2000 GT

1. The mainshaft has to be dismantled before some of the synchroniser rings can be inspected. For dismantling it is best to mount the plain portion of the shaft between two pieces of wood in a vice.

2. From the forward end of the mainshaft pull off the caged roller bearing (2) and the synchro ring (8). (Fig.6.4).

3. With a pair of circlip pliers remove the circlip (3) which holds the third/fourth gear synchroniser hub in place.

4. Ease the hub (38) and third gear (13) forward by gentle leverage with a pair of long nosed pliers.

5. The hub (38) and synchro ring (12) are then removed from the mainshaft.

6. Then slide off third gear. Nothing else can be removed from this end of the mainshaft because of the raised lip on the shaft.

7. Move to the other end of the mainshaft and remove the small circlip then slide off the speedometer drive taking care not to loose the ball which locates in a groove in the gear and a small recess in the mainshaft.

8. Remove the circlip (21), and then gently lever off the large bearing with the aid of two tyre levers as shown in the photo.

9. The bearing followed by the large thrust washer (28) can then be pulled off. Follow these items by pulling off first gear (29) and the synchroniser ring (30).

10 With a pair of circlip pliers remove the circlip (24) which retains the first and second gear synchroniser assembly in place.

11 The first and second gear synchroniser followed by second gear (14) are then simply slid off the mainshaft. The mainshaft is now completely dismantled.

12 If a new synchroniser assembly is being fitted it is necessary to take it to pieces first to clean off all the preservative. These instructions are also pertinent in instances where the outer sleeve has come off the hub accidentally during dismantling.

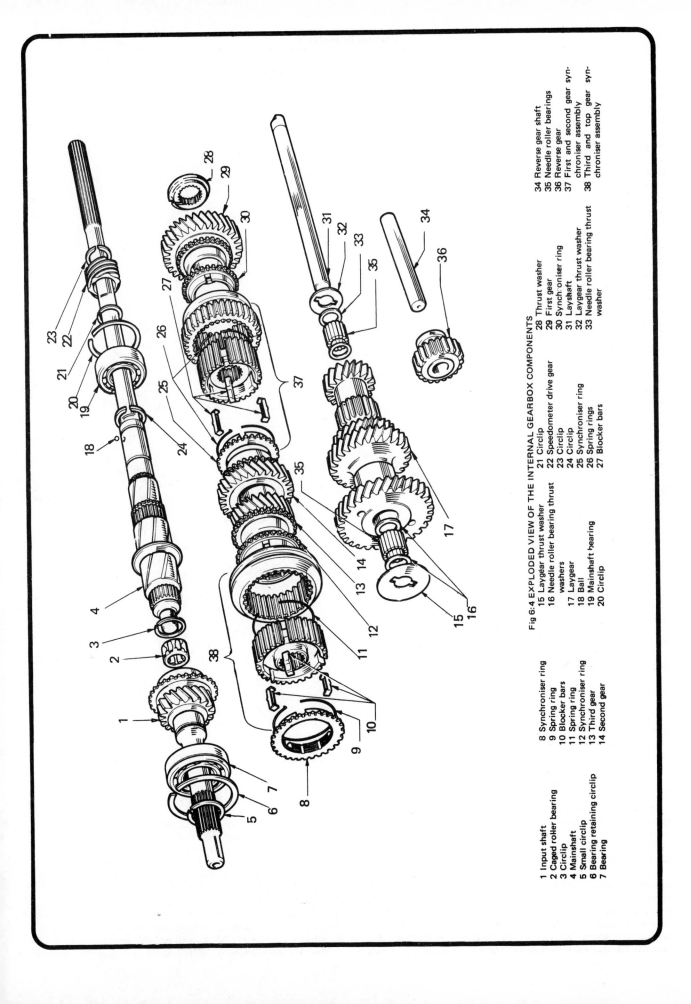

Fig 6:4 EXPLODED VIEW OF THE INTERNAL GEARBOX COMPONENTS

1 Input shaft
2 Caged roller bearing
3 Circlip
4 Mainshaft
5 Small circlip
6 Bearing retaining circlip
7 Bearing

8 Synchroniser ring
9 Spring ring
10 Blocker bars
11 Spring ring
12 Synchroniser ring
13 Third gear
14 Second gear

15 Laygear thrust washer
16 Needle roller bearing thrust washers
17 Laygear
18 Ball
19 Mainshaft bearing
20 Circlip

21 Circlip
22 Speedometer drive gear
23 Circlip
24 Circlip
25 Synchroniser ring
26 Spring rings
27 Blocker bars

28 Thrust washer
29 First gear
30 Synchroniser ring
31 Layshaft
32 Laygear thrust washer
33 Needle roller bearing thrust washer

34 Reverse gear shaft
35 Needle roller bearings
36 Reverse gear
37 First and second gear synchroniser assembly
38 Third and top gear synchroniser assembly

13 To dismantle an assembly for cleaning slide the synchroniser sleeve off the splined hub and clean all the preservative from the blocker bars (27), spring rings (26), the hub itself (A), and the sleeve (B).

14 Oil the components lightly and then fit the sleeve (B) to the hub (A) so the lines marked on them (see Fig.6.5) are in line. Note the three slots in the hub and fit a blocker bar in each.

15 Fit the two springs (26) one on the front and one on the rear face of the inside of the synchroniser sleeve under the blocker bars with the tagged end of each spring locating in the 'U' section of the same bar. One spring must be put on anti-clockwise, and one clockwise when viewed from the side (see Fig.6.6). When either side of the assembly is viewed face on the direction of rotation of the springs should then appear the same.

16 Prior to reassembling the mainshaft read Section 8 of this chapter to ensure that the correct thickness of selective circlips are used. Reassembly commences by replacing second gear (14), gear teeth facing the raised lip and its synchroniser ring (25) on the rear portion of the mainshaft (photo).

17 Next slide on the first and second gear synchroniser assembly (37), (photo A) AND MAKE CERTAIN that the cut-outs in the sycnhroniser ring fit over the blocker bars in the synchroniser hub (photo B); that the marks on the mainshaft and hub are in line (where made); and that the reverse gear teeth cut on the synchroniser sleeve periphery are adjacent to second gear.

18 Replace the circlip (24) which holds the synchroniser hub in place (photo).

19 Then fit another synchroniser ring (30) again ensuring that the cut-outs in the ring fit over the blocker bars in the synchroniser hub.

20 Next slide on first gear (29) so the synchronising cone portion lies inside the synchronising ring just fitted (photo).

21 Fit the splined thrust washer (28) to the front of first gear (photo).

22 The mainshaft bearing is then slid on as far as it will go (photo).

23 To press the bearing fully home, close the jaws of the vice until they are not quite touching the mainshaft, and with the bearing resting squarely against the side of the vice jaws draw the bearing on by tapping the end of the shaft with a hide or plastic hammer (photo).

24 Replace the small circlip retaining the main bearing in place (photo).

25 At this time it is wise to slide over the main bearing the large circlip which retains the mainshaft assembly to the gearbox extension as it will be needed in this position later (photo).

26 Replace the small ball that retains the speedometer drive in its recess in the mainshaft (photo).

27 Slide on the speedometer drive noting that it can only be fitted one way round as the groove in which the ball fits does not run the whole length of the drive (photo).

28 Now fit the circlip to retain the speedometer drive, (photo). Assembly of this end of the mainshaft is now complete.

29 Moving to the short end of the mainshaft slide on third gear (13) so that the machined gear teeth lie adjacent to second gear, then slide on the synchroniser ring (photo).

30 Fit the third and fourth gear synchroniser assembly (38) (photo) again ensuring that the cut-outs on the ring line up with the blocker bars.

31 With a suitable piece of metal tube over the mainshaft, tap the synchroniser fully home onto the mainshaft (photo).

32 Then fit the securing circlip (3) in place (photo). Apart from the needle roller bearing race which rests on the nose of the mainshaft this completes mainshaft reassembly.

8. Selective Circlips - 2000 GT

1. Two of the circlips fitted in the gearbox are available in various thicknesses. This is to ensure that any wear on the mainshaft assembly is taken up and the minimum of endfloat allowed.

2. During reassembly of the mainshaft the first circlip that is a selective one is the bearing retaining circlip (21 in Fig.6.4). It is essential that the thickest circlip that will fit in the groove is used

so that as much endfloat as possible is eliminated. The following thicknesses are available:—

Part No.	Size	Colour Code
2824E-7669-A	.0707 in. (1.795 mm)	Plain
2824E-7669-B	.0719 in. (1.825 mm)	Pink
2824E-7669-C	.0731 in. (1.860 mm)	Magenta
2824E-7669-D	.0743 in. (1.890 mm)	Violet
2824E-7669-E	.0755 in. (1.920 mm)	Green
2824E-7669-F	.0767 in. (1.950 mm)	Blue
2824E-7669-G	.0779 in. (1.980 mm)	Red
2824E-7669-H	.0791 in. (2.010 mm)	Yellow

3. The other circlip which is fitted after selection is the large circlip (20) which holds the bearing in place in the extension housing. Once again it is essential that the thickest circlip that will fit the groove in the housing is used. Although in the mainshaft reassembly it is advised to place this circlip loosely behind the main bearing in the early stages it can in fact be changed when the mainshaft is fitted to the extension housing without any trouble. The following sizes are available:—

Part No.	Size	Colour Code
2824E-7030-A	.0731 in. (1.860 mm)	Yellow
2824E-7030-B	.0720 in. (1.830 mm)	Red
2824E-7030-C	.0708 in. (1.800 mm)	Blue
2824E-7030-D	.0696 in. (1.770 mm)	Violet
2824E-7030-E	.0684 in. (1.737 mm)	Green
2824E-7030-F	.0682 in. (1.732 mm)	Magenta
2824E-7030-G	.0670 in. (1.702 mm)	Plain

9. Gearbox Reassembly - 2000 GT

1. If removed replace the reverse idler gear and selector lever in the gearbox, by tapping in the shaft (34). Once it is through the casing fit the gearwheel (36) so that 1st gear teeth are facing in towards the main gearbox area.

2. Fit the reverse selector lever in the groove in the idler gear then drive the shaft home with a soft headed hammer until it is flush with the gearbox casing.

3. Slide a retaining washer (16) into either end of the laygear (17) so that they abut the internal machined shoulders.

4. Smear thick grease on the laygear orifice and fit the needle rollers (35) one at a time (photo) until all are in place. The grease will hold the rollers in position. Build up the needle roller bearings in the other end of the laygear in a similar fashion.

5. Fit the external washer to each end of the laygear, taking care not to dislodge the roller bearings.

6. Carefully slide in the dummy layshaft used previously for driving out the layshaft in Section 4/16 (photo).

7. Grease the two thrust washers (15 and 32) and position the larger of the two (15) in the front of the gearbox so the tongues fit into the machined recesses.

8. Fit the smaller of the thrust washers (32) to the rear of the gearbox in the same way (photo).

9. Fit the laygear complete with dummy layshaft in the bottom of the gearbox casing taking care not to dislodge the thrust washers, (photo).

10 Now from inside the gearbox slide in the input shaft assembly (1), (photo A) and drive the bearing into place with a suitable drift (photo B).

11 Secure the bearing in position by replacing the circlip (6) (photo).

12 Fit a new gasket to the bearing retainer and smear on some Wellseal or similar sealing compound (photo).

13 Replace the retainer on the input shaft (photo A) ensuring that the oil drain hole is towards the bottom of the gearbox, and tighten down the bolts (photo B).

14 Place the gearbox extension housing in a vice and slide in the mainshaft assembly (photo).

15 Secure the mainshaft to the gearbox extension by locating the circlip already placed loosely behind the main bearing into its groove in the extension (photo A). If it is found to be a loose fit refer to

Fig.6.5. The synchroniser assembly alignment marks

Fig.6.6. The synchroniser hub springs must be put on as shown in the illustration

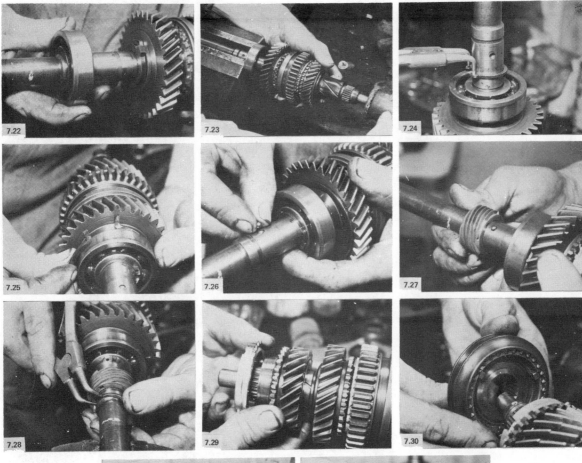

7.22

7.23

7.24

7.25

7.26

7.27

7.28

7.29

7.30

7.31

7.32

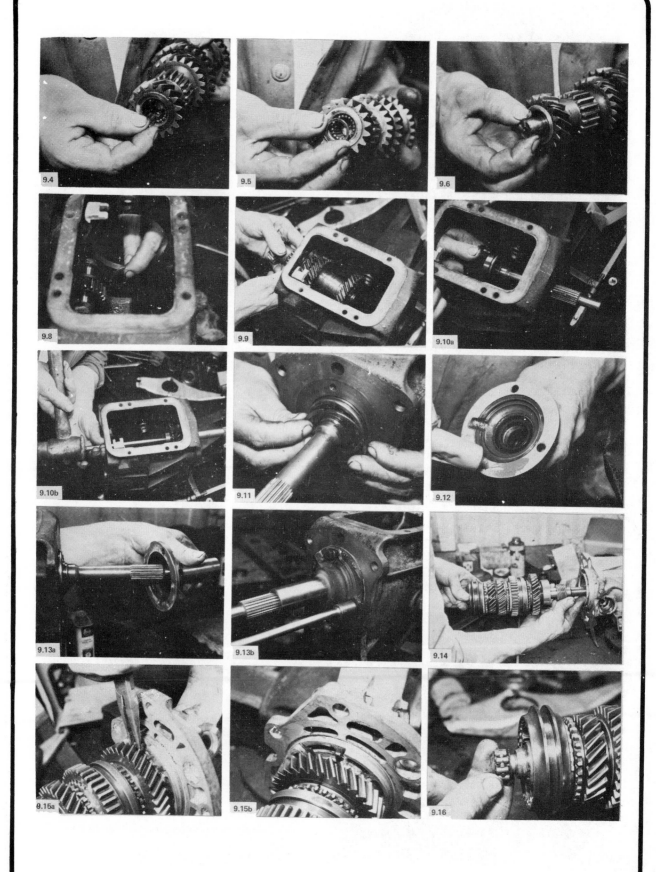

Fig.6.7. Replacing the selector ball, spring and retaining screw

Fig.6.8. Speedometer cable retainer (3000 GT & E)

Section 8 and select a thicker circlip. Photo B shows the circlip correctly located.

16 Fit a new gasket to the extension housing and then replace the small roller bearing on the nose of the mainshaft (photo).

17 Slide the combined mainshaft and housing assembly into the rear of the gearbox and mate up the nose of the mainshaft with the rear of the input shaft (photo).

18 Completely invert the gearbox so that the laygear falls into mesh with the mainshaft gears.

19 Turn the extension housing round until the cut-out on it coincides with the hole for the layshaft (photo). It may be necessary to trim the gasket.

20 Push the layshaft into its hole from the rear thereby driving out the dummy shaft at the same time (photo).

21 Tap the layshaft into position until its front end is flush with the gearbox casing and ensure that the cut-out on the rear end is in the horizontal position so it will fit into its recess in the extension housing flange (photo).

22 Turn the gearbox the right way up again correctly line up the extension housing, and secure it to the gearbox housing by replacing the bolts (photo).

23 The selector forks cannot be replaced until the two synchroniser hubs are pushed by means of a screwdriver or drift to their most forward positions (photos A and B).

24 Now lower the selector forks into position (photo A) and it will be found that they will now drop in quite easily (photo B). Now return the synchroniser hubs to their original positions.

25 Slide the gearchange selector rod into place from the rear of the extension and as it comes into the gearbox housing slide onto it the selector boss and 'C' cam, having just made sure that the cam locates in the cut-outs in the selector fork extension arms.

26 Push the selector rod through the boss and the selector forks until the pin holes on the boss and rail align. Tap the pin into place thereby securing the boss to the selector rod. During this operation ensure that the cut-out on the gearbox end of the selector rail faces to the right.

27 Replace the ball, spring and retaining screw in the top right-hand side of the gearbox casing as shown in Fig.6.7.

28 Apply a small amount of sealer to the blanking plug and gently tap it into position in the rear of the extension housing behind the selector rail.

29 Place a new gasket on the gearbox top cover plate, having applied a layer of Loctite or similar sealer to it and then replace the top cover and tighten down its four retaining bolts.

30 Replace the speedometer drive gear in the extension, smear the edges of its retaining cup with sealing compound and tap the cup into place. Remove the gearbox from the vice and tighten down the drain plug.

31 Replace the bellhousing onto the gearbox and tighten down the retaining bolts, replace the clutch release fork and the clutch release bearing. Reassembly is now complete.

10. Gearbox Removal & Replacement - 3000 GT & E

1. The gearbox can be removed in unit with the engine through the engine compartment as described in Chapter One. Alternatively the gearbox can be separated from the rear of the engine at the bellhousing and the gearbox lowered from the car. The latter method is easier and quicker than the former.

2. Remove the gearbox drain plug from the right-hand lower side of the casing and allow all the oil to drain into a container for at least ten minutes.

3. Jack up the car and fit stands if these are available as a considerable amount of work has to be carried out under the car.

4. Undo and remove the four bolts securing the propeller shaft to the rear axle flange having first marked both flanges to ensure correct alignment on reassembly.

5. Remove the two bolts that hold the centre propeller shaft bearing carrier to its bracket, then slide the propeller shaft out of the gearbox

Fig.6.9. EXPLODED VIEW OF THE CAPRI 3000 GT & E INTERNAL GEARBOX COMPONENTS

1	Synchroniser ring	25	Circlip
2	Spring ring	26	Thrust washer
3	Blocker bar	27	Mainshaft bearing
4	Synchroniser nub	28	Spacer
5	Spring ring	29	Speedometer drive gear
6	Synchroniser sleeve	30	Tab washer
7	Synchroniser ring	31	Mainshaft nut
8	Third gear	32	Mainshaft
9	Second gear	33	Thrust washer
10	Synchroniser ring	34	Needle roller bearing thrust washer
11	Spring	35	Needle roller bearings
12	Blocker bar	36	Needle roller bearing thrust washer
13	Synchroniser hub	37	Laygear
14	Spring ring	38	Needle roller bearing thrust washer
15	Synchroniser sleeve	39	Needle roller bearing
16	Synchroniser ring	40	Needle roller bearing thrust washer
17	First gear	41	Thrust washer
18	Small circlip	42	Layshaft
19	Bearing retaining circlip	43	Reverse gear shaft
20	Bearing	44	Reverse gear
21	Input shaft		
22	Caged roller bearing		
23	Circlip		
24	Ball		

Fig.6.10. EXPLODED VIEW OF THE CAPRI 3000 GT & E GEARBOX EXTERIOR

1	Bolt	23	Bearing housing
2	Spring washer	24	Gearbox extension
3	Bearing retainer	25	Bearing
4	Gasket	26	Oil seal
5	Oil seal	27	Shaft
6	Stud	28	Spring
7	Gearbox casing	29	Sleeve
8	Gasket	30	Spring
9	Pin	31	Oil seals
10	Spring washer	32	Washer
11	Bolt	33	Nut
12	Vent	34	Stud
13	Selector	35	Gasket
14	Pin	36	Gearbox side cover
15	Selector shaft	37	Spring washer
16	Shaft and cam	38	Bolt
17	Dowels	39	Levers
18	Ball	40	Lever
19	Balls	41	Washer
20	Lever and shaft	42	Nut
21	Shaft and cam	43	Washer
22	Selector	44	Nut

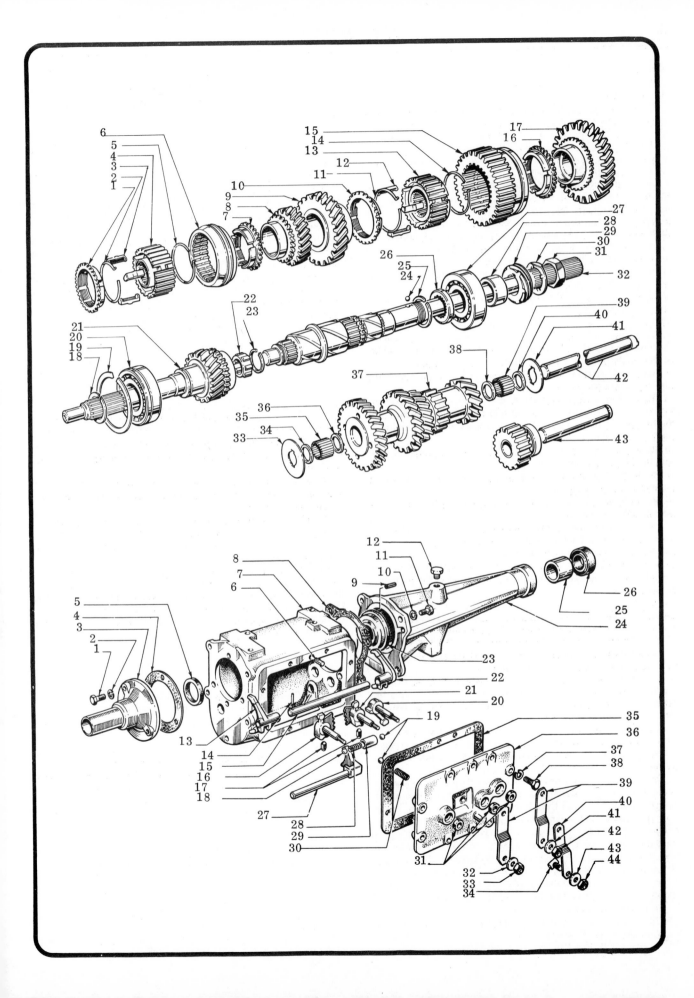

extension.

6. Disconnect the two exhaust pipes from their manifolds by undoing the retaining nuts.

7. Slacken off the adjustment on the clutch cable, remove the rubber gaiter and take the end of the clutch cable out of its slot in the release fork. Tuck the cable out of harms way.

8. Undo the small bolt holding the forked speedometer cable retainer to the gearbox extension, (See Fig.6.8), remove the retainer and pull out the cable from the extension.

9. Disconnect the three gear linkage rods from the operating arms on the left-hand side of the gearbox by removing the spring clips and the single bolts on 1st/2nd and 3rd/4th selector rods. The reverse gear selector rod is retained purely by two spring clips.

10 Disconnect the battery by taking off the earth lead, remove the starter motor terminal lead and then undo its three retaining bolts and remove the starter motor from the car.

11 Undo the bolts round the bellhousing periphery, noting the positions of those that are longer than the rest.

12 Support the rear of the engine by means of a jack or blocks of wood under the sump.

13 Place a jack under the gearbox casing to support its weight, then undo the two bolts found at each end of the rear crossmember. Unscrew the recessed bolt in the centre of the crossmember which holds it to the gearbox extension. Remove the crossmember.

14 Disconnect the reversing light from the gearbox by pulling off the wire at the snap connector.

15 The gearbox on the 3000 GT & E is heavy and on no account should it be allowed to hang on the first motion shaft when it is in the half off position. The best way to remove it is to slide it rearwards supported on a trolley jack.

16 Replacement is a direct reversal of the removal procedure, but note the following points:—

17 Check that the adaptor plate is correctly in place on the rear of the engine before fitting the gearbox.

18 Do not forget that an engine earth strap may be fitted to one of the top bellhousing bolts.

19 Ensure that the mating marks previously made on the propeller shaft and rear axle flanges are in line on reassembly, or vibration may become apparent after reassembly.

20 After refitting, refill the gearbox with the correct amount of Castrol Hypoy Light as listed in the specifications at the beginning of this chapter.

11. Gearbox Dismantling, Reassembly & Examination - 3000 GT & E

1. Remove the selector housing from the left-hand side of the gearbox by undoing the eight bolts and spring washers.

2. Remove the speedometer driven gear and bearing from the gearbox extension then undo the four bolts and spring washers holding the extension to the gearbox casing and carefully withdraw the housing off the mainshaft.

3. Tap the layshaft rearwards with a drift until it is just clear of the front of the gearbox casing. Using a dummy shaft drive the layshaft out and allow the laygear cluster to drop to the bottom of the gearbox.

4. The mainshaft can now be withdrawn from the rear of the gearbox casing. A small roller bearing should come away on the nose of the mainshaft, but if it is not there it will be found in its recess in the input shaft and should be removed at this stage.

5. Moving to the front of the gearbox remove the bolts retaining the input shaft cover and take it off the shaft. Remove the large circlip now exposed and then with a soft headed hammer tap the input shaft towards the rear and remove it from inside the gearbox.

6. The laygear cluster can now be removed from the bottom of the gearbox together with its two thrust washers (one at either end).

7. The reverse idler gear can be removed by screwing a suitable bolt into the end of the shaft and then levering the shaft out with the aid of two large open ended spanners.

8. The gearbox is now stripped right out and must be thoroughly cleaned. Reassembly is a direct reversal of the dismantling procedure.

9. All components of the gearbox should now be examined for damage or wear. To do this follow the basic principles laid out in Section 5 of this chapter.

12. Input Shaft & Mainshaft - Dismantling & Reassembly - 1300 GT & E

1. The basic principles of dismantling and reassembling the input shaft and mainshaft on this gearbox are exactly the same as those listed in Sections 6 and 7 of this chapter covering the 2000 GT gearbox.

2. The one main difference to be found is that the components on the rear end of the mainshaft are held in place by a nut and tab washer and not a circlip.

3. This nut and tab washer must be removed before the speedometer drive gear can be slid off and the other components removed.

4. On reassembly the nut must be tightened to a torque of 25 to 30 lb/ft. (3.5 to 4.2 kg.m) before the tab washer is turned down.

5. When working on either the mainshaft or input shaft it is wise to follow carefully the exploded view of the gearbox internal components in Fig.6.9.

13. Gear Selector Linkage - 3000 GT & E - Adjustments

1. In order to do this task correctly it will be necessary to make up a small tool out of 7/32 inch steel rod to the dimensions shown in Fig.6.11.

2. Slacken off the bolt securing the two uppermost selector rods and remove the spring clip securing the reverse gear selector rod which is the lower of the three.

3. Set the gear lever in the neutral position and lock the selector levers in this position with the alignment tool as shown in Fig.6.12.

4. Set the gearbox operating levers in the neutral position on the side of the gearbox casing.

5. Now tighten the securing bolt on the uppermost selector rods and adjust the reverse gear selector rod by screwing the spigot on the selector rod either in or out as necessary. Once a perfect fit is obtained with the selector lever replace the spring clip.

6. Remove the alignment tool, check that all the gears are obtainable and road test the car.

14. Floor Change Mechanism - 3000 GT & E - Overhaul

1. Jack up the car and fit stands and place the gear lever in the neutral position.

2. Disconnect the gear selector rods from the gearbox operating levers by undoing the retaining bolts and spring clips.

3. Unscrew the gear lever knob and remove the centre console then undo the three bolts holding the floor change mechanism to the centre transmission tunnel.

4. The selector rods can now be removed from the lower end of the selector mechanism.

5. Referring to Fig.6.13, take off the gear lever boot (2) and then the protective dust cover (3) from underneath the assembly.

6. With a drift, drive out the pin (4) which holds the gear lever to the selector lever pivot shaft (6), then lift off the gear lever.

7. Pull the selector levers to the rear until it is possible to slide out the pivot shaft (6).

8. Remove the flat bearing plate (7) the pivot shaft bush (8) and the reverse stop spring (9) and retainer (10).

9. Reassembly is a direct reversal of the dismantling procedure as is the procedure of replacing the assembly in the car.

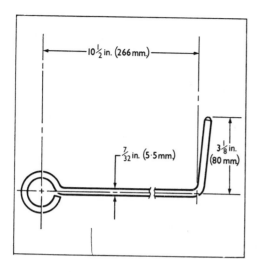

Fig.6.11. Dimensions of selector lever adjustment tool 3000 GT and E (Section 13)

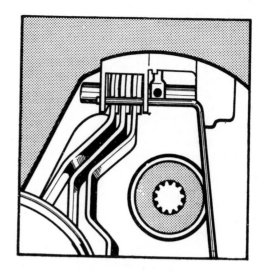

Fig.6.12. Locking the gear selector levers in position, 3000 GT and E (Section 13)

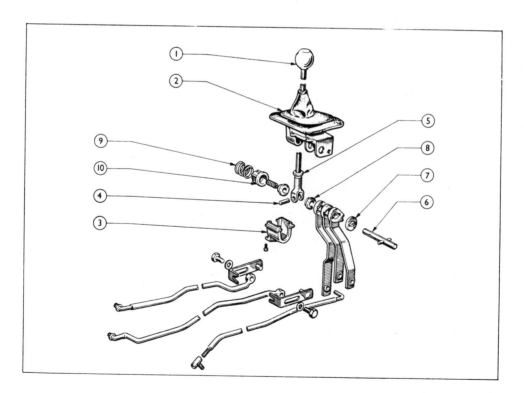

Fig.6.13. EXPLODED VIEW OF THE 3000 GT & E FLOOR CHANGE MECHANISM (Section 14)

1	Gear knob	4	Pin	7	Bearing plate	10 Spring retainer
2	Boot	5	Gear lever	8	Bush	
3	Plastic dust cover	6	Pivot pin	9	Reverse stop spring	

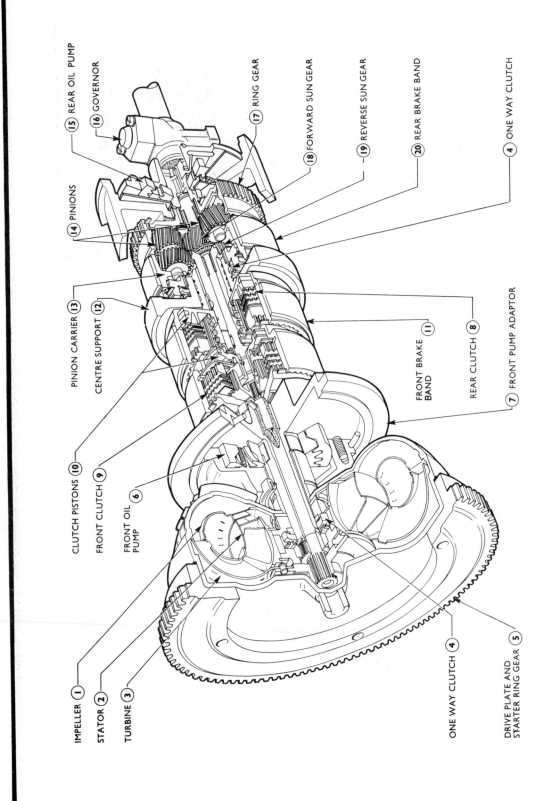

IMPELLER (1)

STATOR (2)

TURBINE (3)

ONE WAY CLUTCH (4)

DRIVE PLATE AND
STARTER RING GEAR (5)

CLUTCH PISTONS (10)

FRONT CLUTCH (9)

FRONT OIL
PUMP (6)

PINION CARRIER (13)

CENTRE SUPPORT (12)

PINIONS (14)

REAR OIL PUMP (15)

GOVERNOR (16)

RING GEAR (17)

FORWARD SUN GEAR (18)

REVERSE SUN GEAR (19)

REAR BRAKE BAND (20)

ONE WAY CLUTCH (4)

FRONT BRAKE
BAND (11)

REAR CLUTCH (8)

FRONT PUMP ADAPTOR (7)

Fig.6.14. THE BORG WARNER TYPE 35 AUTOMATIC TRANSMISSION (Section 15)

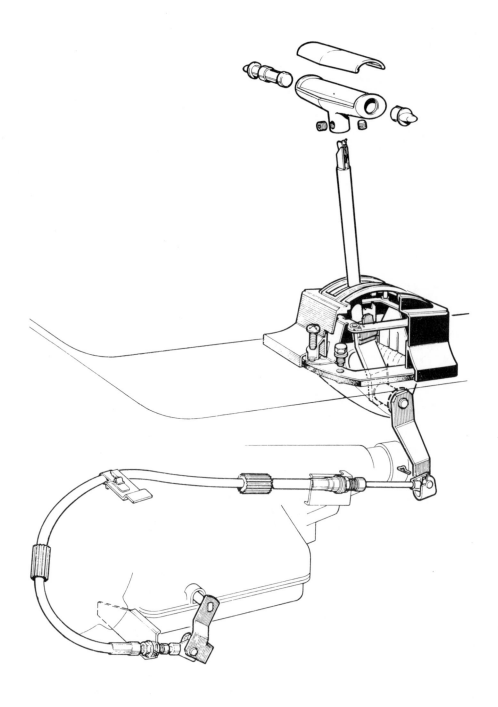

Fig.6.15. View of the selector level and cable assembly with 'A' the adjustment point and 'B' the clevis pin securing the operating arm to the cable end

15. Automatic Transmission - General Description

The automatic transmission available as an optional extra on Capri models is the Borg-Warner Type 35. It consists of a torque converter and a hydraulically controlled automatic epicyclic gearbox with three forward speeds and one reverse.

Selection of the required ratio is obtained by means of a floor mounted lever between the seats. A fixed quadrant at the base of the lever indicates which range has been selected. The quadrant is marked P—R—N—D—2—1.

It is not possible to start the engine unless the gear lever is in the P or N positions. This prevents inadvertent movement of the car and is controlled by an inhibitor switch mounted on the gearbox. To prevent possible damage to the gearbox or engine certain selections cannot be made without depressing the spring loaded button on the side of the 'T' shaped gear stick. These are P to R, R to P, D to 2, 2 to 1, N to R.

Due to the extreme complexity of the automatic gearbox, if the performance is not up to standard or overhaul is necessary this should be entrusted to your local Ford main agents who will have the necessary equipment and special tools essential to sort out most problems.

16. Automatic Transmission - Routine Maintenance

1. Every 6,000 miles check the automatic transmission fluid level. With the engine at its normal operating temperature, move the gear selector to the P position and allow the engine to idle for two minutes or so. Remove the dipstick, wipe it clean and with the engine still idling insert the dipstick and quickly withdraw it again. Top up if necessary down the dipstick tube with Castrol TQF automatic transmission fluid. The difference between the two marks on the dipstick is approximately one pint.

17. Automatic Transmission - Removal & Replacement

1. Open the bonnet and disconnect the negative earth lead from the battery.
2. Detach the downshift cable from its bracket on the rocker cover and also from the throttle linkage.
3. Undo and remove the four uppermost bolts holding the torque converter housing to the engine. One of these bolts also retains the automatic transmission dipstick tube.
4. Jack up the car and fit stands. Then working underneath the car remove the retaining clip and bolt and withdraw the speedometer cable from the transmission.
5. Remove the starter motor which may be held in position by either two or three bolts according to type.
6. Through the hole available after removing the starter motor undo all the bolts securing the drive plate to the torque converter. The crankshaft will have to be rotated to bring each bolt into a position where it can be removed.
7. Remove the stiffening bracket between the engine and the transmission unit and then remove the torque converter dust cover and drain the transmission fluid by removing the drain plug.
8. Disconnect the selector cable from the operating arm on the left-hand side of the transmission and also from its support bracket.
9. Remove the propeller shaft as described in Chapter Seven.

10 Place a trolley jack under the gearbox to support the weight of the latter, and then remove the rear crossmember by undoing the four bolts holding it to the underframe and the one recessed bolt securing it to the gearbox extension.
11 Note the wiring positions on the inhibitor switch then disconnect them. If fitted disconnect the reversing lamp black earthing wire from the rear of the gearbox by undoing one of the gearbox to extension housing bolts.
12 Disconnect the exhaust pipes from the manifolds then remove the dipstick and tube assembly. It may be necessary to slightly lower the gearbox on its jack to do this task.
13 Undo and remove the two remaining bolts securing the torque converter housing to the engine, support the front of the engine with a jack and then slide the gearbox assembly rearwards preferably on a trolley jack and then pull it out from under the car.
14 The torque converter can now be removed. If required the converter housing can be removed from the gearbox casing by undoing the six bolts and spring washers.
15 Replacement of the automatic transmission is a reversal of the removal procedure, but the following torque wrench settings should be observed:—
Gearbox case to torque converter housing 8 to 13 lb/ft. (1.11 to 1.80 kg.m).
Rear crossmember to gearbox 10 to 18 lb/ft. (1.38 to 2.49 kg.m).
Gearbox drain plug 9 to 12 lb/ft. (1.40 to 1.66 kg.m).
Drive plate to torque converter 25 to 30 lb/ft. (3.45 to 4.14 kg.m).

18. Downshift Cable Adjustment

1. This method of adjusting the downshift cable can only be applied if the accelerator linkage is in perfect condition and the original crimped collar is still on the downshift valve cable. If you are in doubt consult your local Ford agent who will have the special equipment to carry out this task on older models with slightly worn linkages.
2. If all is well proceed as follows:— run the engine until it is hot, ensure that the gearbox is topped up with fluid and ensure that the accelerator linkage is set correctly.
3. Slacken off the downshift cable adjuster locknut then adjust the outer cable length with the adjusting nut until the crimped collar on the inner cable contacts the outer cable adjust with the inner cable taut. Retighten the locknut.

19. Selector Linkage Adjustment

1. Jack up the front of the car and fit stands, then working under the car on the right hand side of the gearbox remove the small clip and clevis pin which hold the lower end of the selector cable to the operating arm on the gearbox.
2. Put the selector lever in the car in the 'I' position and pull the operating arm on the gearbox as far to the rear as it will go.
3. Slacken the locknut on the lower bracket and by using the adjusting nut adjust the length of the cable until the clevis pin holes on the gearbox operating arm and the hole in the end of the cable are perfectly lined up. Tighten the locknut.
4. Lightly grease the clevis pin and reassemble it to the operating arm and cable. Secure it in place with its retaining clip.
5. Before lowering the car to the ground, check that all gear selector positions can be obtained.

Symptom	Reason/s	Remedy
Ineffective synchromesh.	Worn baulk rings or synchro hubs.	Dismantle and renew.
Jumps out of one or more gears (on drive or over-run)	Weak detent springs or worn selector forks or worn gears.	Dismantle and renew.
Noisy, rough, whining and vibration.	Worn bearings and/or laygear thrust washers (initially) resulting in extended wear generally due to play and blacklash.	Dismantle and renew.
Noisy and difficult engagement of gears.	Clutch fault.	Examine clutch operation.

NOTE: It is sometimes difficult to decide whether it is worthwhile removing and dismantling the gearbox for a fault which may be nothing more than a minor irritant. Gearboxes which howl, or where the synchromesh can be 'beaten' by a quick gear change, may continue to perform for a long time in this stage. A worn gearbox usually needs a complete rebuild to eliminate noise because the various gears, if re-aligned on new bearings will continue to howl when different wearing surfaces are presented to each other.

The decision to overhaul therefore, must be considered with regard to time and money available, relative to the degree of noise or mal-function that the driver has to suffer.

Fig.6.16. Gear selector rod adjusting bolt 3000 GT & E.

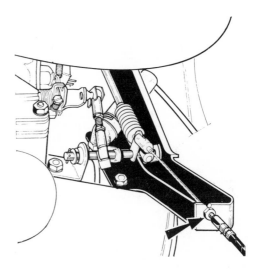

Fig.6.17. Downshift cable adjusting point (Section 18).

Chapter 7 Propeller shaft and universal joints

Contents

1. General Description

The Capri 2000 GT, 3000 GT and 3000 E models all fit as standard equipment a split two piece propeller shaft. The propeller shaft is supported in the centre by a rubber insulated bearing which is bolted to the underframe.

The universal joints at either end of the propeller shaft and the one on the rear of the centre bearing are serviceable as a kit. All universal joints are of the sealed type and require no maintenance.

2. Propeller Shaft - Removal & Replacement

1. Jack up the rear of the car, or position the rear of the car over a pit or on a ramp.
2. If the rear of the car is jacked up supplement the jack with support blocks so that danger is minimised, should the jack collapse.
3. If the rear wheels are off the ground place the car in gear or put the handbrake on to ensure that the propeller shaft does not turn when an attempt is made to loosen the four nuts securing the propeller shaft to the rear axle.
4. Unscrew and remove the four self-locking nuts, bolts and securing washers which hold the flange on the propeller shaft to the flange on the rear axle.
5. The propeller shaft is carefully balanced to fine limits and it is important that it is replaced in exactly the same position it was in prior to its removal. Scratch a mark on the propeller shaft and rear axle flanges to ensure accurate mating when the time comes for reassembly.
6. Undo and remove the two bolts holding the centre bearing housing to the underframe.
7. Slightly push the shaft forward to separate the two flanges at the rear, then lower the end of shaft and pull it rearwards to disengage it from the gearbox mainshaft splines.
8. Place a large can or tray under the rear of the gearbox extension to catch any oil which is likely to leak through the spline lubricating holes when the propeller shaft is removed.
9. Replacement of the two piece propeller shaft is a reversal of the above procedure. Ensure that the mating marks scratched on the propeller shaft and rear axle flanges line up.

3. Propeller Shaft, Centre Bearing - Removal & Replacement

1. Prior to removing the centre bearing from the front section of the two piece propeller shaft, carefully scratch marks on the rear yoke and on the shaft just forward of the bearing housing to ensure

correct alignment on reassembly.
2. Knock back the tab washer on the centre bolt located in the jaws of the rear yoke. Slacken off the nut and remove the 'U' washer from under it.
3. With the 'U' washer removed the rear yoke can now be drawn off the splines of the front section. The centre bolt and its washer remain attached to the splined front section.
4. Slide the bearing housing with its rubber insulator from the shaft. Bend back the six metal tabs on the housing and remove the rubber insulator.
5. The bearing and its protective caps should now be withdrawn from the splined section of the propeller shaft by careful levering with two large screwdrivers or tyre levers. If a suitable puller tool is available this should always be used in preference to any other method as it is less likely to cause damage to the bearing.
6. To replace the bearing, select a piece of piping or tubing that is just a fraction smaller in diameter than the bearing, place the splined part of the drive shaft upright in a vice, position the bearing on the shaft and using a soft hammer on the end of the piece of tubing drive the bearing firmly and squarely onto the shaft.
7. Replace the rubber insulator in the bearing housing ensuring that the boss on the insulator is at the top of the housing and will be adjacent to the underframe when the propeller shafts are replaced.
8. When the insulator is correctly positioned bend back the six metal tabs and slide the housing and insulator assembly over the bearing.
9. Slide the splined end of the shaft into the rear yoke ensuring that the previously scribed mating marks are correctly aligned.
10 Replace the 'U' washer under the centre bolt with its smooth surface facing the front section of the propeller shaft. Tighten down the centre bolt to a torque of 28 lb/ft. and bend up its tab washer to secure it.

4. Universal Joints - Inspection & Repair

1. Wear in the needle roller bearings is characterised by vibration in the transmission, 'clonks' on taking up the drive, and in extreme cases of lack of lubrication, metallic squeaking, and ultimately grating and shrieking sounds as the bearings break up.
2. It is easy to check if the needle roller bearings are worn with the propeller shaft in position, by trying to turn the shaft with one hand, the other hand holding the rear axle flange when the rear universal is being checked, and the front half coupling when the front universal is being checked. Any movement between the propeller shaft and the front and the rear half couplings is indicative of considerable wear. If worn, the old bearings and spiders will have to

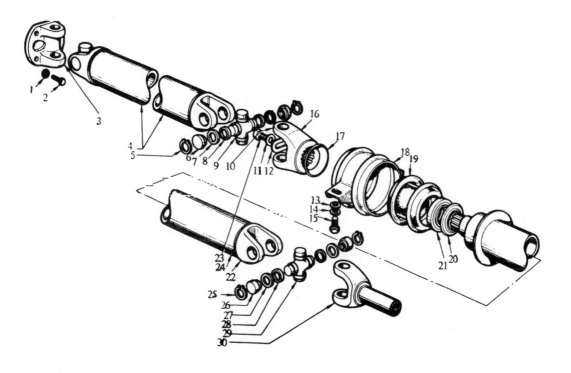

Fig.7.1. EXPLODED VIEW OF THE TWO PIECE PROPELLER SHAFT

1	Lock washer	9	Spider	17	Bearing cup	25	Circlip
2	Bolt	10	Splined centre yoke	18	Bearing housing	26	Needle roller bearing
3	Drive shaft flange yoke	11	Washer	19	Rubber insulator		and cap
4	Rear section propeller shaft	12	'U' washer	20	Bearing cup	27	Oil seal
5	Circlip	13	Washer	21	Bearing	28	Oil sealer retainer
6	Needle roller bearing & cap	14	Lock washer	22	Front section yoke	29	Spider
7	Oil seal	15	Bolt	23	Bolt	30	Splined universal joint
8	Oil seal retainer	16	Yoke	24	Front section propeller shaft		knuckle

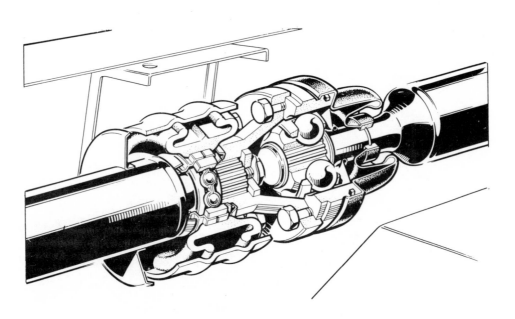

Fig.7.2. Cut-away view of the constant velocity joint

be discarded and a repair kit, comprising new universal joint spiders, bearings, oil seals, and retainers purchased. Check also by trying to lift the shaft and noticing any movement in the joints.

3. Examine the propeller shaft splines for wear. If worn it will be necessary to purchase a new front half coupling, or if the yokes are badly worn, an exchange propeller shaft. It is not possible to fit oversize bearings and journals to the trunnion bearing holes.

5. Universal Joints - Dismantling

1. Clean away all traces of dirt and grease from the circlips located on the ends of the bearing cups, and remove the clips by pressing their open ends together with a pair of pliers (photo), and lever them out with a screwdriver. NOTE: If they are difficult to remove tap the bearing cup face resting on top of the spider with a mallet which will ease the pressure on the circlip.

2. Take off the bearing cups on the propeller shaft yoke. To do this select two sockets from a socket spanner set, one large enough to fit completely over the bearing cup and the other smaller than the bearing cup (photo).

3. Open the jaws of the vice and with the sockets opposite each other and the U.J. in between tighten the vice and so force the narrower socket to move the opposite cup partially out of the yoke (photo) into the larger socket.

4. Remove the cup with a pair of pliers (photo). Remove the opposite cup, and then free the yoke from the propeller shaft.

5. To remove the remaining two cups now repeat the instructions in paragraph 3, or use a socket and hammer as illustrated.

6. Universal Joints - Reassembly

1. Thoroughly clean out the yokes and journals.

2. Fit new oil seals and retainers on the spider journals, place the spider on the propeller shaft yoke, and assemble the needle rollers in the bearing races with the assistance of some thin grease. Fill each bearing about a third full with Castrol LM and fill the grease holes in the spider journal making sure all air bubbles are eliminated.

3. Refit the bearing cups on the spider and tap the bearings home so they lie squarely in position. Replace the circlips.

7. Constant Velocity Joint - Removal & Replacement

1. On some models a constant velocity joint may be fitted in place of the centre bearing on the propeller shaft. This does away with the universal joint on the rear of the bearing.

2. With the propeller shaft removed from the car remove the six bolts and washers holding the two halves of the joint together and separate the bearing cage from the flange.

3. Free the dust cover from the rear of the bearing cage assembly by loosening the metal strap then remove the circlip holding the bearing cage in place and withdraw the bearing assembly from the splines.

4. When replacing a new bearing assembly pack the cage with Castrol MS3 grease leaving an air gap for expansion of the grease then reassemble in the reverse order to dismantling. The six bolts must be tightened down to a torque of 21 to 24 lb/ft. (2.9 to 3.4 kg.m).

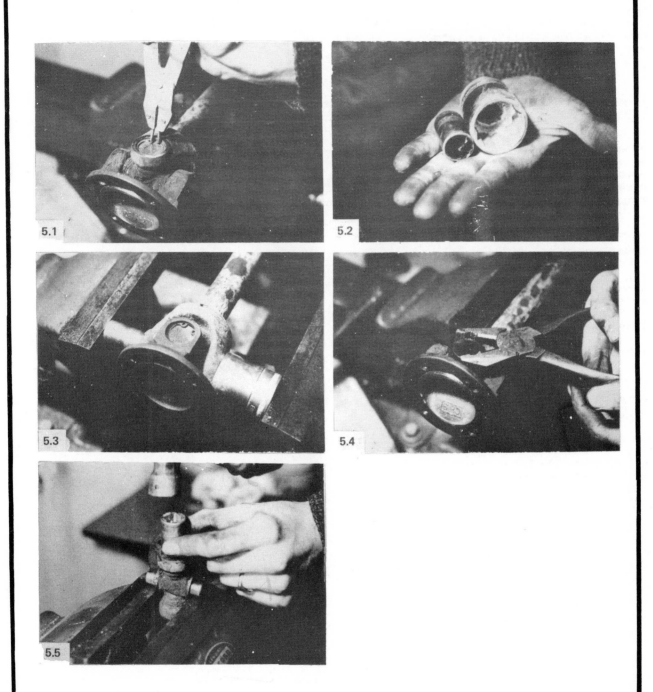

Dismantling universal joints (Section 5.1 to 5.5)

Chapter 8 Rear axle

Contents

Specifications

Type	Semi-floating hypoid
Ratios - 2000 GT	3.44 to 1
- 3000 GT	3.22 to 1
- 3000 GT &3000 E 1971 on	3.09 to 1

Number of Teeth

Crownwheel - 2000 GT	31
- 3000 GT	29
Pinion - 2000 GT	9
- 3000 GT	9

Pinion/Crownwheel backlash	.047 to .086 in. (.12 to .22 mm)
Differential bearing pre-load	.0012 to .0031 in. (.03 to .08 mm)
Differential side gear play	.0004 to .006 in. (.01 to .15 mm)

Rear axle oil capacity...	1.9 pints (2.3 US pints, 1.1 litres)
Grade of oil	Castrol Hypoy

Torque Wrench Settings

Crownwheel to differential	58 to 63 lb/ft. (8.0 to 8.7 kg.m)
Differential bearing cap bolts	43 to 49 lb/ft. (6.0 to 6.8 kg.m)
Axle shaft bearing retainer bolts	20 to 23 lb/ft. (2.7 to 3.2 kg.m)
Pinion flange retaining nut	72 to 87 lb/ft. (10. to 12 kg.m)
Rear cover bolts	22 to 29 lb/ft. (3.0 to 4.0 kg.m)

1. General Description

The rear axle fitted to the Capri 2000 and 3000 differs from that used on other Capri models in that the crownwheel, pinion and differential assembly is no longer removed from the front of the casing. These components are now accessible by removing a cover plate from the rear of the axle housing. The axle is held in place by two semi-elliptic springs and two radius arms. These provide the necessary lateral and longitudinal support for the axle.

As the rear axle is a particularly sensitive piece of equipment needing a variety of special tools to set it up correctly, it is not recommended for the owner to attempt any ambitious repairs. It is simpler and probably cheaper in the long run to fit a guaranteed secondhand axle from a car breakers yard than attempt only complicated repair work.

Should a differential unit cause trouble this can easily be replaced without removing the axle from the car thus reducing dismantling to a minimum. All nuts and bolts on this axle assembly are metric

threads so get hold of some metric sockets and spanners before starting work.

2. Rear Axle - Routine Maintenance

1. Every 6,000 miles remove the filler plug in the rear axle casing and top up with Castrol Hypoy. After topping up do not replace the plug for five minutes or so to allow any excess oil to run out. If the axle is overfilled there is a possibility that oil will leak out of the ends of the axle casing and ruin the rear brake linings.
2. Every 36,000 miles drain the oil from the rear axle when hot, by removing the rear cover as described in Section 6. Refill the axle with 1.9 pints (2.3 US pints, 1.1 litres) of Castrol Hypoy. This is not a factory recommended maintenance task, as there will have been no deterioration in the condition of the oil. However, the oil with time will become contaminated with minute particles of metal and for this reason the author prefers to change the rear axle oil once every three years or 36,000 miles rather than leave it in for the life of the car.

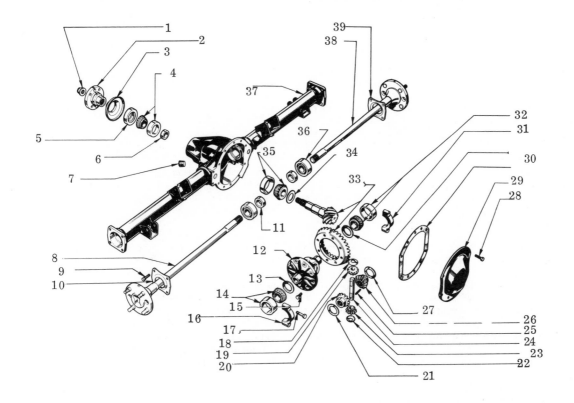

Fig.8.1 EXPLODED VIEW OF THE REAR AXLE

1	Pinion nut	11	Retainer ring	21	Selective spacer	31	Bearing cap
2	Flange	12	Differential housing	22	Pinion thrust washer	32	Bearing assembly
3	Deflector	13	Selective spacer	23	Differential pinion	33	Crown wheel and
4	Bearing assembly	14	Bearing assembly	24	Spider shaft		pinion assembly
5	Seal	15	Bolt	25	Pinion shaft lock pin	34	Selective spacer
6	Selective spacer	16	Bearing cap	26	Differential gear	35	Bearing assembly
7	Filler/level plug	17	Bolt	27	Selective spacer	36	Half shaft bearing
8	Half shaft	18	Pinion thrust washer	28	Bolt	37	Axle housing
9	Bolt	19	Differential pinion	29	Rear axle housing cover	38	Half shaft
10	Bearing retainer	20	Differential gear	30	Selective spacer	39	Bearing retainer

 Fig.8.2. Removing the differential assembly from the axle housing with two tapered pieces of wood

3. Rear Axle - Removal & Replacement

1. Place the car on level ground chock the front wheels, and loosen the rear wheel nuts.

2. Raise and support the rear of the body and the differential casing with chocks or jacks so that the rear wheels are clear of the ground. This is most easily done by placing a jack under the centre of the differential, jacking up the axle and then fitting chocks under the mounting points at the front of the rear springs to support the body.

3. Remove both rear wheels and place the wheel nuts in the hub caps for safe keeping.

4. Mark the propeller shaft and differential drive flanges to ensure replacement in the same relative positions. Undo and remove the nuts and bolts holding the two flanges together.

5. Release the handbrake and by undoing the adjusting nut, disconnect the cable at the pivot point at the rear of the axle casing.

6. Unscrew the union on the brake pipe at the junction on the rear axle and have handy either a jar to catch the hydraulic fluid or a plug to block the end of the pipe.

7. Undo the nuts and bolts holding the shock absorber attachments to the spring seats and remove the bolts thus freeing the shock absorbers. It will probably be necessary to adjust the jack under the axle casing to free the bolts.

8. Unscrew the nuts and withdraw the through bolts holding the radius arms to the rear axle casing.

9. Unscrew the nuts from under the spring retaining plates. These nuts screw onto the ends of the inverted 'U' bolts which retain the axle to the spring.

10 The axle will now be resting free on the jack and can now be removed by lifting it through one of the wheel arches.

11 Reassembly is a direct reversal of the removal procedure, but various points must be carefully noted.

12 The nuts on the 'U' bolts must be tightened to a torque of 18 to 26 lb/ft. (2.49 to 3.60 kg.m).

13 The radius arm nuts on the axle casing must not be fully tightened down until the car is resting on its wheels. This also applies to the shock absorber lower mounting bolts. The torque settings are:—

    Radius arms 22 to 27 lb/ft. (3.04 to 3.73 kg.m).

    Shock absorbers 40 to 45 lb/ft. (5.54 to 6.22 kg.m).

14 Bleed the brakes after reassembly as described in Chapter 9, Section 3.

4. Half Shafts - Removal & Replacement

1. Place the car on level ground, chock the front wheels, loosen the rear wheel nuts on the side being worked on, or both sides if both half shafts are to be removed, then jack up the rear of the car and remove the wheels.

2. Release the handbrake then remove the brake drum securing screw and take off the brake drum.

3. Undo and remove the four bolts retaining the half shaft bearing housing to the axle casing. These bolts are accessible with a socket on an extension through the holes in the half shaft flange.

4. It should be possible at this stage to remove the half shaft by simply pulling on the flange, but if this fails replace the road wheel on the studs and tighten down two opposite nuts just enough to prevent movement of the wheel on the studs.

5. Sitting on the ground, with one leg either side of the wheel and braced on the spring, get a firm hold on the outer edge of the tyre

and pull straight outwards as hard as possible.

6. Care must be taken not to damage the splines on the end of the half shaft when withdrawing by this method as its release from the axle casing may be a bit sudden.

7. Replacement is a reversal of the removal procedure, but once again care should be taken not to damage the splines on the end of the half shaft. The half shaft bearing housing bolts should be replaced at a torque of 20 to 23 lb/ft. (2.7 to 3.2 kg.m).

5. Half Shaft Combined Bearing & Oil Seal - Removal & Replacement

1. The owner is not recommended to attempt to do this job unless the proper Ford tools are available, as the correct fitting of the bearing and oil seal is of vital importance to its efficiency. The tools required are Tool No.P.4090—2 and 6 which is the bearing remover and replacer and Tool No.370 which is a universal taper base to fit an hydraulic or mechanical press.

2. Locate the adaptors of Tool No.P.4090—6 and a slave ring between the bearing and the half shaft flange then by using the universal taper base No.370 support the whole assembly in an hydraulic press and push the half shaft out of the combined bearing and oil seal.

3. To fit a new bearing locate the bearing retainer plate and the bearing on the half shaft making sure that the oil seal side of the bearing is facing the splined end of the half shaft.

4. Using the adaptors on Tool No.P.4090—2 and a slave ring support the assembly in the bed of an hydraulic press.

5. Press the bearing onto the half shaft right up to the stop then in the same way press the retainer ring onto the axle shaft up to the bearing.

6. Differential - Removal & Replacement

1. Release the handbrake cross cable from the back of each brake drum by pulling out the small spring clips and withdrawing the clevis pins.

2. To give more room to work in, release the handbrake return spring from its bracket on the axle casing then remove the operating lever from the casing.

3. Place a bowl or similar container under the rear axle back plate then remove the back plate and gasket by undoing the retaining bolts and allow the oil to drain into the container.

4. Whilst the oil is draining withdraw the half shafts about four or five inches out of the axle casing as described in Section 4.

5. Working inside the axle casing undo and remove the four bolts holding the two 'U' shaped differential bearing caps in the casing. Remove the bearing caps.

6. Fig.8.2 shows the differential assembly being removed from the axle casing using two pieces of tapered wood. In this case the axle was out of the car, but the same method should be used with the axle in situ.

7. With the differential assembly out of the car the crownwheel can, if required, now be removed from it by undoing the 8 retaining bolts.

8. Replacement is a direct reversal of the removal procedure, but make sure the various bolts are torqued down to the correct settings shown in the Specifications of this chapter.

9. Before replacing the rear cover plate, carefully clean the two mating surfaces and always fit a new gasket.

Castrol GRADES

Castrol Engine Oils

Castrol GTX

An ultra high performance SAE 20W/50 motor oil which exceeds the latest API MS requirements and manufacturers' specifications. Castrol GTX with liquid tungsten† generously protects engines at the extreme limits of performance, and combines both good cold starting with oil consumption control. Approved by leading car makers.

Castrol XL 20/50

Contains liquid tungsten†; well suited to the majority of conditions giving good oil consumption control in both new and old cars.

Castrolite (Multi-grade)

This is the lightest multi-grade oil of the Castrol motor oil family containing liquid tungsten†. It is best suited to ensure easy winter starting and for those car models whose manufacturers specify lighter weight oils.

Castrol Grand Prix

An SAE 50 engine oil for use where a heavy, full-bodied lubricant is required.

Castrol Two-Stroke-Four

A premium SAE 30 motor oil possessing good detergency characteristics and corrosion inhibitors, coupled with low ash forming tendency and excellent anti-scuff properties. It is suitable for all two-stroke motor-cycles, and for two-stroke and small four-stroke horticultural machines.

Castrol CR (Multi-grade)

A high quality engine oil of the SAE-20W/30 multi-grade type, suited to mixed fleet operations.

Castrol CRI 10, 20, 30

Primarily for diesel engines, a range of heavily fortified, fully detergent oils, covering the requirements of DEF 2101-D and Supplement 1 specifications.

Castrol CRB 20, 30

Primarily for diesel engines, heavily fortified, fully detergent oils, covering the requirements of MIL-L-2104B.

Castrol R 40

Primarily designed and developed for highly stressed racing engines. Castrol 'R' should not be mixed with any other oil nor with any grade of Castrol.
†*Liquid Tungsten is an oil soluble long chain tertiary alkyl primary amine tungstate covered by British Patent No. 882,295.*

Castrol Gear Oils

Castrol Hypoy (90 EP)

A light-bodied powerful extreme pressure gear oil for use in hypoid rear axles and in some gearboxes.

Castrol Gear Oils (continued)

Castrol Hypoy Light (80 EP)

A very light-bodied powerful extreme pressure gear oil for use in hypoid rear axles in cold climates and in some gearboxes.

Castrol Hypoy B (90 EP)

A light-bodied powerful extreme pressure gear oil that complies with the requirements of the MIL-L-2105B specification, for use in certain gearboxes and rear axles.

Castrol Hi-Press (140 EP)

A heavy-bodied extreme pressure gear oil for use in spiral bevel rear axles and some gearboxes.

Castrol ST (90)

A light-bodied gear oil with fortifying additives

Castrol D (140)

A heavy full-bodied gear oil with fortifying additives.

Castrol Thio-Hypoy FD (90 EP)

A light-bodied powerful extreme pressure gear oil. This is a special oil for running-in certain hypoid gears.

Automatic Transmission Fluids

Castrol TQF

(Automatic Transmission Fluid)

Approved for use in all Borg-Warner Automatic Transmission Units. Castrol TQF also meets Ford specification M2C 33F.

Castrol TQ Dexron®

(Automatic Transmission Fluid)

Complies with the requirements of Dexron® Automatic Transmission Fluids as laid down by General Motors Corporation.

Castrol Greases

Castrol LM

A multi-purpose high melting point lithium based grease approved for most automotive applications including chassis and wheel bearing lubrication.

Castrol MS3

A high melting point lithium based grease containing molybdenum disulphide.

Castrol BNS

A high melting point grease for use where recommended by certain manufacturers in front wheel bearings when disc brakes are fitted.

Castrol Greases (continued)

Castrol CL

A semi-fluid calcium based grease, which is both waterproof and adhesive, intended for chassis lubrication.

Castrol Medium

A medium consistency calcium based grease.

Castrol Heavy

A heavy consistency calcium based grease.

Castrol PH

A white grease for plunger housings and other moving parts on brake mechanisms. *It must NOT be allowed to come into contact with brake fluid when applied to the moving parts of hydraulic brakes.*

Castrol Graphited Grease

A graphited grease for the lubrication of transmission chains.

Castrol Under-Water Grease

A grease for the under-water gears of outboard motors.

Anti-Freeze

Castrol Anti-Freeze

Contains anti-corrosion additives with ethylene. glycol. Recommended for the cooling systems of all petrol and diesel engines.

Speciality Products

Castrol Girling Damper Oil Thin

The oil for Girling piston type hydraulic dampers.

Castrol Shockol

A light viscosity oil for use in some piston type shock absorbers and in some hydraulic systems employing synthetic rubber seals. It must not be used in braking systems.

Castrol Penetrating Oil

A leaf spring lubricant possessing a high degree of penetration and providing protection against rust.

Castrol Solvent Flushing Oil

A light-bodied solvent oil, designed for flushing engines, rear axles, gearboxes and gearcasings.

Castrollo

An upper cylinder lubricant for use in the proportion of 1 fluid ounce to two gallons of fuel.

Everyman Oil

A light-bodied machine oil containing anti-corrosion additives for both general use and cycle lubrication.

Chapter 9 Braking system

Contents

Specifications

Type of System	Disc at front drum at rear
Footbrake	Hydraulic on all 4 wheels
Handbrake	Mechanical to rear wheels only
Front brake layout	Trailing callipers

Brake Dimensions

Front - Disc diameter	9.625 in. (24.45 cm)
- Disc thickness	.500 in. (1.26 cm)
- Maximum disc run-out	.0035 in.' (.089 mm)
- Cylinder diameter	2.125 in. (5.39 cm)
- Total pad swept area	189.5 sq.in. (1220 sq.cm)
- Early pad colour coding	Green, Red, Red, Red
- Later pad coding - 2000 GT	MNTX M108 GH
- 3000 GT	FER 2430F FF

Rear - Drum dimensions - 2000 GT	9 x 1.75 in. (22.9 x 4.45 cm)
- 3000 GT	9 x 2.25 in. (22.9 x 5.72 cm)
- Total shoe swept area - 2000 GT	99 sq.in. (639 sq.cm)
- 3000 GT	127.3 sq.in. (821.3 sq.cm)
- Rear wheel cylinder diameter - 2000 GT...	.75 in. (1.87 cm)
- 3000 GT...	.70 in. (1.77 cm)
Lining code - 2000 GT	DON 242 FE
- 3000 GT	MNTX M79 GG

Master Cylinder Diameter ... ...   .813 in. (2.06 cm)

Mechanical Servo

Boost ratio	2.2 to 1
Diaphragm area	38 sq.in.

Torque Wrench Settings

Brake calliper to suspension	45 to 50 lb/ft. (6.22 to 6.91 kg.m)
Disc to hub...	30 to 34 lb/ft. (4.15 to 4.70 kg.m)
Rear backplate to axle housing...	15 to 18 lb/ft. (2.07 to 2.49 kg.m)
Hydraulic pipe unions..	5 to 7 lb/ft. (0.7 to 1.0 kg.m)
Bleed valves...	5 to 7 lb/ft. (0.7 to 1.0 kg.m)

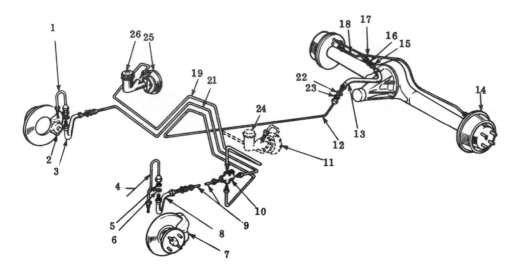

Fig.9.2. DUAL LINE BRAKE PIPE LAYOUT — WITH SERVO

1	Pipe	10	Brake calliper	19	Nut	28 Pipe
2	Calliper	11	Washer	20	Washer	29 Pipe
3	Flexible hose	12	Nut	21	Flexible hose	30 L.H.D. master cylinder
4	Nut	13	Pipe	22	Brake drum	31 Master cylinder
5	Washer	14	Pressure differential valve	23	Washer	32 Servo
6	Pipe	15	L.H.D. pipe	24	Nut	33 Nut
7	Nut	16	L.H.D. pipe	25	Pipe	34 Washer
8	Washer	17	L.H.D. servo	26	Pipe	
9	Flexible hose	18	Pipe	27	Pipe	

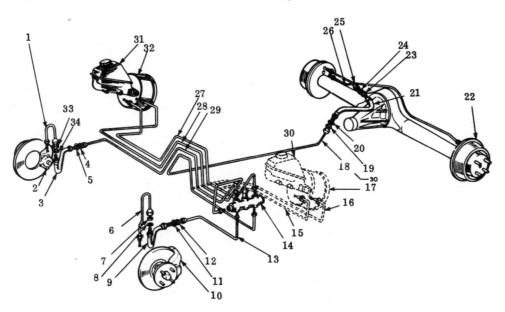

Fig.9.1. SINGLE LINE BRAKE PIPE LAYOUT — WITH SERVO

1	Pipe	8	Flexible hose	15	Washer	23 Nut
2	Brake calliper	9	Pipe	16	Nut	24 L.H.D. master cylinder
3	Flexible hose	10	Four-way connector	17	Pipe	25 Servo
4	Pipe	11	L.H.D. servo	18	Pipe	26 Master cylinder
5	Nut	12	Pipe	19	Pipe	
6	Washer	13	Flexible hose	21	Pipe	
7	Brake calliper	14	Brake drum	22	Washer	

1. Disc/Drum Brakes - General Description

Disc brakes are fitted to the front wheels of all models together with single leading shoe drum brakes at the rear. The mechanically operated handbrake works on the rear wheels only.

The brakes fitted to the front wheels are of the rotating disc and static calliper type, with one calliper per disc, each calliper containing two piston operated friction pads, which on application of the footbrake pinch the disc rotating between them. The front brakes are of the trailing calliper type to minimise the entry of water.

Application of the footbrake creates hydraulic pressure in the master cylinder and fluid from the cylinder travels via steel and flexible pipes to the cylinders in each half of the callipers, thus pushing the pistons, to which are attached the friction pads, into contact with either side of the disc.

Two seals are fitted to the operating cylinders, the outer seal prevents moisture and dirt entering the cylinder, while the inner seal which is retained in a groove inside the cylinder, prevents fluid leakage.

As the friction pads wear so the pistons move further out of the cylinders and the level of the fluid in the hydraulic reservoir drops. Disc pad wear is therefore taken up automatically and eliminates the need for periodic adjustment by the owner.

All Capri models use a floor mounted handbrake located between the front seats.

A single cable runs from the lever to a compensator mechanism on the back of the rear axle casing. From the compensator a single cable runs to the rear brake drums. As the rear brake shoes wear the handbrake cables operate a self adjusting mechanism in the rear brake drums thus doing away with the necessity for the owner to adjust the brakes on each rear wheel individually. The only adjustment required is on the handbrake compensator mechanism, due to wear in the linkage.

A suspended vacuum type servo is fitted as standard equipment on all models.

On certain models, in particular those cars for export to the U.S.A. a dual braking system is fitted providing separate hydraulic circuits for the front and rear brakes. Should one circuit fail the other circuit is unaffected and the car can still be stopped. A warning light is fitted on the fascia which illuminates, should either circuit fail. The bulb in the light can also be tested by means of the switch provided.

2. Brake - Maintenance

1. Every 3,000 miles or more frequently if necessary, carefully clean the top of the brake master cylinder reservoir, remove the cap, and inspect the level of the fluid which should be ¼ inch below the bottom of the filler neck. Check that the breathing holes in the cap are clear.
2. If the fluid is below this level, top up the reservoir with Castrol Girling brake fluid or any approved fluid conforming to SAE J1703A or SAE J700R3. It is vital that no other brake fluid is used. Use of a non-standard fluid may result in brake failure caused by the perishing of special seals in the master cylinder and brake cylinders. If topping up becomes frequent, then check the metal piping and flexible hoses for leaks, and check for worn brake or master cylinders which can also cause loss of fluid.
3. Every 6,000 miles check the front brake disc pads and the rear brake shoes for wear and renew them if necessary. Also check the adjustment on the handbrake cable and adjust if necessary. Due to the self adjusting rear brakes it should not be necessary to adjust the handbrake cable unless wear has taken place in the linkage.
4. Every 36,000 miles or three years whichever comes sooner it is advisable to change the fluid in the braking system and at the same time renew all hydraulic seals and flexible hoses.

3. Bleeding the Hydraulic System

1. Removal of all the air from the hydraulic system is essential to the correct working of the braking system, and before undertaking this, examine the fluid reservoir cap to ensure that both vent holes, one on top and the second underneath but not in line, are clear; check the level of fluid and top up if required.
2. Check all brake line unions and connections for possible seepage, and at the same time check the condition of the rubber hoses, which may be perished.
3. If the condition of the wheel cylinders is in doubt, check for possible signs of fluid leakage.
4. If there is any possibility of incorrect fluid having been put into the system, drain all the fluid out and flush through with methylated spirits. Renew all piston seals and cups since these will be affected and could possibly fail under pressure.
5. Gather together a clean jam jar, a 9 inch length of tubing which fits tightly over the bleed nipples, and a tin of the correct brake fluid.
6. To bleed the system, clean the areas around the bleed valves, and start on the front brakes first by removing the rubber cup over the bleed valve, if fitted, and fitting a rubber tube in position.
7. Place the end of the tube in a clean glass jar containing sufficient fluid to keep the end of the tube underneath during the operation.
8. Open the bleed valve with a spanner and quickly press down the brake pedal. After slowly releasing the pedal, pause for a moment to allow the fluid to recoup in the master cylinder and then depress again. This will force air from the system. Continue until no more air bubbles can be seen coming from the tube. At intervals make certain that the reservoir is kept topped up, otherwise air will enter at this point again.
9. Repeat this operation on the other front brake and the left-hand rear brake, there being no bleed valve on the right-hand rear brake. When completed, check the level of the fluid in the reservoir and then check the feel of the brake pedal, which should be firm and free from any 'spongy' action, which is normally associated with air in the system.

4. Rear Brake Shoes - Inspection, Removal & Replacement

After high mileages it will be necessary to fit replacement brake shoes with new linings. Refitting new brake linings to old shoes is not always satisfactory, but if the services of a local garage or workshop with brake lining equipment is available, then there is no reason why your own shoes should not be successfully relined.

1. Remove the hub cap, loosen off the wheel nuts, then securely jack up the car, and remove the road wheel. Chock the front wheels and fully release the handbrake.
2. Undo the single domed screw retaining the brake drum and then pull off the drum.
3. Remove the small holding down springs from each shoe by turning two small top washers through 90°.
4. Pull out the ends of each shoe from their locating slots in the fixed pivot on one side of the drum and the wheel cylinder on the other side. When removing the shoes from their slots in the wheel cylinder great care should be taken not to allow the piston to fall out of the wheel cylinder. This can be kept in place by an elastic band.
5. Remove the shoes with the return springs still attached. then take off the return springs noting that they are of different lengths and the positions in which they are fitted.
6. Take the self adjusting ratchet wheel assembly off the wheel cylinder and turn the ratchet wheel until it is right up against the end of the slot headed bolt on which it rotates. This has the effect of adjusting the rear brake to the fully off position. If this is not done it may be found difficult to get the brake drum to fit over the new shoes when reassembling.
7. The brake linings should be examined and must be renewed if they

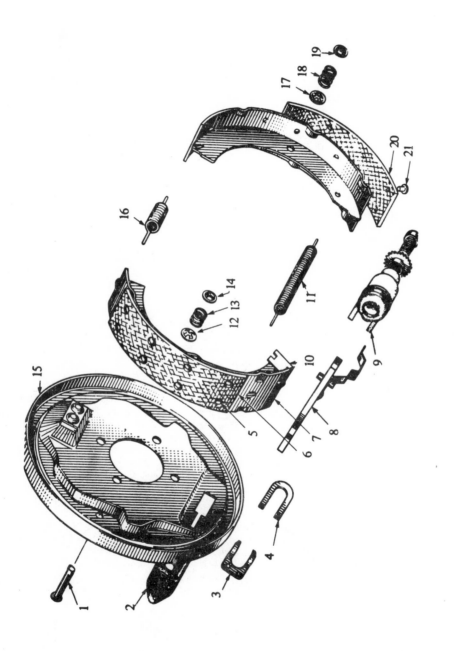

Fig.9.3. EXPLODED VIEW OF THE REAR BRAKE ASSEMBLY

1 Pin
2 Dust cover
3 Cylinder retaining clip
4 Cylinder retaining clip
5 Rivet
6 Lining material

7 Shoe
8 Handbrake lever
9 Wheel cylinder
10 Shoe support plate
11 Return spring
12 Spring seating washer

13 Spring
14 Pin retainer
15 Backplate
16 Return spring
17 Spring seating washer
18 Spring

19 Pin retainer
20 Lining material
21 Rivet

are so worn that the rivet heads are flush with the surface of the lining. If bonded linings are fitted these must be renewed when the material has worn down to 1/32nd inch at its thinnest point.

8. Replacement of the shoes is a direct reversal of the removal procedure but great care must be taken to ensure that the return springs are correctly fitted.

9. When replacement of the shoes is complete, operate the handbrake several times to allow the rear brake self adjusting mechanism to bring the shoes into the correct position, then road test the car to ensure the brakes are operating correctly.

5. Flexible Hoses - Inspection, Removal & Replacement

1. Inspect the condition of the flexible hydraulic hoses leading from under the front wings to the brackets on the front suspension units, and also the single hose on the rear axle casing. If they are swollen, damaged or chafed, they must be renewed.

2. Undo the locknuts at both ends of the flexible hoses and then holding the hexagon nut on the flexible hose steady undo the other union nut and remove the flexible hose and washer.

3. Replacement is a reversal of the removal procedure, but carefully check that all the securing brackets are in a sound condition and that the locknuts are tight.

4. After replacing a flexible hose bleed the brakes as described in Section 3.

6. Rear Brake Seals - Inspection & Overhaul

If hydraulic fluid is leaking from one of the rear brake cylinders it will be necessary to dismantle the cylinder and replace the dust cover and piston sealing rubber. If brake fluid is found running down the side of the wheel, or it is noticed that a pool of liquid forms alongside one wheel and the level in the master cylinder has dropped, and the hoses are in good order proceed as follows:—

1. Remove the offending brake drum and shoes as described in Section 4.

2. Remove the small metal clip holding the rubber dust cap in place then prise off the dust cap.

3. Take the piston complete with its seal out of the cylinder bore and then withdraw the spring from the bore as well. Should the piston and seal prove difficult to remove gentle pressure on the brake pedal will push it out of the bore. If this method is used, place a quantity of rag under the brake backplate to catch the hydraulic fluid as it pours out of the cylinder.

4. Inspect the cylinder bore for score marks caused by impurities in the hydraulic fluid. If any are found the cylinder and piston will require renewal together as an exchange unit.

5. If the cylinder bore is sound thoroughly clean it out with fresh hydraulic fluid.

6. The old rubber seal will probably be visibly worn or swollen. Detach it from the piston, smear a new rubber seal with hydraulic fluid and assemble it to the piston with the flat face of the seal next to the piston rear shoulder.

7. Reassembly is a direct reversal of the above procedure. If the rubber dust cap appears to be worn or damaged this should also be replaced.

8. Replenish the hydraulic fluid, replace the brake shoes and drum and bleed the braking system as described in Section 3.

7. Rear Wheel Cylinders - Removal & Replacement

1. Remove the left or right-hand brake drum and brake shoes as required, as described in Section 4.

2. To avoid having to completely drain the hydraulic system screw down the master cylinder reservoir cap tightly over a piece of polythene.

3. Free the hydraulic pipe from the wheel cylinder at the union, (there are two unions on the right-hand brake plate).

4. Working on the inside of the brake backplate remove the spring clip and clevis pin from the handbrake link.

5. From the back of the brake backplate prize off and remove the rubber boot on the back of the wheel cylinder.

6. Pull off the two 'U' shaped retainers holding the wheel cylinder to the backplate noting that the spring retainer is fitted from the handbrake link end of the wheel cylinder and the flat retainer from the other end, the flat retainer being located between the spring retainer and the wheel cylinder.

7. Now the wheel cylinder together with the handbrake link can be removed from the brake backplate.

8. Before commencing replacement smear the area where the wheel cylinder slides on the backplate and the brake shoe support pads with Castrol PH white brake grease or other approved brake grease.

9. Replacement is a straightforward reversal of the removal sequence, but the following points should be checked with extra care.

10 After fitting the rubber boot, check that the wheel cylinder can slide freely in the carrier plate and that the handbrake link operates the self adjusting mechanism correctly.

11 It is important to note that the self adjusting ratchet mechanism on the right-hand rear brake is right-hand threaded and the mechanism on the left-hand rear brake is left-hand threaded.

12 When replacement is complete, bleed the braking system as described in Section 3.

8. Brake Master Cylinder - Removal & Replacement

1. Working under the bonnet, disconnect the single hydraulic pipe leading to the master cylinder by undoing the union. Plug the end of the pipe to prevent any dirt entering.

2. Undo the nuts and washers holding the master cylinder to the front of the servo unit and remove the master cylinder.

3. Replacement is a reversal of the removal procedure: bleed the brakes after replacement.

9. Brake Master Cylinder - Dismantling & Reassembly

1. To dismantle the master cylinder, pull off the rubber dust cover where the pushrod enters the master cylinder then with a pair of long nosed pliers remove the circlip holding the pushrod in place in the cylinder and remove the pushrod.

2. Now withdraw the piston and valve assembly complete from the master cylinder. The piston is held in the spring retainer by a tab which engages under a shoulder on the front of the piston. Gently lift this tab and remove the piston.

3. Carefully compress the spring and move the spring retainer to one side. This will release the end of the valve stem from the retainer.

4. Slide the valve spacer and shim off the valve stem. Remove the rubber seal from the piston and the valve seal off the other end of the valve stem.

5. Examine the bore of the cylinder carefully for any scores or ridges, and if this is found to be smooth all over, new seals can be fitted. If there is any doubt as to the condition of the bore, then a new cylinder must be fitted.

6. If examination of the seals shows them to be apparently oversize, or very loose on their seats, suspect oil contamination in the system. Oil will swell these rubber seals, and if one is found to be swollen, it is reasonable to assume that all seals in the braking system will need attention.

7. Before reassembly wash all parts in methylated spirit, commercial alcohol or approved brake fluid. Do not use any other type of oil or cleaning liquid or the seals will be damaged.

8. To reassemble the master cylinder start by fitting the piston seal to the piston with the sealing lips towards the narrow end and fit the valve seal to the valve stem with the lip towards the front of the valve, Fig.9.5. clearly shows the correct fitting of the seals.

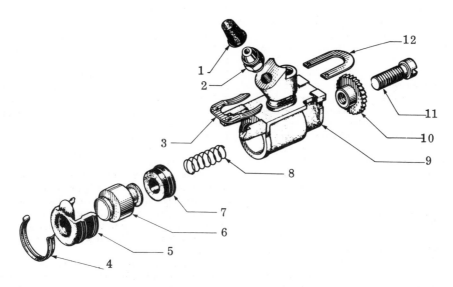

Fig.9.4. EXPLODED VIEW OF THE REAR WHEEL BRAKE CYLINDER

1 Dust cap	4 Spring clip	7 Seal	10 Adjusting wheel
2 Bleed nipple	5 Dust cover	8 Spring	11 Screw
3 Retaining clip	6 Piston	9 Body	12 Retaining clip

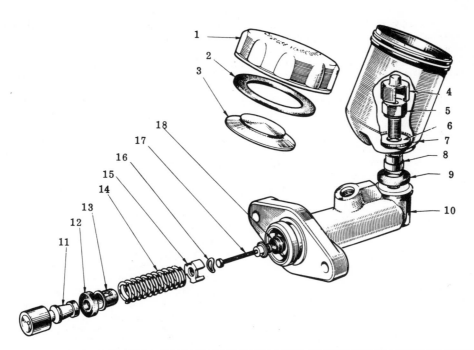

Fig.9.5. EXPLODED VIEW OF THE SINGLE LINE SERVO ASSISTED BRAKE MASTER CYLINDER

1 Reservoir cap	6 Washer	11 Piston	16 Spring washer
2 Cap seal	7 Reservoir body	12 Piston seal	17 Valve stem
3 Seal retainer	8 Sleeve	13 Spring retainer	18 Valve seal
4 Baffle	9 Seal	14 Spring	
5 Filler opening adaptor	10 Master cylinder body	15 Valve spacer	

9. Place the shim washer on the valve stem ensuring that the convex face abuts the shoulder flange on the valve stem. Fit the seal spacer onto the valve stem so that the legs of the spacer are facing the valve seal.

10 Refit the spring to the valve stem then insert the spring retainer into the open end of the spring. Compress the spring and engage the small boss on the end of the valve stem into its recess in the spring retainer.

11 Place the narrow end of the piston in its slot in the spring retainer and secure it there by pressing down the tab.

12 Dip the complete assembly in clean approved hydraulic fluid and with the valve leading slide it into the cylinder taking extra care not to damage the piston cylinder as it goes into the cylinder.

13 Replace the piston in the master cylinder and secure it with the circlip. Finally replace the rubber dust cap. The master cylinder can now be refitted to the car as described in Section 8.

10. Handbrake Linkage - Adjustment

1. Fit chocks under front wheels to prevent the car moving then release the handbrake and jack up the rear of the car.

2. Before making any adjustments check that the cable from the handbrake and that the transverse cable are correctly located in their guides and that the guides are well greased.

3. Slacken the locknut on the main handbrake cable on the relay lever on the rear of the back axle, and turn the adjusting nut until the main cable is reasonably taut.

4. The relay lever should be just clear of the stop on the banjo rear axle casing.

5. To adjust the single transverse cable, slacken the locknut on the end of the cable next to the right-hand rear brake. Check carefully that both handbrake operating levers are back on their stops and in the fully 'off' position then adjust the cable until it is reasonably taut. Check the handbrake operating levers again and finally tighten down the locknut.

6. The effect of adjusting the transverse cable may have upset the adjustment of the main cable so this should be checked again and adjusted as necessary and the locknut tightened down.

7. At frequent intervals during the adjustments it is advisable to check that the handbrake operating levers on both rear brakes have not moved off their stops. If they do move and are left in that position any adjustments made will be of no use and in fact the car will be motoring with the rear brakes partially applied all the time thus causing excessive wear to the brake linings.

11. Pedals - Removal & Replacement

1. Disconnect the servo pushrod from the brake pedal by removing the small spring clip from the clevis pin then withdrawing the clevis pin and bushes.

2. Take off the spring clip holding the clutch cable to the top of its pedal and withdraw the short pivot pin.

3. Remove the circlip from its groove on the pivot pin between the two pedals. The groove is situated between the brake pedal and the right-hand side of the pedal mounting bracket.

4. Withdraw the pedal pivot pin from the clutch pedal end, then remove the two pedals carefully, noting the position of the bushes at either end and the single spacer washer.

5. Replacement is a direct reversal of the removal procedure detailed above, but when refitting the servo pushrod to the brake pedal ensure that the yellow paint mark on the pushrod yoke is facing towards the centre line of the car.

12. Disc Brake Friction Pads - Inspection, Removal & Replacement

1. Remove the front wheels and inspect the amount of friction material left on the friction pads. The pads must be renewed when the thickness of the material has worn down to 1/16th inch.

2. With a pair of pliers pull out the two small wire clips that hold the main retaining pins in place (See photo).

3. Remove the main retaining pins which run through the calliper the metal backing of the pads and the shims. (See photo).

4. The friction pads and shims can now be removed from the calliper. If they prove difficult to move by hand a pair of long nosed pliers can be used (see photo).

5. Carefully clean the recesses in the calliper in which the friction pads and shims lie, and the exposed faces of each piston from all traces of dirt and rust.

6. Remove the cap from the hydraulic fluid reservoir and place a large rag underneath the unit. To make it easier to fit the new pads and shims, press the pistons in each half of the calliper in as far as they will go. This will cause the fluid level in the reservoir to rise and possibly spill over onto the protective rag.

7. Fit new friction pads and shims: the shims can be fitted either way up.

8. Insert the main pad retaining pins, and secure them in position with the small wire clips. Make sure when replacing the clips that their exposed portions are facing away from the piston seal so as to prevent damage to the seal.

9. Press on the brake pedal several times to bring the pads into contact with the disc then check that they are free to move slightly thus ensuring that the retaining pins are not fouling the pads in any way.

10 Check the level in the master cylinder and top up with approved fluid if necessary then having replaced the wheels test the brakes on the road to ensure all is well.

13. Brake Calliper - Removal, Dismantling & Reassembly

1. Jack up the car and remove the road wheel, remove the friction pads and shims as described in the previous section and disconnect the hydraulic fluid pipe at either the back of the calliper or at the bracket on the suspension unit.

2. If it is intended to dismantle the calliper after removal; before disconnecting the hydraulic pipe depress the brake pedal to bring the calliper pistons into contact with the disc. This will make it much easier to remove the pistons when the calliper is removed.

3. Knock back the locking tabs on the calliper mounting bolts (see Fig.9.9), undo the bolts and remove the calliper from the disc.

4. Remove the circlip which retains the sealing bellows to the calliper then carefully prize the sealing bellows from the groove in which they fit in the piston skirt.

5. The piston can now be removed from its bore . If it proves difficult to move a small amount of air pressure applied at the hydraulic pipe union will push it out.

6. Pull the other end of the sealing bellows out of their machined location in the cylinder bore and withdraw the piston sealing ring from the cylinder bore. The operation can now be repeated on the other piston and cylinder.

7. The pistons and piston bores should be carefully cleaned with approved brake fluid and examined for signs of wear, score marks or damage. All rubber seals and sealing bellows should be replaced as a matter of course.

8. Reassembly is a direct reversal of the removal sequence but great care should be taken when passing the piston through the rubber bellows into the cylinder bore as it is very easy at this stage to damage the bellows.

9. Once the calliper has been reassembled, fit it over the disc and using a new locking tab, tighten down the securing bolts to a torque of 45 to 50 lb/ft. (6.22 to 6.91 kg.m).

10 Reconnect the pipe and bleed the system (Section 3).

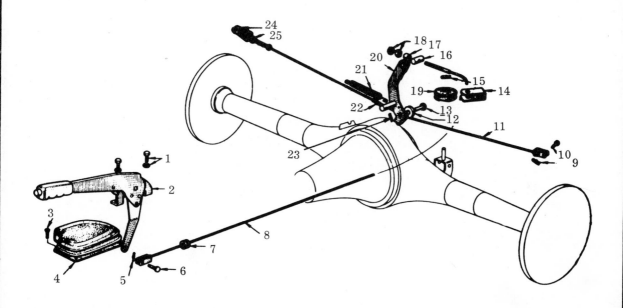

Fig 9:6. EXPLODED VIEW OF THE HANDBRAKE MECHANISM

1	Bolt and washer	8	Cable	15	Retaining pin
2	Handbrake lever	9	Retaining pin	16	Pin
3	Screw	10	Clevis pin	17	Spacer
4	Dust cover	11	Transverse cable	18	Adjusting and locknuts
5	Retaining pin	12	Cable pulley	19	Pulley
6	Clevis pin	13	Clevis pin	20	Compensator
7	Cable guide	14	Pulley retainer	21	Spring

22	Retaining pin
23	Retaining pin
24	Clevis
25	Adjusting nut

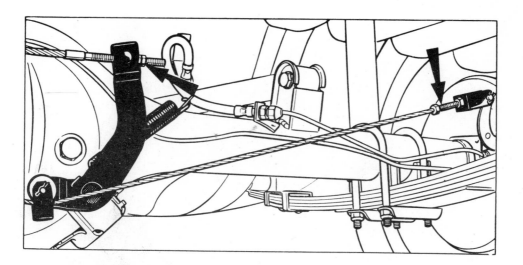

Fig.9.7. The handbrake linkage adjustment points

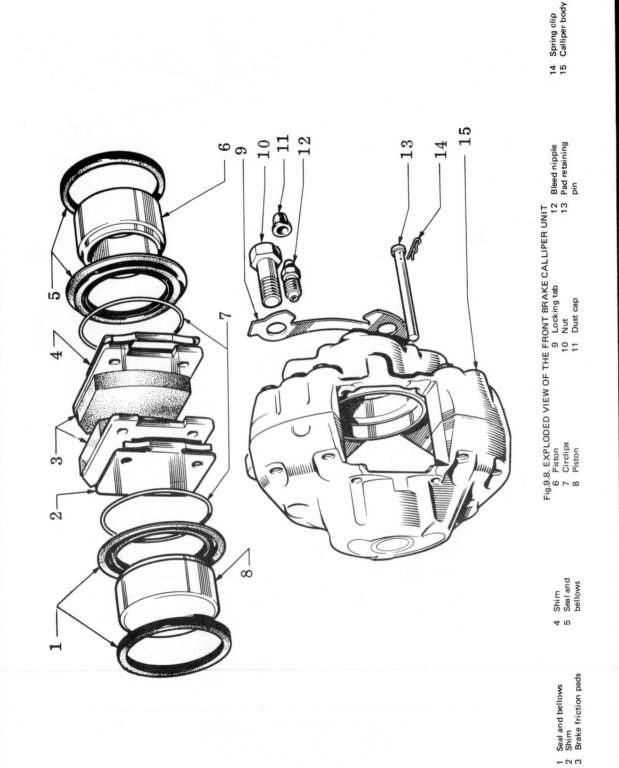

Fig.9.8. EXPLODED VIEW OF THE FRONT BRAKE CALLIPER UNIT

1 Seal and bellows
2 Shim
3 Brake friction pads

4 Shim
5 Seal and bellows

6 Piston
7 Circlips
8 Piston

9 Locking tab
10 Nut
11 Dust cap

12 Bleed nipple
13 Pad retaining pin

14 Spring clip
15 Calliper body

12.2

12.3

12.4

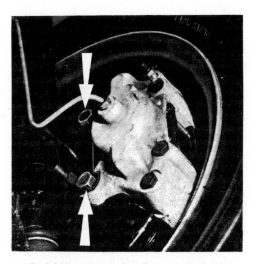

Fig 9:9 View of the brake caliper mounting bolts

14. Brake Disc - Removal & Replacement

1. The brake disc is not normally removed from the hub unless it is to be replaced with a new disc.
2. Remove the hub and disc assembly complete as described in Chapter 11, Section 4.
3. Separate the hub from the disc by knocking back the locking tabs and undoing the four bolts. Discard the disc, bolts, and locking tabs.
4. Before fitting a new disc to the hub, thoroughly clean the mating surfaces of both components. If this is not done properly and dirt is allowed to get between the hub and the disc this will seriously affect the disc brake run-out when it is checked after reaseembly.
5. Align the mating marks on the new disc and the hub and fit the two together using new locking tabs and nuts. Tighten the nuts down to a torque of 30 to 34 lb/ft. (4.15 to 4.70 kg.m) and bend up the locking tabs.
6. Replace the disc and hub assembly and check the disc brake run-out as described in Chapter 11, Section 4.

15. Dual Braking System - General Description

1. Certain models of the Capri 2000 and 3000, in particular those built for certain overseas markets are fitted with separate front and rear braking systems. This is also available as an optional extra on models for the home market. By using this system, hydraulic failure should it occur is never complete, only the front or rear brakes going out of action at any one time.
2. A tandem master cylinder is used and both the front and rear systems are connected to the opposite sides of a pressure differential warning actuator. Should either the front or the rear brakes fail the pressure drop on one side of the warning actuator causes a shuttle valve to move from its normal mid position so actuating an electrical switch which brings on a warning light on the fascia.
3. It is possible to check the bulb in the warning light by operating a switch on the fascia.

16. Pressure Differential Warning Actuator - Centralisation

1. If the shuttle in the pressure differential actuator has moved, either because air has got into one of the braking circuits or because one of the circuits has failed it will be necessary to centralise the shuttle.
2. This can be done by getting hold of an old screwdriver and cutting it down or grinding it into a tool of the dimensions shown in Fig.9.10.
3. The rubber cover should be removed from the bottom of the pressure differential warning actuator and the tool inserted through the hole where it will engage in a slot in the larger piston thus drawing it into a central position.
4. During bleeding of the brakes the piston must be held in this position throughout the operation or it will prove very difficult to get the warning light to go out and stay out.

17. Pressure Differential Warning Actuator - Dismantling, Examination and Reassembly

1. Disconnect the five hydraulic pipes at their unions on the pressure differential warning actuator and to prevent too much loss of hydraulic fluid either place a piece of polythene under the cap of the master cylinder and screw it down tightly or plug the ends of the two pipes leading from the master cylinder.
2. Referring to Fig.9.11, disconnect the wiring from the switch assembly (2).
3. Undo the single bolt holding the assembly to the rear of the engine compartment and remove it from the car.

4. To dismantle the assembly start by undoing the end plug (4) and discarding the copper gasket (5). Then undo the adaptor (8) and also discard its copper gasket as they must be replaced.
5. Unscrew the switch assembly (2) from the top of the unit then push the small and large pistons (7) out of their bores taking extreme care not to damage the bores during this operation.
6. Take the small seals (1 and 3) from their pistons making a careful note that the seals are slightly tapered and that the large diameter on each seal is fitted to the slotted end of the pistons. Discard the seals as they must be replaced.
7. Pull the dust cover (6) off the bottom of the unit and also discard this component for the same reasons as above.
8. Carefully examine the pistons (7) and the bore of the actuator for score marks scratches or damage; if any are found the complete unit must be exchanged.
9. To test if the switch assembly (2) is working correctly reconnect the wiring and press the plunger against any part of the bare metal of the engine or the bodywork when the warning light should come on. If it does not come on check the switch by substitution and also check the warning lamp bulb.
10 To reassemble the unit, start by fitting new seals (1 and 3) to the pistons (7) making sure that they are correctly fitted as detailed in paragraph 6 of this section.
11 With the slotted end outwards, gently push the larger piston into the bore until the groove in the other end of the piston is opposite the hole in which the switch assembly (2) is fitted.
12 Screw the switch assembly (2) into position and tighten it down to a torque or 2 to 2.5 lb/ft. (0.28 to 0.34 kg.m). Then gently push the shorter piston, with the slotted end outwards into the other end of the actuator.
13 Fit new copper washers (5) to the adaptor (8) and the end plug (4) and replace them in the assembly tightening them down to a torque of 16 to 20 lb/ft. (2.22 to 2.80 kg.m). Fit a new dust cover (6) over the bottom aperture.
14 Replacement of the pressure differential warning actuator on the car is a direct reversal of the removal sequence. The brakes must be bled after replacement.

18. Tandem Master Cylinder - Dismantling, Examination & Reassembly

1. The tandem master cylinder comprises two piston assemblies, one behind the other operating in a common bore. There are two outlets from the master cylinder, one to the front brakes and one to the rear brakes, both going via the pressure differential warning actuator.
2. To remove the tandem master cylinder, disconnect the pushrod from the brake pedal, detach the two hydraulic pipes at their unions with the side of the master cylinder and undo the two nuts and spring washers holding the master cylinder to the bulkhead. Plug the loose pipes to prevent entry of dirt.
3. To dismantle the unit, pull off the rubber dust cover and remove the circlip and washer under the dust cover which holds the pushrod in place. Remove the pushrod.
4. Take the hydraulic fluid reservoir off the cylinder assembly by undoing the two screws on either side of the cylinder.
5. From the top of the cylinder remove the circlip and spring from the primary recuperating valve and with a suitable hexagon headed key take out the plug which holds this valve in place, then remove the valve assembly.
6. Fit plugs to the two outlet holes and also to the primary recuperating valve aperture, then using a suitable air line blow gently into the other hole on the top of the cylinder. This will remove from the cylinder bore the primary piston and spring, the secondary piston and the secondary recuperating valve assemblies.
7. Remove the piston seal from the primary piston. Lift the tab on the secondary piston spring retainer and remove the piston. Compress the secondary piston spring, move the retainer to one side and remove the secondary recuperating valve stem from the retainer.

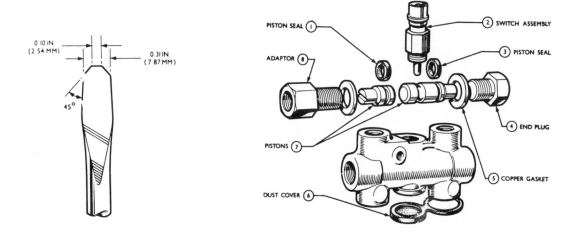

0 10 IN.
(2 54 MM)

0 31 IN.
(7 87 MM)

45°

Fig.9.10. Screwdriver special tool dimensions

PISTON SEAL ①

SWITCH ASSEMBLY ②

ADAPTOR ⑧

③ PISTON SEAL

④ END PLUG

PISTONS ⑦

⑤ COPPER GASKET

DUST COVER ⑥

Fig.9.11. Exploded view of the valve and switch assembly unit

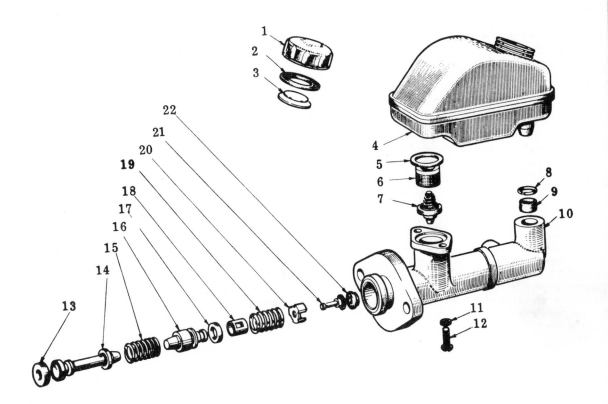

Fig.9.12. EXPLODED VIEW OF THE DUAL LINE BRAKE MASTER CYLINDER

1	Reservoir cap	7	Tipping valve	13	Seal	19	Spring
2	Cap seal	8	Circlip	14	Primary piston	20	Spring retainer
3	Seal retainer	9	Gasket	15	Spring	21	Valve
4	Reservoir	10	Master cylinder body	16	Secondary piston	22	Seal
5	Sealing ring	11	Washer	17	Seal		
6	Tipping valve retainer	12	Screw	18	Spring retainer		

Then slide the valve spacer and shim from the valve stem, noting the way in which the shim is fitted.

8. Remove the small rubber valve seal and also the secondary piston seal. Examine all the rubber seals for signs of loose fitting or swelling and renew as necessary. Also examine the state of the cylinder bore for signs of scoring or corrosion. If this is damaged in any way a replacement master cylinder must be fitted. It is also advisable to replace all rubber seals as a matter of course whether they are damaged or not.

9. Clean all parts with approved hydraulic fluid prior to reassembly in the cylinder bore.

10 Fit a new seal onto the secondary piston and a new seal to the valve stem. Replace the shim on the valve stem making sure that the convex side faces towards the seal spacer which is fitted next, with its legs towards the vave seal.

11 Refit the secondary piston spring over the valve stem, insert the spring retainer, compress the spring and fit the boss in the valve stem into its location in the spring retainer.

12 Place the narrow end of the secondary piston into the spring retainer and secure it in place by pressing down the tab. Dip the now complete secondary assembly in approved hydraulic fluid and carefully slide it into the cylinder bore with the secondary recuperating valve leading.

13 Place the primary piston spring into the cylinder, fit a new rubber seal to the primary piston, dip it in approved fluid and carefully slide it into the cylinder, drilled end first.

14 Fit the pushrod into the end of the primary piston and retain it with the washer and circlip.

15 Place the primary recuperating valve into its location in the top of the cylinder and check that it is properly located by moving the pushrod up and down a small amount. Screw the retaining plug into position and refit the spring and circlip to the valve plunger.

16 Move the pushrod in and out of the cylinder and check that the recuperating valve opens when the rod is fully withdrawn and closes again when it is pushed in.

17 Check the condition of the front and rear reservoir gaskets and if there is any doubt as to their condition they must be replaced. Refit the reservoir to the cylinder with its two retaining screws.

18 Refitting the master cylinder to the car is a reversal of the removal instructions. When replacement is complete bleed the brakes and road test the car.

19. Vacuum Servo Unit - Removal & Replacement

1. Remove the vacuum supply pipe from the servo unit and then undo the brake fluid pipes from the master cylinder. Block the ends of the pipes to prevent the entry of dirt.

2. Take the master cylinder off the front of the servo unit by undoing the two retaining nuts and washers.

3. Detach the servo pushrod from the brake pedal by removing the spring clip, clevis pin and clevis pin bushes.

4. Undo the four nuts and washers that hold the rear end of the servo unit mounting bracket to the rear bulkhead and lift away the mounting bracket and servo unit complete.

5. Remove the servo unit from its mounting bracket by undoing the four retaining nuts and washers.

6. Replacement of the servo unit and its mounting bracket is a direct reversal of the above procedure, but note the following points:

7. When fitted correctly the pushrod that is attached to the brake pedal must have the yellow paint mark on the clevis yoke facing towards the centre of the car.

8. As shown in Fig.9.14, measure the distance between the centre of the brake pushrod hole and the face of the servo mounting bracket. This dimension should be between 6.16 to 6.28 inch (156.5 to 159.5 mm). If found to be incorrect the length of the pushrod can be adjusted at the clevis yoke 'A'.

9. After replacement, bleed the hydraulic system as described in Section 3.

20. Vacuum Servo Unit - Dismantling, Examination & Reassembly

1. Before starting to dismantle the servo unit it will be necessary to make up two pieces of angle iron or similar metal flat rod about three feet long each with holes drilled in them to fit over the four studs on the pushrod side of the servo unit. You will also require another piece of angle iron about one foot long with holes drilled to coincide with the master cylinder attachment bolts.

2. Scribe marks on both halves of the servo unit so that the shells can be refitted in exactly the same position on reassembly.

3. Fit the three pieces of angle iron to the servo unit as shown in Fig.9.15 and clamp the one foot long piece in a vice so that the servo non-return valve is accessible and pointing downwards. Ensure that the nuts on the angle irons are tight.

4. As it is not possible to separate the two shells with the spring pressure still on the diaphragm it is necessary to create a vacuum behind the diaphragm. This is done by connecting a suitable length of hose to the servo non-return valve and the engine manifold and starting up the engine.

5. It will probably be necessary to get two assistants to help with the next operation, one to steady the servo unit in the vice and one on the end of one of the longer angle irons. Using the top angle irons as leverage turn the servo top shell in an anti-clockwise direction until a mark on the top shell aligns with a cut-away on the bottom shell. At this point the shells should separate, but if they fail to do so they can be gently tapped with a soft headed hammer. It is important to keep the vacuum going all the time or the two shells will fly apart under the action of the diaphragm spring causing possible injury and damage.

6. Once the two shells have been separated the vacuum can be released and the diaphragm and diaphragm plate assembly, which includes the control rod and the valve assembly, can be withdrawn.

7. The control rod and valve assembly should now be removed from the plate and the diaphragm taken from its plate by carefully pulling its centre from its locating groove in the plate.

8. Take off and discard the air filter which is found in the extension flange on the rear edge of the diaphragm plate.

9. Withdraw the seal from the larger front shell and also the internal pushrod and remove the slotted disc from the diaphragm plate.

10 With a screwdriver, prize off the seal retainer from the smaller rear shell and take out the seal.

11 With a suitable spanner, unscrew the non-return valve and its seal from the larger front shell.

12 Carefully examine and clean all parts of the servo before reassembly, and as a matter of course replace all rubber parts including the diaphragm. The control and valve assembly are replaced as a unit and should not be broken down.

13 Commence reassembly by fitting a new seal to the non-return valve and replacing the valve in the front shell.

14 Place a new seal into its recess in the rear shell and fit the seal retainer which can be forced into place with a socket just smaller than the retainer.

15 Fit a new air filter to the rear of the diaphragm plate then insert the control rod and valve assembly into the centre of the diaphragm plate and apply a suitable lubricant such as Part No.EM-1C-14 to the bearing surfaces of the control rod and valve assembly. Secure the complete assembly in the plate with the stop key, (see photo).

16 Assemble the new diaphragm to its plate making sure that its centre is correctly located in the groove on the plate. It is advisable to lightly grease the areas of the diaphragm that contact the shells with a grease such as Ford Part No.EM-1C-15. This will help during reassembly and also during later dismantling operations. This grease must not be allowed to come into contact with any of the hydraulic brake system seals or damage will result.

17 Refit the lengths of angle iron as in paragraph 3 and replace the unit in the vice. Reconnect the vacuum pipe, check that the two shells are correctly lined up and start the engine.

18 With the help of the vacuum created and by applying further pressure to the rear shell completely engage the two shells together

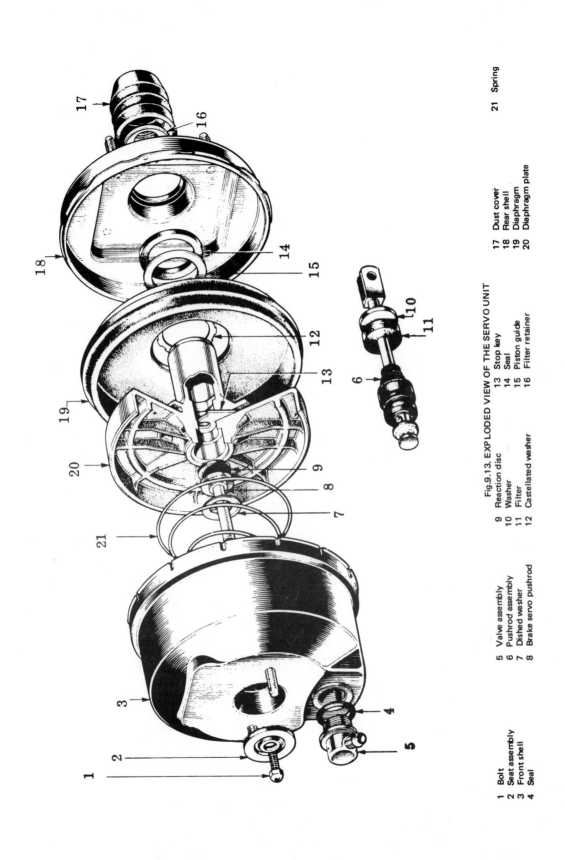

Fig.9.13. EXPLODED VIEW OF THE SERVO UNIT

1	Bolt	9	Reaction disc	17 Dust cover
2	Seat assembly	10	Washer	18 Rear shell
3	Front shell	11	Filter	19 Diaphragm
4	Seal	12	Castellated washer	20 Diaphragm plate
5	Valve assembly	13	Stop key	21 Spring
6	Pushrod assembly	14	Seal	
7	Dished washer	15	Piston guide	
8	Brake servo pushrod	16	Filter retainer	

and with the aid of the angle irons turn the rear shell in a clockwise direction until the scribe marks made prior to dismantling are in line.

19 With the vacuum still being applied, check how far the pushrod extends beyond the front shell. This must be from 0.011 to 0.016 inch (0.28 to 0.40 mm).

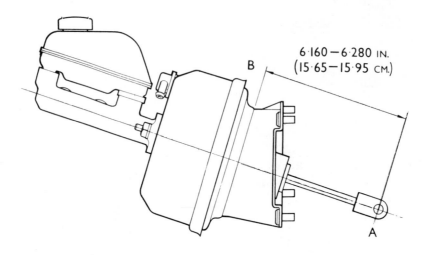

6·160 — 6·280 IN.
(15·65 — 15·95 CM.)

Fig.9.14. Correct fitted dimensions of servo unit. Adjust pushrod at 'A' to give dimensions as shown at 'B'.

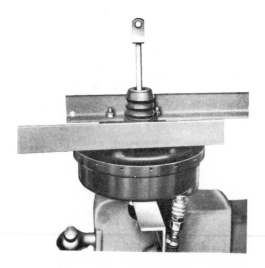

Fig.9.15. Method of separating the front and rear shells ot tne servo unit

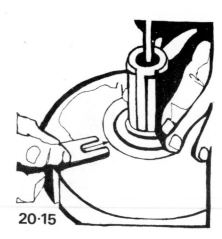

20·15

Before diagnosing faults from the following chart, check that any braking irregularities are not caused by:—

1. Uneven and incorrect tyre pressures.
2. Incorrect 'mix' of radial and cross-ply tyres.
3. Wear in the steering mechanism.
4. Defects in the suspension and dampers.
5. Misalignment of the body frame.

Symptom	Reason/s	Remedy
Stopping ability poor, even though pedal pressure is firm.	Linings and/or drums badly worn or scored.	Dismantle, inspect and renew as required.
	One or more wheel hydraulic cylinders seized, resulting in some brake shoes not pressing against the drums (or pads against discs).	Dismantle and inspect wheel cylinders. Renew as necessary.
	Brake linings contaminated with oil.	Renew linings and repair source of oil contamination.
	Wrong type of linings fitted (too hard).	Verify type of material which is correct for the car and fit it.
	Brake shoes wrongly assembled.	Check for correct assembly.
	Servo unit not functioning	Check and repair as necessary.
Car veers to one side when the brakes are applied.	Brake pads or linings on one side are contaminated with oil.	Renew pads or linings and stop oil leak.
	Hydraulic wheel cylinder(s) on one side partially or fully seized.	Inspect wheel cylinders for correct operation and renew as necessary.
	A mixture of lining materials fitted between sides.	Standardize on types of linings fitted.
	Unequal wear between sides caused by partially seized wheel cylinders.	Check wheel cylinders and renew linings and drums as required.
Pedal feels spongy when the brakes are applied.	Air is present in the hydraulic system.	Bleed the hydraulic system and check for any signs of leakage.
Pedal feels springy when the brakes are applied.	Brake linings not bedded into the drums (after fitting new ones).	Allow time for new linings to bed in
	Master cylinder or brake backplate mounting bolts loose.	Re-tighten mounting bolts.
	Severe wear in brake drums causing distortion when brakes are applied.	Renew drums and linings.
Pedal travels right down with little or no resistance and brakes are virtually non-operative.	Leak in hydraulic system resulting in lack of pressure for operating wheel cylinders.	Examine the whole of the hydraulic system and locate and repair source of leaks. Test after repairing each and every leak source.
	If no signs of leakage are apparent the master cylinder internal seals are failing to sustain pressure.	Overhaul master cylinder. If indications are that seals have failed for reasons other than wear all the wheel cylinder seals should be checked also and the system completely replenished with the correct fluid.
Binding, juddering overheating.	One or a combination of causes given in the foregoing sections.	Complete and systematic inspection of the whole braking system.

Chapter 10 Electrical system

Contents

Specifications

Battery

Type	Lead Acid 12 volt	
Earthed terminal	Negative '−'	
Capacity at 20 hr rate	2000	3000
Standard	38 amp/hr	44 amp/hr
Cold climate	54 amp/hr	55 amp/hr
Cold climate heavy duty...	−	66 amp/hr

Plates per cell:

Standard	9	9
Cold climate...	13	11
Cold climate heavy duty	−	13

Specific gravity charged	1.275 to 1.290

Electrolyte capacity:

Standard	4.5 pints (5.4 US pints, 2.5 litres)
Cold climate...	6.4 pints (7.7 US pints, 3.6 litres)
Cold climate H.D (3000 only)	7.7 pints (9.3 US pints, 4.3 litres)

Dynamo (2000 only)	Lucas C40 (C40/L cold start models)
Maximum charge	22 amps (25 amps with C40/L)
Number of brushes	2
Brush length new	.718 in. (18.23 mm)
Brush spring tension	18 to 24 oz.
Field resistance	6.0 ohms

Alternator	2000 optional	3000 standard
Type...	Lucas 15 ACR	Lucas 17 ACR

Speed (ratio to engine)	1.88 to 1	1.88 to 1
Maximum charge	28 amps	35 amps
Brush spring tension	7 to 10 oz	7 to 10 oz

Starter Motor Inertia Type (2000 only)

Number of brushes	4
Minimum brush length	.4 in. (10.3 mm)
Brush spring tension ... ... ,...	34 oz. (.96 kg)
Gear ratio	13.4 to 1
Teeth on pinion	9
Teeth on ring gear	121
Lock torque	6.4 lb./ft. (.884 kg.m)

NOTE: A pre-engaged type of starter motor is fitted as standard on all 3000 models and 2000 models with 'cold start' equipment. It can also be purchased as an optional extra on standard 2000 models.

Starter Motor Pre-engaged Type

Number of brushes	4
Minimum brush length - 2000	.25 in. (6.4 mm)
- 3000	.30 in. (7.5 mm)
Brush spring tension - 2000	40 oz. (1.15 kg)
- 3000	32 oz. (.90 kg)
Gear ratio	13.4 to 1
Teeth on pinion	9
Teeth on ring gear	121
Lock torque - 2000	9 lb/ft. (1.24 kg.m)
- 3000	14.5 lb/ft. (2.3 kg.m)

Regulator/Control Box (2000 with dynamo only)

Type	Lucas RB340 or Autolite	
Cut in voltage	12.6 to 13.4 volts	
Drop off voltage	9.25 to 11.25 volts	
Cut-out:	Lucas	Autolite
Armature to core air gap	.035 to .045 in. (.9 to 1.1 mm)	.025 to .037 in. (.64 to .94 mm)
Current regulator, on load setting	Max. generator output ± 1½ amps	
Current regulator:	Lucas	Autolite
Armature to core air gap	.045 in. to .049 in. (1.14 to 1.24 mm)	.014 to .019 in. (.36 to .48 mm)
Voltage regulator:		
Open circuit setting	14.4 to 15.6 volts at 20°C (68°F)	
Armature to core air gap	.045 to .049 in. (1.14 to 1.24 mm)	.024 to .028 in. (.61 to .71 mm)
Reverse current	3.0 to 5.0 amps	
Voltage setting at 2,000 r.p.m	10°C (50°F) 14.5 to 15.8 volts	
	20°C (68°F) 14.5 to 15.5 volts	
	30°C (86°F) 14.3 to 15.3 volts	
	40°C (104°F) 14.3 to 15.0 volts	

Fuse Unit

Number of fuses	6
Number of spare fuses in box	1

Bulbs

Headlamps	60/45 watt, sealed beam
Sidelamps	5 watt wedge base
Indicator lamps	24 watt bayonet fitting
Tail and stop light...	24/6 watt bayonet fitting
Number plate light	5 watt wedge base
Interior light	6 watt festoon
Warning lights	2.2 watt wedge base
Panel light	2.2 watt wedge base
Clock	1.2 watt wedge base

Torque Wrench Setting

Starter motor retaining bolts	20 to 25 lb/ft. (2.76 to 3.46 kg.m)
Generator pulley	14 to 17 lb/ft. (1.93 to 2.35 kg.m)
Generator mounting bolts	15 to 18 lb/ft. (2.07 to 2.49 kg.m)
Generator mounting bracket	20 to 25 lb/ft. (2.76 to 3.46 kg.m)

1. General Description

The electrical system is of the 12 volt type and the major components comprise: a 12 volt battery with the negative terminal earthed; a dynamo or alternator; a control box, if a dynamo is fitted and a starter motor.

A Lucas dynamo is fitted to the 2000 cc model but a Lucas 15ACR alternator is available as an optional extra. The 3000 cc models fit a Lucas 17ACR alternator as standard. The alternators have their own integral regulator units but if a dynamo is fitted a three bobbin control box of either Lucas or Autolite manufacture is used.

The starter motor which is of the inertia type on the 2000 GT and of the pre-engaged type on the 3000 models is mounted to the clutch bellhousing on the left-hand side of the engine. As an optional extra it is possible to have a pre-engaged starter motor fitted to the 2000 GT.

The 12 volt battery gives a steady supply of current for the ignition, lighting and other electrical circuits, and provides a reserve of electricity when the current consumed by the electrical equipment exceeds that being produced by the dynamo or alternator.

The dynamo is of the two brush type and works in conjunction with the voltage regulator and cut-out. The dynamo is cooled by a multi-bladed fan mounted behind the dynamo pulley, and blows air through cooling holes in the dynamo end brackets. The output from the dynamo is controlled by the voltage regulator which ensures a high output if the battery is in a low state of charge or the demands from the electrical equipment high, and a low output if the battery is fully charged and there is little demand from the electrical equipment.

The regulator mechanism in the 15 and 17ACR alternators operates in a similar manner.

2. Battery - Removal & Replacement

1. The battery is positioned on a tray in the front of the engine compartment forward of the nearside suspension.
2. Disconnect the earthed negative lead and then the positive lead by slackening the retaining nuts and bolts or, by unscrewing the retaining screws if these are fitted.
3. Remove the battery clamp and carefully lift the battery off its tray. Hold the battery vertical to ensure that no electrolyte is spilled.
4. Replacement is a direct reversal of this procedure. NOTE: Replace the positive lead and the negative (earth) lead, smearing the terminals with petroleum jelly (vaseline) to prevent corrosion. NEVER use an ordinary grease as applied to other parts of the car.

3. Battery - Maintenance & Inspection

1. Normal weekly battery maintenance consists of checking the electrolyte level of each cell to ensure that the separators are covered by ¼ inch of electrolyte. If the level has fallen top up the battery using distilled water only. Do not overfill. If a battery is overfilled or any electrolyte spilled, immediately wipe away the excess as electrolyte attacks and corrodes any metal it comes into contact with very rapidly.
2. As well as keeping the terminals clean and covered with petroleum jelly, the top of the battery, and esepcially the top of the cells, should be kept clean and dry. This helps prevent corrosion and ensures that the battery does not become partially discharged by leakage through dampness and dirt.
3. Once every three months remove the battery and inspect the battery securing bolts, the battery clamp plate, tray, and battery leads for corrosion (white fluffy deposits on the metal which are brittle to touch). If any corrosion is found, clean off the deposits with ammonia and paint over the clean metal with an anti-rust/anti-acid paint.

4. At the same time inspect the battery case for cracks. If a crack is found, clean and plug it with one of the proprietary compounds marketed by firms such as Holts for this purpose. If leakage through the crack has been excessive then it will be necessary to refill the appropriate cell with fresh electrolyte as detailed later. Cracks are frequently caused to the top of the battery cases by pouring in distilled water in the middle of winter AFTER instead of BEFORE a run. This gives the water no chance to mix with the electrolyte and so the former freezes and splits the battery case.
5. If topping up the battery becomes excessive and the case has been inspected for cracks that could cause leakage, but none are found, the battery is being overcharged and the voltage regulator will have to be checked and reset.
6. With the battery on the bench at the three monthly interval check, measure its specific gravity with a hydrometer to determine the state of charge and condition of the electrolyte. There should be very little variation between the different cells and if a variation in excess of 0.025 is present it will be due to either:—
a) Loss of electrolyte from the battery at sometime caused by spillage or a leak resulting in a drop in the specific gravity of the electrolyte, when the deficiency was replaced with distilled water instead of fresh electrolyte.
b) An internal short circuit caused by buckling of the plates or a similar malady pointing to the likelihood of total battery failure in the near future.
7. The specific gravity of the electrolyte for fully charged conditions at the electrolyte temperature indicated, is listed in Table A. The specific gravity of a fully discharged battery at different temperatures of the electrolyte is given in Table B.

Table A
Specific Gravity - Battery Fully Charged

1.268 at	100°F or 38°C
1.272 at	90°F or 32°C
1.276 at	80°F or 27°C
1.280 at	70°F or 21°C
1.284 at	60°F or 16°C
1.288 at	50°F or 10°C
1.292 at	40°F or 4°C
1.296 at	30°F or -1.5°C

Table B
Specific Gravity - Battery Fully Discharged

1.098 at	100°F or 38°C
1.102 at	90°F or 32°C
1.106 at	80°F or 27°C
1.110 at	70°F or 21°C
1.114 at	60°F or 16°C
1.118 at	50°F or 10°C
1.122 at	40°F or 4°C
1.126 at	30°F or -1.5°C

4. Electrolyte Replenishment

1. If the battery is in a fully charged state and one of the cells maintains a specific gravity reading which is 0.025 or more lower than the others, and a check of each cell has been made with a voltage meter to check for short circuits (a four to seven second test should give a steady reading of between 1.2 to 1.8 volts), then it is likely that electrolyte has been lost from the cell with the low reading at sometime.
2. Top up the cell with a solution of 1 part sulphuric acid to 2.5 parts of water. If the cell is already fully topped up draw some electrolyte out of it with a pipette. The total capacity of each cell is ¾ pint.
3. When mixing the sulphuric acid and water NEVER ADD WATER TO SULPHURIC ACID — always pour the acid slowly onto the water in a glass container. IF WATER IS ADDED TO SULPHURIC ACID IT WILL EXPLODE.
4. Continue to top up the cell with the freshly made electrolyte and then recharge the battery and check the hydrometer readings.

5. Battery Charging

1. In winter time when heavy demand is placed upon the battery, such as when starting from cold, and much electrical equipment is continually in use, it is a good idea occasionally to have the battery fully charged from an external source at the rate of 3.5 to 4 amps.

2. Continue to charge the battery at this rate until no further rise in specific gravity is noted over a four hour period.

3. Alternatively, a trickle charger charging at the rate of 1.5 amps can be safely used overnight.

4. Specially rapid 'boost' charges which are claimed to restore the power of the battery in 1 to 2 hours are most dangerous as they can cause serious damage to the battery plates through over-heating.

5. While charging the battery, note that the temperature of the electrolyte should never exceed 100°F.

6. Dynamo - Routine Maintenance

1. Routine maintenance consists of checking the tension of the fan belt, and lubricating the dynamo rear bearing once every 6,000 miles.

2. The fan belt should be tight enough to ensure no slip between the belt and the dynamo pulley. If a shrieking noise comes from the engine when the unit is accelerated rapidly, it is likely that it is the fan belt slipping. On the other hand, the belt must not be too taut or the bearings will wear rapidly and cause dynamo failure or bearing seizure. Ideally ½ inch of total free movement should be available at the fan belt midway between the fan and the dynamo pulley.

3. To adjust the fan belt tension slightly slacken the three dynamo retaining bolts, and swing the dynamo on the upper two bolts outwards to increase the tension, and inwards to decrease it.

4. It is best to leave the bolts fairly tight so that considerable effort has to be used to move the dynamo; otherwise it is difficult to get the correct setting. If the dynamo is being moved outwards to increase the tension and the bolts have only been slackened a little, a long spanner acting as a lever placed behind the dynamo with the lower end resting against the block works very well in moving the dynamo outwards. Retighten the dynamo bolts and check that the dynamo pulley is correctly aligned with the fan belt.

5. Lubrication on the dynamo consists of inserting three drops of SAE.30 engine oil in the small oil hole in the centre of the commutator end bracket. This lubricates the rear bearing. The front bearing is pre-packed with grease and requires no attention.

7. Dynamo - Testing in Position

1. If, with the engine running, no charge comes from the dynamo, or the charge is very low, first check that the fan belt is in place and is not slipping. Then check that the leads from the control box to the dynamo are firmly attached and that one has not come loose from its terminal.

2. The lead from the 'D' terminal on the dynamo should be connected to the 'D' terminal on the control box, and similarly the 'F' terminals on the dynamo and control box should also be connected together. Check that this is so and that the leads have not been incorrectly fitted.

3. Make sure none of the electrical equipment (such as the lights or radio) is on and then pull the leads off the dynamo terminals marked 'D' and 'F', join the terminals together with a short length of wire.

4. Attach to the centre of this length of wire the positive clip of a 0-20 volts voltmeter and run the other clip to earth on the dynamo yoke. Start the engine and allow it to idle at approximately 750 r.p.m. At this speed the dynamo should give a reading of about 15 volts on the voltmeter. There is no point in raising the engine speed above a fast idle as the reading will then be inaccurate.

5. If no reading is recorded then check the brushes and brush connections. If a very low reading of approximately 1 volt is observed then the field winding may be suspect.

6. If a reading of between 4 to 6 volts is recorded it is likely that the armature winding is at fault.

7. With the Lucas C40—1 windowless yoke dynamo it must be removed and dismantled before the brushes and commutator can be attended to.

8. If the voltmeter shows a good reading, then with the temporary link still in position, connect both leads from the control box to 'D' and 'F' on the dynamo ('D' to 'D' and 'F' to 'F'). Release the lead from the 'D' terminal at the control box and clip one lead from the voltmeter to the end of the cable, and the other lead to a good earth. With the engine running at the same speed as previously, an identical voltage to that recorded at the dynamo should be noted on the voltmeter. If no voltage is recorded then there is a break in the wire. If the voltage is the same as recorded at the dynamo then check the 'F' lead in similar fashion. If both readings are the same as at the dynamo then it will be necessary to test the control box.

8. Dynamo - Removal & Replacement

1. Slacken the two dynamo retaining bolts, and the nut on the sliding link, and move the dynamo in towards the engine so that the fan belt can be removed.

2. Disconnect the two leads from the dynamo terminals.

3. Remove the nut from the sliding link bolt, and remove the two upper bolts. The dynamo is then free to be lifted away from the engine.

4. Replacement is a reversal of the above procedure. Do not finally tighten the retaining bolts and the nut on the sliding link until the fan belt has been tensioned correctly. See 10/6.2 for details.

9. Dynamo - Dismantling & Inspection

1. Mount the dynamo in a vice and unscrew and remove the two through bolts from the commutator end bracket. (See photo).

2. Mark the commutator end bracket and the dynamo casing so the end bracket can be replaced in its original position. Pull the end bracket off the armature shaft. NOTE: Some versions of the dynamo may have a raised pip on the end bracket which locates in a recess on the edge of the casing. If so, marking the end bracket and casing is not necessary. A pip may also be found on the drive end bracket at the opposite end of the casing. (See photo).

3. Lift the two brush springs and draw the brushes out of the brush holders (arrowed in photo).

4. Measure the brushes and, if worn down to 9/32 inch or less, unscrew the screws holding the brush leads to the end bracket. Take off the brushes complete with leads. Old and new brushes are compared in the photo.

5. If no locating pip can be found, mark the drive end bracket and the dynamo casing so the drive end bracket can be replaced in its original position. Then pull the drive end bracket complete with armature out of the casing (see photo).

6. Check the condition of the ball bearing in the drive end plate by firmly holding the plate and noting if there is visible side movement of the armature shaft in relation to the end plate. If play is present the armature assembly must be separated from the end plate. If the bearing is sound there is no need to carry out the work described in the following two paragraphs.

7. Hold the armature in one hand (mount it carefully in a vice if preferred) and undo the nut holding the pulley wheel and fan in place. Pull off the pulley wheel and fan.

8. Next remove the woodruff key (arrowed) from its slot in the armature shaft and also the bearing locating ring.

9. Place the drive end bracket across the open jaws of a vice with the armature downwards and gently tap the armature shaft from the bearing (see photo) in the end plate with the aid of a suitable drift.

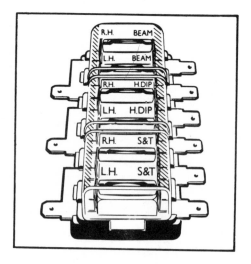

Fig.10.1. View of the fuse block

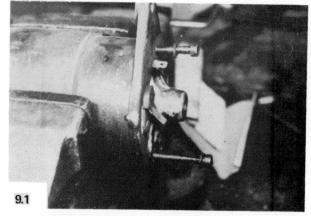

9.1

9.2

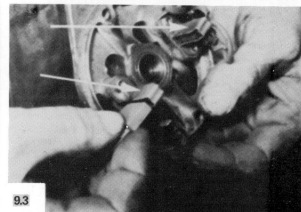

9.3

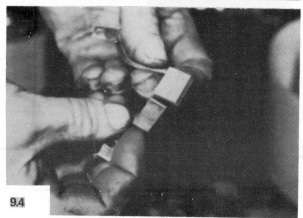

9.4

9.5

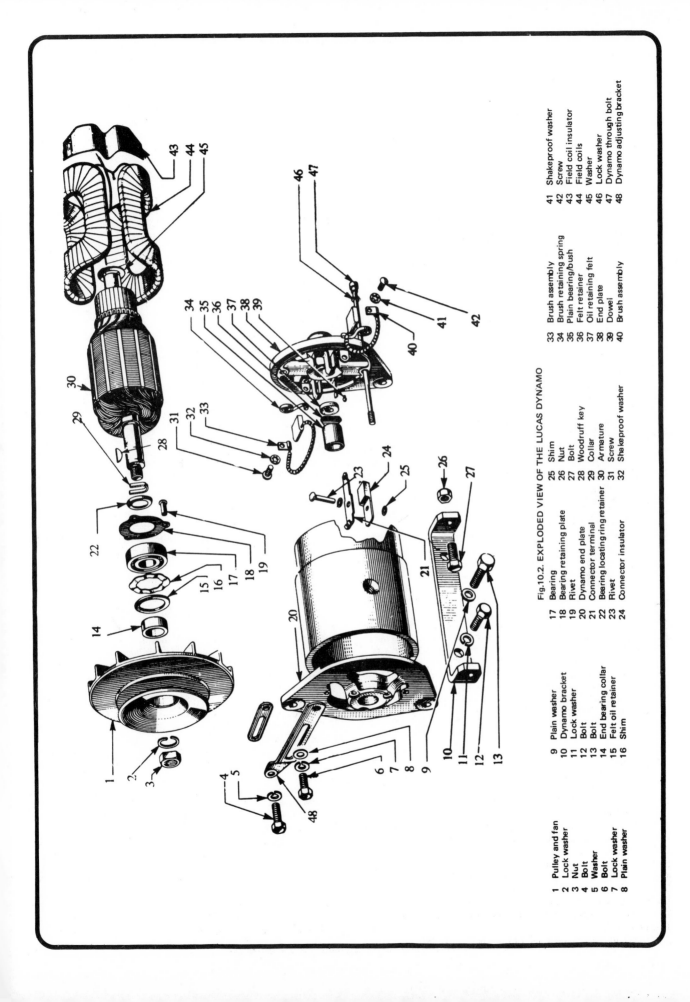

Fig.10.2. EXPLODED VIEW OF THE LUCAS DYNAMO

1 Pulley and fan
2 Lock washer
3 Nut
4 Bolt
5 Washer
6 Bolt
7 Lock washer
8 Plain washer
9 Plain washer
10 Dynamo bracket
11 Lock washer
12 Bolt
13 Bolt
14 End bearing collar
15 Felt oil retainer
16 Shim
17 Bearing
18 Bearing retaining plate
19 Rivet
20 Dynamo end plate
21 Connector terminal
22 Bearing locating ring retainer
23 Rivet
24 Connector insulator
25 Shim
26 Nut
27 Bolt
28 Woodruff key
29 Collar
30 Armature
31 Screw
32 Shakeproof washer
33 Brush assembly
34 Brush retaining spring
35 Plain bearing/bush
36 Felt retainer
37 Oil retaining felt
38 End plate
39 Dowel
40 Brush assembly
41 Shakeproof washer
42 Screw
43 Field coil insulator
44 Field coils
45 Washer
46 Lock washer
47 Dynamo through bolt
48 Dynamo adjusting bracket

10 Carefully inspect the armature and check it for open or short circuited windings. It is a good indication of an open circuited armature when the commutator segments are burnt. If the armature has short circuited the commutator segments will be very badly burnt, and the overheated armature windings badly discoloured. If open or short circuits are suspected then test by substituting the suspect armature for a new one (see photo).

11 Check the resistance of the field coils. To do this, connect an ohmmeter between the field terminal and the yoke and note the reading on the ohmmeter which should be about 6 ohms. If the ohmmeter reading is infinity this indicates an open circuit in the field winding. If the ohmmeter reading is below 5 ohms this indicates that one of the field coils is faulty and must be replaced.

12 Field coil replacement involves the use of a wheel operated screwdriver, a soldering iron, caulking and riveting and this operation is considered to be beyond the scope of most owners. Therefore, if the field coils are at fault either purchase a rebuilt dynamo, or take the casing to a Ford dealer or electrical engineering works for new field coils to be fitted.

13 Next check the condition of the commutator (arrowed). If it is dirty and blackened as shown clean it with a petrol dampened rag. If the commutator is in good condition the surface will be smooth and quite free from pits or burnt areas, and the insulated segments clearly defined.

14 If, after the commutator has been cleaned, pits and burnt spots are still present, wrap a strip of glass paper round the commutator taking great care to move the commutator ¼ of a turn every ten rubs till it is thoroughly clean. (See photo).

15 In extreme cases of wear the commutator can be mounted in a lathe and with the lathe turning at high speed, a very fine cut may be taken off the commutator. Then polish the commutator with glass paper. If the commutator has worn so that the insulators between the segments are level with the top of the segments, then undercut the insulators to a depth of 1/32 inch (.8 mm). The best tool to use for this purpose is half a hacksaw blade ground to a thickness of the insulator, and with the handle end of the blade covered in insulating tape to make it comfortable to hold. This is the sort of finish the surface of the commutator should have when finished, (photo).

16 Check the bush bearing (arrowed) in the commutator end bracket for wear by noting if the armature spindle rocks when placed in it. If worn it must be renewed.

17 The bush bearing can be removed by a suitable extractor or by screwing a 5/8 inch tap four or five turns into the bush. The tap complete with bush is then pulled out of the end bracket.

18 NOTE: Before fitting the new bush bearing that it is of the porous bronze type, and it is essential that it is allowed to stand in SAE.30 engine oil for at least 24 hours before fitment. In an emergency the bush can be immersed in hot oil (100°C) for 2 hours.

19 Carefully fit the bush into the end plate, pressing it in until the end of the bearing is flush with the inner side of the end plate. If available, press the bush in with a smooth shouldered mandrel the same diameter as the armature shaft.

10. Dynamo - Repair & Reassembly

1. To renew the ball bearing fitted to the drive end bracket drill out the rivets which hold the bearing retainer plate to the end bracket and lift off the plate.

2. Press out the bearing from the end bracket and remove the corrugated and felt washers from the bearing housing.

3. Thoroughly clean the bearing housing, and the new bearing and pack with high melting-point grease.

4. Place the felt washer and corrugated washer in that order in the end bracket bearing housing (see photo).

5. Then fit the new bearing as shown.

6. Gently tap the bearing into place with the aid of a suitable drift. (See photo).

7. Replace the bearing plate and fit three new rivets. (See photo)

8. Open up the rivets with the aid of a suitable cold chisel. (See photo).

9. Finally pein over the open end of the rivets with the aid of a ball hammer as illustrated.

10 Refit the drive end bracket to the armature shaft. Do not try and force the bracket on but with the aid of a suitable socket abutting the bearing tap the bearing on gently, so pulling the end bracket down with it. (See photo).

11 Slide the spacer up the shaft and refit the woodruff key. (See photo).

12 Replace the fan and pulley wheel and then fit the spring washer and nut and tighten the latter. The drive bracket end of the dynamo is now fully assembled as shown.

13 If the brushes are little worn and are to be used again then ensure that they are placed in the same holders from which they were removed. When refitting brushes, either new or old, check that they move freely in their holders. If either brush sticks, clean with a petrol moistened rag and, if still stiff, lightly polish the sides of the brush with a very fine file until the brush moves quite freely in its holders.

14 Tighten the two retaining screws and washers which hold the wire leads to the brushes in place (see photo).

15 It is far easier to slip the end piece with brushes over the commutator if the brushes are raised in their holders as shown and held in this position by the pressure of the springs resting against their flanks (arrowed).

16 Refit the armature to the casing and then the commutator end plate and screw up the two through bolts.

17 Finally, hook the ends of the two springs off the flanks of the brushes and onto their head so the brushes are forced down into contact with the armature.

11. Alternators - General Description

The Lucas 15ACR alternator is available as an optional extra on the Capri 2000 GT. On the 3000 GT a Lucas 17ACR alternator is fitted as standard. The alternator's main advantage is its ability to provide a high charge at low revolutions and it will ensure that a charge reaches the battery with all the electrical equipment in use.

An important feature of the alternator is its built-in output control regulator, based on 'thick film' hybrid integrated microcircuit techniques, which results in the alternator being a self contained generating and control unit.

The system provides for direct connection of a charge indicator light, and eliminates the need for a field switching relay or warning light control unit, necessary with a dynamo.

The alternator is of rotating field, ventilated design. It comprises principally: A laminated stator on which is wound a star-connected 3-phase output winding: A 12-pole rotor carrying the field windings. Each end of the rotor shaft runs in ball race bearings which are lubricated for life; Natural finish aluminium die cast end brackets, incorporating the mounting lugs: A rectifier pack for converting the a.c. output of the machine to d.c. for battery charging: An output control regulator.

The rotor is belt driven from the engine through a pulley keyed to the rotor shaft. A pressed steel fan adjacent to the pulley draws cooling air through the machine. This fan forms an integral part of the alternator specification. It has been designed to provide adequate air flow with a minimum of noise, and to withstand the high stresses associated with maximum speed. Rotation is clockwise viewed on the drive end. Maximum continuous rotor speed is 12,500 rev/min.

Rectification of alternator output is achieved by six silicon diodes housed in a rectifier pack and connected as a 3-phase full-wave bridge. The rectifier pack is attached to the outer face of the slip ring end bracket and contains also three 'field' diodes; at normal operating speeds, rectified current from the stator output windings flows through these diodes to provide self-excitation of the rotor field, via brushes bearing on face-type slip rings.

The slip rings are carried on a small diameter moulded drum attached to the rotor shaft outboard of the slip ring end bearing.

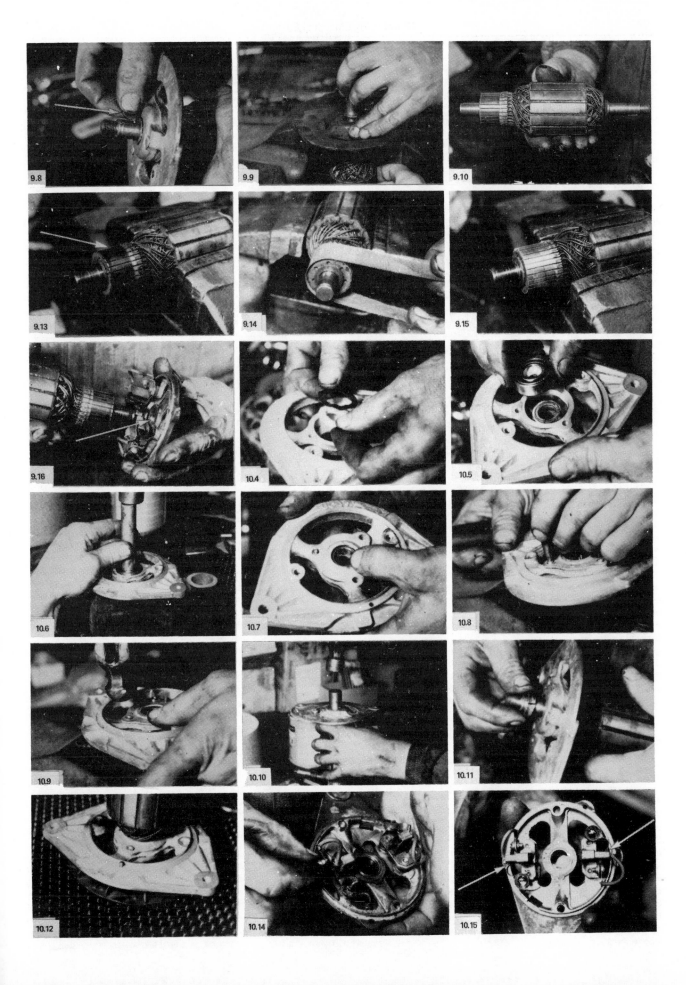

The inner ring is centred on the rotor shaft axis, while the outer ring has a mean diameter of ¾ inch approximately. By keeping the mean diameter of the slip rings to a minimum, relative speeds between brushes and rings, and hence wear, are also minimal. The slip rings are connected to the rotor field winding by wires carried in grooves in the rotor shaft.

The brushgear is housed in a moulding screwed to the outside of the slip ring end bracket. This moulding thus encloses the slip ring and brushgear assembly, and together with the shielded bearing, protects the assembly against the entry of dust and moisture.

The regulator is set during manufacture and requires no further attention. Briefly, the 'thick film' regulator comprises resistors and conductors screen printed onto a 1 inch square alumina substrate. Mounted on the substrate are Lucas semi-conductor dice consisting of three transistors, a voltage reference diode and a field recirculation diode, and also two capacitors. The internal connections between these components and the substrate are made by special Lucas patented connectors. The whole assembly is 1/16 inch thick, and is housed in a recess in an aluminium heat sink, which is attached to the slip ring end bracket. Complete hermetic sealing is achieved by a silicone rubber encapsulant to provide environmental protection.

Electrical connections to external circuits are brought out to Lucar connector blades, these being grouped to accept a moulded connector socket which ensures correct connections.

12. Alternator - Routine Maintenance

1. The equipment has been designed for the minimum amount of maintenance in service. The only items subject to wear being the brushes and bearings.
2. Brushes should be examined after about 75,000 miles, and renewed if necessary. The bearings are pre-packed with grease for life, and should not require any further attention.

13. Alternators - Special Procedures

1. A replacement alternator must always be checked to ensure that polarity connections are correct. They are clearly marked and wrong connections can damage the equipment.
2. Never reverse battery connections. The rectifiers could be damaged.
3. Always connect up the battery earth terminal first.
4. Disconnect the alternator/control unit whenever the battery is being charged in position, as a safety precaution.
5. Never disconnect the battery with the engine running, or run the alternator with the output cable disconnected or any other alternator circuits disconnected.
6. The cable between the battery and alternator is always 'live'. Take care not to short to earth.

14. Alternator - Removal & Replacement

1. Disconnect the battery by removal of the negative earth terminal.
2. Unplug the leads on the rear of the alternator.
3. Slacken the three alternator securing bolts and tilt the alternator towards the engine.
4. Remove the fan belt.
5. Remove the alternator securing bolts and detach the alternator.
6. Replacement is the reversal of the above procedure, but ensure the fan belt has ½ inch (13 mm) free movement at a point midway between the alternator and water pump pulleys after the alternator securing bolts are secured.

15. Alternator - Dismantling & Inspection (Brushes Only)

1. Referring to Fig.10.3. remove the end cover by undoing the screws.
2. To inspect the brushes correctly the brush holder moulding should be removed complete by undoing the two bolts and disconnecting the 'Lucar' connection to the diode plates.
3. With the brush holder moulding removed and the brush assemblies still in position check that they protrude from the face of the moulding by at least 0.2 inches (5 mm). Also check that when depressed, the spring pressure is 7—10 ozs. when the end of the brush is flush with the face of the brush moulding. To be done with any accuracy this requires a push type spring gauge.
4. Should either of the foregoing requirements not be fulfilled the spring assemblies should be replaced.
5. This can be done by simply renewing the holding screws of each assembly and replacing them.
6. With the brush holder moulding removed the slip rings on the face end of the rotor are exposed. These can be cleaned with a petrol soaked cloth and any signs of burning may be removed very carefully with fine glass paper. On no account should any other abrasive be used or any attempt at machining be made.
7. When the brushes are refitted they should slide smoothly in their holders. Any sticking tendency may first be rectified by wiping with a petrol soaked cloth, or if this fails, by carefully polishing with a very fine file where any binding marks may appear.
8. Reassemble in the reverse order of dismantling. Ensure that leads which may have been connected to any of the screws are reconnected correctly. NOTE:
1. If the charging system is suspect, first check the fan belt tension and condition - refer to Chapter 10/6.2 for details.
2. Check the battery - refer to Chapter 10/3 for details.
3. With an alternator the ignition warning light control feed comes from the centre point of a pair of diodes in the alternator via a control unit similar in appearance to an indicator flasher unit. Should the warning light indicate lack of charge, check this unit and if suspect replace it.
4. Should all the above prove negative then proceed to check the alternator.

16. Inertia Type Starter Motor - General Description

The engine is started by the starter motor pinion engaging with the flywheel ring gear or, on automatic transmission cars, with the torque converter inertia ring.

The starter motor is held in position by three bolts which also clamp the bellhousing flange.

The motor is of the four field coil, four pole piece type, and utilises four spring-loaded commutator brushes. Two of these brushes are earthed, and the other two are insulated and attached to the field coil ends.

17. Starter Motor - Testing on Engine

1. If the starter motor fails to operate then check the condition of the battery by turning on the headlamps. If they glow brightly for several seconds and then gradually dim, the battery is in an uncharged condition.
2. If the headlamps glow brightly and it is obvious that the battery is in good condition, then check the tightness of the battery wiring connections (and in particular the earth lead from the battery terminal to its connection on the bodyframe). If the positive terminal on the battery becomes hot when an attempt is made to work the starter, this is a sure sign of a poor connection on the battery terminal. To rectify remove the terminal, clean the inside of the cap and the terminal post thoroughly and reconnect. Check the tightness of the connections at the relay switch and at the starter

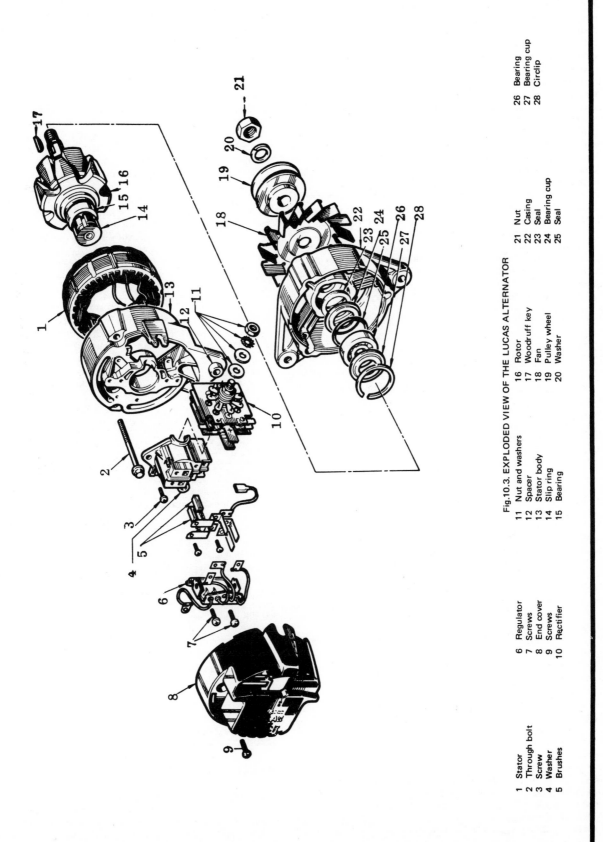

Fig.10.3. EXPLODED VIEW OF THE LUCAS ALTERNATOR

1	Stator	6	Regulator	11	Nut and washers	16	Rotor	21	Nut	26	Bearing
2	Through bolt	7	Screws	12	Spacer	17	Woodruff key	22	Casing	27	Bearing cup
3	Screw	8	End cover	13	Stator body	18	Fan	23	Seal	28	Circlip
4	Washer	9	Screws	14	Slip ring	19	Pulley wheel	24	Bearing cup		
5	Brushes	10	Rectifier	15	Bearing	20	Washer	25	Seal		

motor. Check the wiring with a voltmeter for breaks or shorts.

3. If the wiring is in order then check that the starter motor is operating. To do this, press the rubber covered button in the centre of the solenoid under the bonnet. If it is working the starter motor will be heard to 'click' as it tries to rotate. Alternatively check it with a voltmeter.

If the battery is fully charged, the wiring in order, and the switch working and the starter motor fails to operate, then it will have to be removed from the car for examination. Before this is done, however, ensure that the starter pinion has not jammed in mesh with the flywheel. Check by turning the square end of the armature shaft with a spanner. This will free the pinion if it is stuck in engagement with the flywheel teeth.

18. Starter Motor - Removal & Replacement

1. Disconnect the battery earth lead from the negative terminal.
2. Disconnect the starter motor cable from the terminal on the starter motor end plate.
3. Remove the upper starter motor securing bolt.
4. Working under the car loosen, and then remove, the two lower starter motor securing bolts taking care to support the motor so as to prevent damage to the drive components.
5. Lift the starter motor out of engagement with the flywheel ring and lower it out of the car.
6. Replacement is a straightforward reversal of the removal procedure.

19. Starter Motor - Dismantling & Reassembly

1. With the starter motor on the bench, loosen the screw on the cover band and slip the cover band off. With a piece of wire bent into the shape of a hook, lift back each of the brush springs in turn and check the movement of the brushes in their holders by pulling on the flexible connectors. If the brushes are so worn that their faces do not rest against the commutator, or if the ends of the brush leads are exposed on their working face, they must be renewed.
2. If any of the brushes tend to stick in their holders then wash them with a petrol moistened cloth and, if necessary, lightly polish the sides of the brush with a very fine file, until the brushes move quite freely in their holders.
3. If the surface of the commutator is dirty or blackened, clean it with a petrol dampened rag. Secure the starter motor in a vice and check it by connecting a heavy gauge cable between the starter motor terminal and a 12v battery.
4. Connect the cable from the other battery terminal to earth in the starter motor body. If the motor turns at high speed it is in good order.
5. If the starter motor still fails to function, or if it is wished to renew the brushes, it is necessary to further dismantle the motor.
6. Lift the brush springs with the wire hook and lift all four brushes out of their holders one at a time.
7. Remove the terminal nuts and washer from the terminal post on the commutator end bracket.
8. Unscrew the two through bolts which hold the end plates together and pull off the commutator end bracket. Also remove the driving end bracket which will come away complete with the armature.
9. At this stage, if the brushes are to be renewed, their flexible connectors must be unsoldered and the connectors of new brushes soldered in their place. Check that the new brushes move freely in their holders as detailed above. If cleaning the commutator with petrol fails to remove all the burnt areas and spots, then wrap a piece of glass paper round the commutator and rotate the armature. If the commutator is very badly worn, remove the drive gear as detailed in the following section. Then mount the armature in a lathe and with the lathe turning at high speed, take a very fine cut-out of the commutator and finish the surface by polishing with glass paper. DO NOT UNDERCUT THE MICA INSULATORS BETWEEN THE COMMUTATOR SEGMENTS.

10 With the starter motor dismantled, test the four field coils for an open circuit. Connect a 12 volt battery with a 12 volt bulb in one of the leads between the field terminal post and the tapping point of the field coils to which the brushes are connected. An open circuit is proved by the bulb not lighting.

11 If the bulb lights, it does not necessarily mean that the field coils are in order, as there is a possibility that one of the coils will be earthing to the starter yoke or pole shoes. To check this, remove the lead from the brush connector and place it against a clean portion of the starter yoke. If the bulb lights the field coils are earthing. Replacement of the field coils calls for the use of a wheel operated screwdriver, a soldering iron, caulking and riveting operations and is beyond the scope of the majority of owners. The starter yoke should be taken to a reputable electrical engineering works for new field coils to be fitted. Alternatively, purchase an exchange starter motor.

12 If the armature is damaged this will be evident after visual inspection. Look for signs of burning, discolouration, and for conductors that have lifted away from the commutator. Reassembly is a straightforward reversal of the dismantling procedure.

20. Starter Motor Drive - General Description

1. The starter motor drive is of the outboard type. When the starter motor is operated the pinion moves into contact with the flywheel gear ring by moving in towards the starter motor.
2. If the engine kicks back, or the pinion fails to engage with the flywheel gear ring when the starter motor is actuated no undue strain is placed on the armature shaft, as the pinion sleeve disengages from the pinion and turns independently.

21. Starter Motor Drive - Removal & Replacement

1. When the starter motor is removed the drive should be well washed in petrol or paraffin to remove any grease or oil which may be the cause of a sticking pinion. Under no circumstances should these parts be lubricated.
2. To dismantle the drive, compress the drive spring and cup employing a press for this purpose, and then extract the locking device, pin or circlip.
3. Ease the press and remove the drive spring cup, spring and retaining washer. Pull the drive pinion barrel assembly from the armature shaft. If the pinion is badly worn or broken, this must be replaced as an assembly. When refitting the pinion barrel assembly must be fitted with the pinion teeth toward the armature windings.

22. Pre-Engaged Starter Motors - General Description

This type of starter motor is normally only fitted as original equipment to the Capri 3000 GT and E or 2000 GT models with 'cold start' specifications, but it is available as an optional extra on the standard 2000 GT model.

Two types of motor may be used, the first type being exactly the same as the inertia type described in the previous sections. The second type is a wave wound motor and uses an end-face commutator instead of the normal drum type. On both types a solenoid is attached to the top of the starter motor which actuates a one way clutch when the starter button is pressed, thus engaging the motor to the pinion which is permanently in mesh with the starter ring on the flywheel. The drive to the pinion therefore remains fully engaged until the solenoid is deactivated. The starter motor is attached to the bell-housing by two bolts only and not three as in the inertia type.

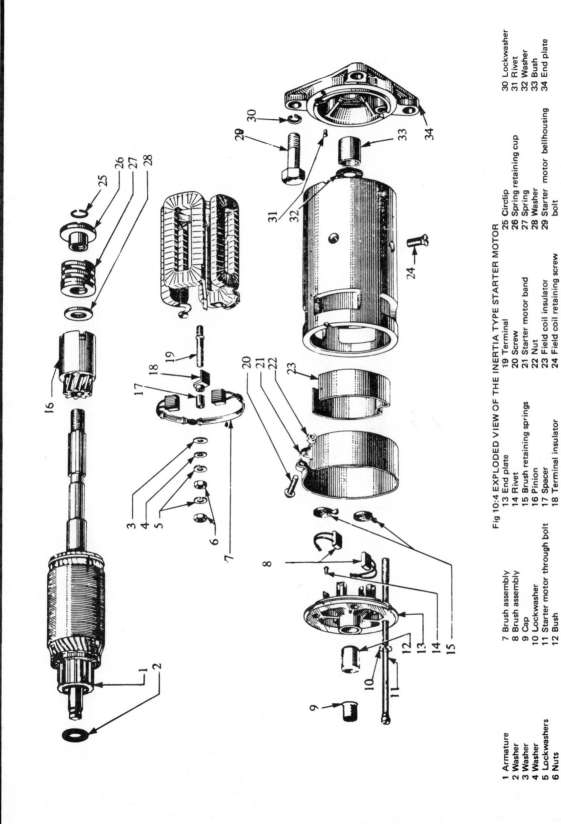

Fig 10:4 EXPLODED VIEW OF THE INERTIA TYPE STARTER MOTOR

1 Armature	13 End plate	25 Circlip
2 Washer	14 Rivet	26 Spring retaining cup
3 Washer	15 Brush retaining springs	27 Spring
4 Washer	16 Pinion	28 Washer
5 Lockwashers	17 Spacer	29 Starter motor bellhousing
6 Nuts	18 Terminal insulator	bolt
7 Brush assembly	19 Terminal	30 Lockwasher
8 Brush assembly	20 Screw	31 Rivet
9 Cap	21 Starter motor band	32 Washer
10 Lockwasher	22 Nut	33 Bush
11 Starter motor through bolt	23 Field coil insulator	34 End plate
12 Bush	24 Field coil retaining screw	

23. Pre-Engaged Starter Motors - Removal & Replacement

1. Disconnect the battery by removing the earth lead from the negative terminal.
2. Disconnect the starter motor cable from the terminal on the starter motor end plate.
3. Remove the two solenoid retaining nuts and the connecting strap and lift off the solenoid.
4. Remove the upper starter motor retaining bolt.
5. Working under the car, remove the lower retaining bolt taking care to support the motor so as to prevent damage to the drive components.
6. Withdraw the starter motor from the bellhousing and lower it from the car.
7. Replacement is a straightforward reversal of the removal procedure.

24. Endface Commutator Starter Motor - Dismantling & Reassembly

Due to the fact that this type of starter motor uses a face commutator, on which the brushes make contact end on, a certain amount of thrust is created along the armature shaft. A thrust bearing is therefore incorporated in the motor at the commutator end.
1. Remove the split pin from the end of the shaft and slide off the shims, washer and thrust plate.
2. Remove the two screws which retain the end plate and pull off the end plate complete with the brush holders and brushes.
3. Should the brushes have to be renewed follow the instructions given in Section 19, paragraph 9 of this chapter.
4. To remove the armature, unscrew the nuts on the holding studs at the drive end bracket.
5. Withdraw the armature complete with the drive and the one way clutch operating lever.
6. Reassembly is a direct reversal of the above procedure, but the armature end float should be measured as indicated in Fig.10.6. The correct end float should be .010 inch (.254 mm) with an 8 volt current activating the solenoid. If the end float is found to be incorrect it can be corrected by fitting an appropriate sized shim or shims between the thrust plate and the split pin. NOTE: Never use the same split pin more than once.

25. Control Box - General Description

1. The control box is positioned on the left-hand wing valance and comprises three units; two separate vibrating armature type single contact regulators and a cut-out relay. One of the regulators is sensitive to change in current and the other to changes in voltage.
2. Adjustments can only be made with a special tool which resembles a screwdriver with a multi-toothed blade. This can be obtained through Lucas or Ford agents.
3. The regulators control the output from the dynamo depending on the state of the battery and the demands of the electrical equipment, and ensure that the battery is not overcharged. The cut-out is really an automatic switch and connects the dynamo to the battery when the dynamo is turning fast enough to produce a charge. Similarly it disconnects the battery from the dynamo when the engine is idling or stationary so that the battery does not discharge through the dynamo.

26. Cut-Out & Regulator Contacts - Maintenance

1. Every **12,000** miles check the cut-out and regulator contacts. If they are dirty or rough or burnt place a piece of fine glass paper (DO NOT USE EMERY PAPER OR CARBORUNDUM PAPER) between the cut-out contacts, close them manually and draw the glass paper through several times.

2. Clean the regulator contacts in exactly the same way, but use emery or carborundum paper and not glass paper. Carefully clean both sets of contacts from all traces of dust with a rag moistened in methylated spirits.

27. Voltage Regulator Adjustment

1. The regulator requires very little attention during its service life, and should there be any reason to suspect its correct functioning, tests of all circuits should be made to ensure that they are not the reason for the trouble.
2. These checks include the tension of the fan belt, to make sure that it is not slipping and so providing only a very low charge rate. The battery should be carefully checked for possible low charge rate due to a faulty cell, or corroded battery connections.
3. The leads from the generator may have been crossed during replacement, and if this is the case then the regulator points will have stuck together as soon as the generator starts to charge. Check for loose or broken leads from the generator to the regulator.
4. If after a thorough check it is considered advisable to test the regulator, this should only be carried out by an electrician who is well acquainted with the correct method using test bench equipment.
5. Pull off the Lucar connections from the two adjacent control box terminals 'B'. To start the engine it will now be necessary to join together the ignition and battery leads with a suitable wire.
6. Connect a 0—30 volt voltmeter between terminal 'D' on the control box and terminal 'WL'. Start the engine and run it at 2,000 r.p.m. The reading on the voltmeter should be steady and lie between the limits detailed in the specification.
7. If the reading is unsteady this may be due to dirty contacts. If the reading is outside the specified limits stop the engine and adjust the voltage regulator in the following manner.
8. Take off the control box cover and start and run the engine at 2,000 r.p.m. Using the correct tool turn the voltage adjustment cam anti-clockwise to raise the setting and clockwise to lower it. To check that the setting is correct, stop the engine, and then start it and run it at 2,000 r.p.m. noting the reading. Refit the cover and the connections to the 'WL' and 'D' terminals.

28. Current Regulator Adjustment

1. The output from the current regulator should equal the maximum output from the dynamo which is 22 amps. To test this it is necessary to by-pass the cut-out by holding the contacts together.
2. Remove the cover from the control box and with a bulldog clip hold the cut-out contacts together. (See Fig.10.7).
3. Pull off the wires from the adjacent terminals 'B' and connect a 0—40 moving coil ammeter to one of the terminals and to the leads.
4. All the other load connections including the ignition must be made to the battery.
5. Start the engine and increase the speed to approximately 3,000 r.p.m. The ammeter should read the rated generator 'output ±1 amp' (22 amp standard, 25 amp C40—L dynamo). If the needle flickers it is likely that the points are dirty. If the reading is too low, turn the special Lucas tool clockwise to raise the setting and anti-clockwise to lower it. Decrease and increase engine speed to previous specification and recheck the setting.

29. Cut-Out Adjustment

1. Check the voltage required to operate the cut-out by connecting a voltmeter between the control box terminals 'D' and 'WL'. Remove the control box cover, start the engine and gradually increase its speed until the cut-outs close. This should occur when the reading is between 12.6 to 13.4 volts.
2. If the reading is outside these limits turn the cut-out adjusting cam (1 in the illustration) by means of the adjusting tool, a fraction

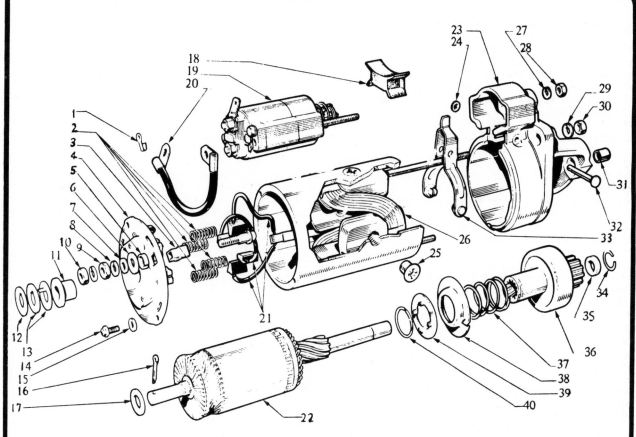

Fig.10.5. EXPLODED VIEW OF THE END FACE COMMUTATOR PRE—ENGAGED TYPE STARTER MOTOR

1	Hook	12	Washers	23	Starter drive cover and
2	Brush springs	13	Tabbed washer		starter motor endplate
3	Insulator	14	Bolt	24	Pin retaining ring
4	Endplate & brush holder	15	Washer	25	Field coil retaining screw
5	Spacer	16	Split pin	26	Field coils
6	Washer	17	Washer	27	Washer
7	Washer	18	Grommet	28	Nut
8	Lockwasher	19	Solenoid assembly	29	Lockwasher
9	Nut	20	Cable assembly	30	Nut
10	Nut	21	Brush assembly	31	Bush
11	Bush	22	Armature	32	Lever swivel pin

33	Actuating lever
34	Circlip
35	Spacer
36	Pinion
37	Spring
38	Clutch assembly
39	Clutch assembly
40	Retaining ring

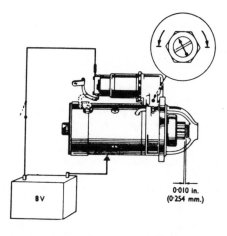

0·010 in.
(0·254 mm.)

8 V

Fig.10.6. Measuring armature end float.

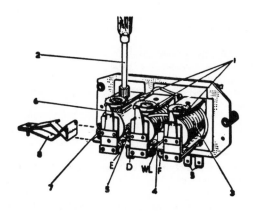

Fig.10.7. THE CONTROL BOX (COVER REMOVED)

1	Adjustment cams	5	Current regulator contacts
2	Setting tool	6	Voltage regulator
3	Cut-out relay	7	Voltage regulator contacts
4	Current regulator	8	Clip

at a time clockwise to raise the voltage, and anti-clockwise to lower it.

3. To adjust the drop off voltage bend the fixed contact blade carefully. The adjustment to the cut-out should be completed within 30 seconds of starting the engine as otherwise heat build-up from the shunt coil will affect the readings.

4. If the cut-out fails to work, clean the contacts, and if there is still no response, renew the cut-out and regulator unit.

30. Fuse Block - Removal & Replacement

1. Open bonnet and pull off two non-reversible wiring plugs on the fuse block.

2. Pull off the transparent fuse cover, remove the two screws securing the fuse block to the body and remove the fuse block.

3. Replacement is a direct reversal of the above but check operation of lighting circuits after replacement.

31. Flasher Circuit - Fault Tracing & Rectification

1. The flasher unit is a small cylindrical metal container located under the dashboard on top of the steering column brace and is held in place by a clip. The unit is actuated by the direction indicator switch.

2. If the flasher unit fails to operate, or works very slowly or rapidly, check out the flasher indicator circuit as detailed below, before assuming that there is a fault in the unit.

a) Examine the direction indicator bulbs both front and rear for broken filaments.

b) If the external flashers are working but either of the internal flasher warning lights have ceased to function, check the filaments in the warning light bulbs and replace with a new bulb if necessary.

c) If a flasher bulb is sound but does not work check all the flasher circuit connections with the aid of the wiring diagram found at the end of this chapter.

d) With the ignition switched on check that the current is reaching the flasher unit by connecting a voltmeter between the 'plus' terminal and earth. If it is found that current is reaching the unit connect the two flasher unit terminals together and operate the direction indicator switch. If one of the flasher warning lights comes on this proves that the flasher unit itself is at fault and must be replaced as it is not possible to dismantle and repair it.

32. Windscreen Wiper Mechanism - Maintenance

1. Renew the windscreen wiper blades at approximately 12,000 mile intervals, or more frequently if necessary.

2. The washer round the wheelbox spindle can be lubricated with several drops of glycerine every 6,000 miles. The windscreen wiper links can be lightly oiled at the same time.

33. Windscreen Wiper Blades - Removal & Replacement

1. Lift the wiper arm away from the windscreen and remove the old blade by turning it in towards the arm and then disengage the arm from the slot in the blade.

2. To fit a new blade, slide the end of the wiper arm into the slotted spring fastening in the centre of the blade. Push the blade firmly onto the arm until the raised portion of the arm is fully home in the hole in the blade.

34. Windscreen Wiper Arms - Removal & Replacement

1. Before removing a wiper arm, turn the windscreen wiper switch on and off to ensure the arms are in their normal parked position

parallel with the bottom of the windscreen.

2. To remove an arm pivot the arm back and pull the wiper arm head off the splined drive. If the arm proves difficult to remove, a screwdriver with a large blade can be used to lever the wiper arm head off the splines. Care must be taken not to damage the splines.

3. When replacing an arm position it so it is in the correct relative parked position and then press the arm head onto the splined drive until it is fully home on the splines.

35. Windscreen Wiper Mechanism - Fault Diagnosis & Rectification

1. Should the windscreen wipers fail, or work very slowly, then check the terminals on the motor for loose connections, and make sure the insulation of all the wiring is not cracked or broken thus causing a short circuit. If this is in order then check the current the motor is taking by connecting an ammeter in the circuit and turning on the wiper switch. Consumption should be between 2.3 to 3.1 amps.

2. If no current is passing through the motor, check that the switch is operating correctly.

3. If the wiper motor takes a very high current check the wiper blades for freedom of movement. If this is satisfactory check the gearbox cover and gear assembly for damage.

4. If the motor takes a very low current ensure that the battery is fully charged. Check the brush gear and ensure the brushes are bearing on the commutator. If not, check the brushes for freedom of movement and, if necessary, renew the tension springs. If the brushes are very worn they should be replaced with new ones. Check the armature by substitution if this unit is suspect.

36. Windscreen Wiper Motor & Linkage - Removal & Replacement

1. Disconnect the battery by removing the negative earth lead and then remove the wiper blades and arms as described in Sections 33 and 34.

2. Undo and remove the two nuts holding the wiper spindles to the bodywork in front of the windscreen.

3. Remove the parcel shelf by taking off the two spring clips at either end and by undoing the single screw on the drivers side and the two screws on the passengers side.

4. To gain better access to the wiper motor disconnect the flexible hoses from the heater to the demister vents above the dash and also the aeroflow flexible pipes.

5. Disconnect the two control cables on the heater at the heater end, making a careful note of their correct fitting in relation to the positions of the heater controls on the fascia. Tuck the cables out of the way under the fascia.

6. Remove the single screw holding the wiper motor to its mounting bracket and lower the motor and linkage just enough to be able to see the wires running to the motor.

7. Disconnect the wires at their connectors on the motor making a note of their relative positions for reassembly purposes.

8. Now lower the complete wiper motor and linkage assembly down in front of the heater and remove it from the car.

9. Reassembly is a direct reversal of the removal procedure, but the screw securing the wiper motor to its mounting bracket should not be fully tightened down until the wiper spindle nuts have been replaced thus ensuring correct alignment of the linkage.

37. Windscreen Wiper Motor - Dismantling, Inspection & Reassembly

1. Start by removing the linkage mechanism from the motor. Carefully prize the short wiper link off the motor operating arm and remove the plastic pivot bush.

2. Undo the three screws which hold the linkage to the wiper motor and separate the two.

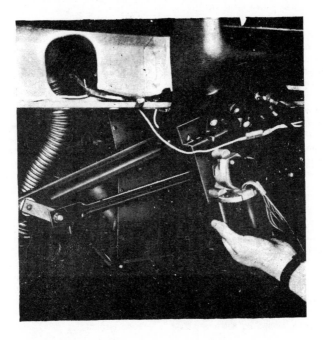

Fig.10.8. Lowering the windscreen wiper motor and linkages out of the car

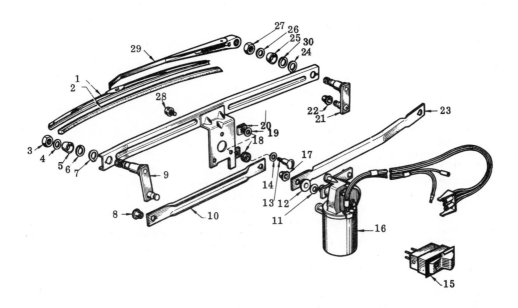

Fig.10.9. EXPLODED VIEW OF THE WINDSCREEN WIPER MECHANISM

1	Blade holder	9	Arm and pivot shaft	17	Bushing	25	Spacer
2	Wiper blade	10	Link arm	18	Grommet	26	Washer
3	Nut	11	Spring washer	19	Washer	27	Nut
4	Washer	12	Bushing	20	Screw clip	28	Nut and washer
5	Spacer	13	Screw	21	Arm & pivot shaft	29	Wiper arm
6	Seal	14	Washer	22	Bushing	30	Seal
7	Ring	15	Switch assembly	23	Link arm		
8	Bushing	16	Wiper motor	24	Ring		

3. Unscrew the two bolts which hold the motor case to the gearbox housing and withdraw the motor case complete with the armature.
4. Take the brushes out of their holders and remove the brush springs.
5. Undo the three screws which hold the brush mounting plate to the wiper gearbox and withdraw the brush mounting plate.
6. Remove the earth wire on the gearbox cover plate by undoing the screw nearest the motor case. Undo the other screw on the gearbox cover plate and remove the cover plate and switch assembly.
7. Pull the spring steel armature stop out of the gearbox casing. Then remove the spring clip and washer which retain the wiper pinion gear in place and withdraw the gear and washer.
8. Undo the nut securing the wiper motor operating arm and remove the lockwasher, arm, wave washer and flat washer in that order.
9. Having removed the operating arm withdraw the output gear, park switch assembly and washer from the gearbox casing.
10 Carefully examine all parts for signs of wear or damage and replace as necessary.
11 Reassembly is a direct reversal of the above procedure.

38. Horn - Fault Tracing & Rectification

1. If the horn works badly or fails completely, check the wiring leading to the horn plug which is located on the body panel next to the horn itself. Also check that the plug is properly pushed home and is in a clean condition free from corrosion etc.
2. Check that the horn is secure on its mounting and that there is nothing lying on the horn body.
3. If the fault is not an external one, remove the horn cover and check the leads inside the horn. If these are sound, check the contact breaker contacts. If these are burnt or dirty clean them with a fine file and wipe all traces of dirt and dust away with a petrol moistened rag.

39. Headlamp & Sidelamp Unit - Removal & Replacement

1. Disconnect the battery by removing the negative earth lead.
2. Open the bonnet and remove the two small screws securing the top of the headlamp bezel to the bodywork.
3. Remove the two lower securing screws from the bezel and lift it away.
4. Remove the four screws holding the sealed beam unit to the body and carefully lift the unit a short distance away from the car.
5. Pull off the wiring plug from the rear of the sealed beam unit and remove the sidelamp bulb which is located just below the plug. Also disconnect the wire leading to the indicator light at its connector. The unit can now be lifted clear of the car.
6. Replacement is a direct reversal of the removal procedure.

40. Headlamp Alignment

1. It is always advisable to have the headlamps aligned on proper optical beam setting equipment but if this is not available the following procedure may be used.
2. Position the car on level ground 10 feet in front of a dark wall or board. The wall or board must be at right angles to the centre line of the car.
3. Draw a vertical line on the board in line with the centre line of the car.
4. Bounce the car on its suspension to ensure correct settlement and then measure the height between the ground and the centre of the headlamps.
5. Draw an horizontal line across the board at this measured height. On this horizontal line mark a cross 21.6 inch (54.8 cm) either side of the vertical centre line.
6. Remove the two head and sidelamp bezels by undoing the four screws on either side and switch the headlamps onto full beam.

7. By carefully adjusting the horizontal and vertical adjusting screws on each lamp, align the centres of each beam onto the crosses which you have previously marked on the horizontal line, 43.2 inch (109.7 cm) apart.
8. Bounce the car on its suspension again and check that the beams return to the correct positions. At the same time check the operation of the dip switch, replace the outer bezels.

41. Front Indicator Lamp Glass & Bulb - Removal & Replacement

1. Disconnect the battery by removing the negative earth lead, then remove the headlamp bezel as described in Section 40.
2. Remove the two screws running through the top and bottom of the lens, lift the lens away and remove the bulb by pushing it in and turning anti-clockwise to release the pins.
3. Replacement is a direct reversal of the removal procedure.

42. Rear Indicator, Stop & Tail Lamp Bulbs - Removal & Replacement

1. Disconnect battery by removal of the negative earth lead.
2. Open the luggage compartment lid and pull off rear lamp trim cover.
3. Pull out the spring-loaded rear and indicator bulb holder and remove the bulbs.
4. Replacement is a direct reversal of the above procedure.

43. Rear Licence Plate Lamp - Removal & Replacement

1. Disconnect battery by removal of negative earth lead.
2. Disconnect the earth and feed wires inside the luggage compartment and pull the wires through the hole in the floor.
3. Press the retaining levers inwards from underneath the bumper and lift off the assembly.
4. Remove the bulb from the assembly.
5. Replacement is a direct reversal of the above procedure, then check the operation of the lamp.

44. Interior Light - Removal & Replacement

1. Disconnect the battery by removal of the negative earth lead.
2. Carefully prize the light assembly from its location above the door.
3. If the bulb is defective it can now be removed by gently pulling it from its spring loaded position.
4. Finally, to remove the complete assembly simply disconnect the wires from the back of the light taking note of their correct positions for reassembly purposes.
5. Replacement of the complete assembly, or the bulb is a direct reversal of the removal sequence.

45. Instrument Panel & Instruments - Removal & Replacement

1. Undo and remove the two bolts holding the steering column to the underside of the dash panel and lower the column out of the way.
2. Remove the five cross-head screws holding the instrument panel to the bulkhead and pull the panel a short distance into the car so as to expose the wiring.
3. Disconnect the speedometer cable from the speedometer by squeezing the knurled portion of the retaining clip and withdraw the cable.
4. Make a careful note of all the wiring positions then disconnect them at their plugs and connectors and withdraw the panel into the car.

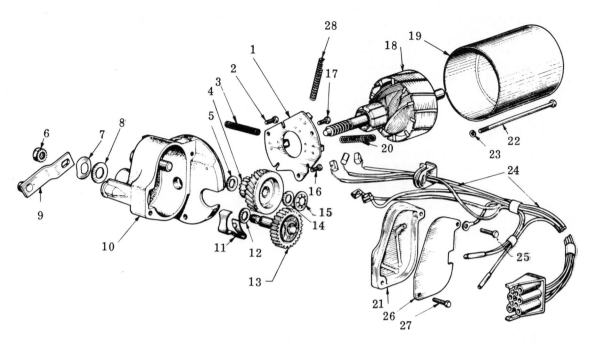

Fig.10.10. EXPLODED VIEW OF THE WINDSCREEN WIPER MOTOR

1	Brush holder plate	9	Output arm	16	Screw	23	Locking washers
2	Screw	10	Housing	17	Screw	24	Wiring loom and brush
3	Spring	11	Stop assembly	18	Armature		assembly
4	Wiper gear and pinion	12	Washer	19	Casing and magnet	25	Screw
5	Washer	13	Shaft & circuit assembly	20	Spring	26	Switch wiring cover
6	Nut	14	Washer	21	Switch & cover assembly	27	Screw
7	& 8 washers	15	Clip	2	Through bolt	28	Spring

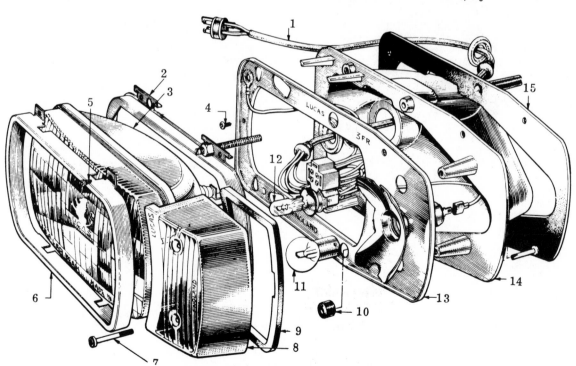

Fig.10.11. EXPLODED VIEW OF THE HEADLAMP ASSEMBLY

1	Wiring	5	Screw	9	Gasket	13	Frame
2	Inner bezel	6	Outer bezel	10	Grommet	14	Lamp body
3	Sealed beam unit	7	Screw	11	Flasher bulb	15	Bracket
4	Screw	8	Flasher lens	12	Sidelamp bulb		

Fig.10.12. Removing the headlamp unit bulb

Fig.10.13. Removing the front indicator lens and bulb

Fig.10.14. Removing the rear side, stop and indicator lamp assembly

Fig.10.15. Removing the licence plate lamp

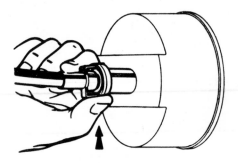

Fig.10.16. Disconnecting the cable from the back of the speedometer

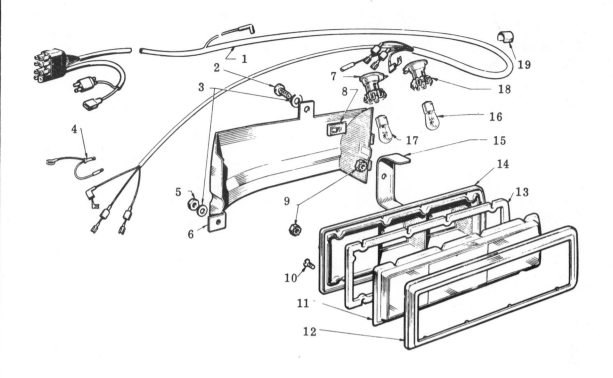

Fig.10.17. EXPLODED VIEW OF THE REAR LAMP ASSEMBLY

1	Wiring	6	Trim cover	11	Lens	16	Bulb
2	Screw	7	Bulb holder	12	Bezel	17	Bulb
3	Washer	8	Screw clip	13	Gasket	18	Bulb holder
4	Connector	9	Nuts and washers	14	Frame	19	Clip
5	Nut	10	Screw	15	Bracket		

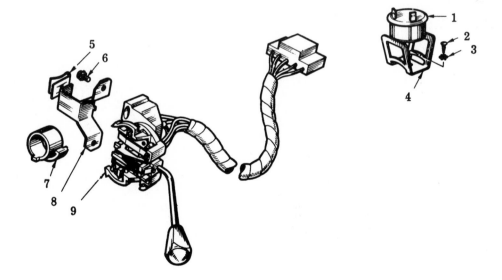

Fig.10.18. EXPLODED VIEW OF THE COMBINED DIRECTION INDICATOR, HEADLAMP FLASHER AND DIPPER SWITCH

1	Flasher unit	4	Bracket	6	Screw and washer	8	Bracket
2	Screw	5	Screw clip	7	Cancelling cam	9	Switch assembly
3	Shakeproof washer						

5. Separate the instrument box from the panel by removing the screws at each corner; four in all.

6. The instruments themselves are held to the box by either two small bolts or screws and can easily be removed and replaced as required.

7. Replacement of the instruments and instrument panel is a direct reversal of the removal procedure.

46. Instrument Voltage Regulator - Removal & Replacement

1. Remove the instrument panel from the car as described in Section 45.

2. The voltage regulator is located on the back of the speedometer and is removed by undoing a single retaining bolt and disconnecting the wires running to it.

3. Replacement is a straightforward reversal of the removal procedure.

47. Direction Indicator, Headlamp Flasher & Horn Switch Assembly Removal & Replacement

1. Disconnect the battery by removing the negative earth lead.

2. Remove the bolts securing the column to the underside of the fascia panel and lower the column.

3. Remove two securing screws on the column shrouds and remove the shrouds.

4. Remove two screws securing the switch to the column.

5. Disconnect the multi pin plug and remove the switch.

6. Replacement is a direct reversal of the removal procedure.

48. Light, Panel Light & Windscreen Wiper Switches - Removal & Replacement

1. Disconnect the battery by removing the negative earth lead.

2. Working under the dash pull off the multi pin plug from whichever switch is being removed.

3. By applying gentle pressure to the back of the switch on one side, carefully ease it into the car.

4. Replacement is a direct reversal of the removal procedure.

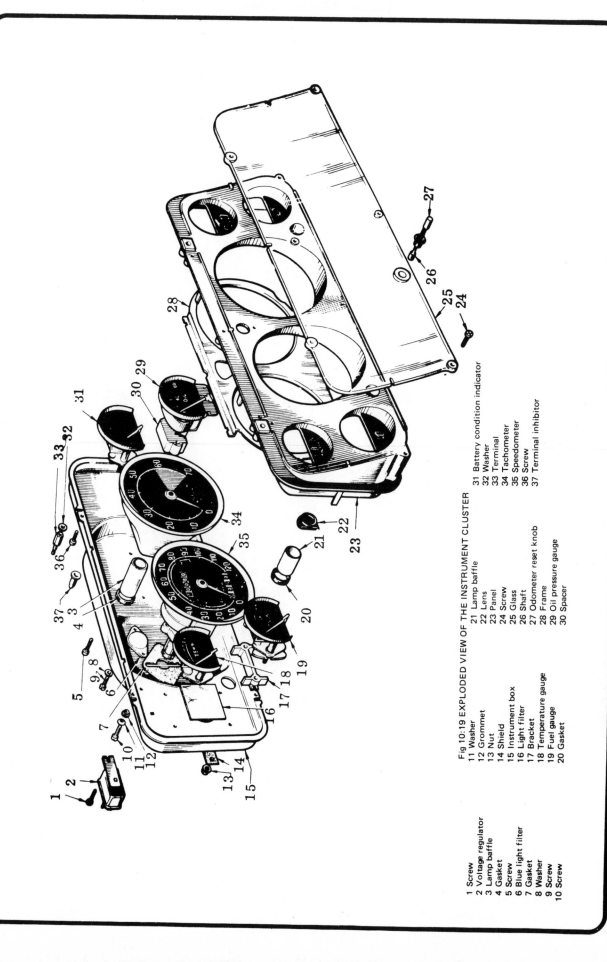

Fig 10:19 EXPLODED VIEW OF THE INSTRUMENT CLUSTER

1 Screw	11 Washer	21 Lamp baffle	31 Battery condition indicator
2 Voltage regulator	12 Grommet	22 Lens	32 Washer
3 Lamp baffle	13 Nut	23 Panel	33 Terminal
4 Gasket	14 Shield	24 Screw	34 Tachometer
5 Screw	15 Instrument box	25 Glass	35 Speedometer
6 Blue light filter	16 Light filter	26 Shaft	36 Screw
7 Gasket	17 Bracket	27 Odometer reset knob	37 Terminal inhibitor
8 Washer	18 Temperature gauge	28 Frame	
9 Screw	19 Fuel gauge	29 Oil pressure gauge	
10 Screw	20 Gasket	30 Spacer	

ALL FOUR WIRING DIAGRAMS USE THE SAME COLOUR CODING & KEY

CODE	WIRING COLOUR
R	Red
Bk	Black
Bl	Blue
W	White
Br	Brown
G	Green

CODE	WIRING COLOUR
Y	Yellow
LG	Light Green
P	Purple
O	Orange
Pk	Pink
S	Slate

CODE	ITEM
1.	R.H. turn signal lamp (front)
2.	L.H. turn signal lamp (front)
3.	R.H. side lamp (front)
4.	L.H. side lamp (front)
5.	R.H. headlamp
6.	L.H. headlamp
7.	R.H. front loom connector
8.	L.H. front loom connector
9.	R.H. side flasher (R.P.O.)
10.	L.H. side flasher (R.P.O.)
11.	Engine compartment loom connector
12.	Engine compartment loom connector (R.P.O.)
13.	Horn
14.	Dual horn (R.P.O.)
15.	Road lamp (R.P.O.)
16.	Fog lamp (R.P.O.)
17.	Battery (L.H.D.)
18.	Battery (R.H.D.)
19.	Ignition coil
20.	Distributor
21.	Oil pressure switch
22.	Temperature sender unit
23.	Generator
24.	Alternator (R.P.O.)
25.	Starter solenoid (automatic transmission)
26.	Starter solenoid (manual transmission)
27.	Pre-engaged starter motor - automatic transmission (R.P.O.)
28.	Inertia starter motor - automatic transmission
29.	Inertia starter motor - manual transmission
30.	Pre-engaged starter motor - manual transmission (R.P.O.)
31	Regulator
32.	Fuse block
33.	R.H. bulkhead wiring connector
34.	L.H. bulkhead wiring connector
35.	Stop lamp switch
36.	Brake fluid low pressure switch (R.P.O.)
37.	Windscreen wiper motor
38.	Windscreen wiper motor - 2 speed (R.P.O.)
39.	Heater motor
40.	Heater resistance
41.	Reversing lamp switch - manual transmission (R.P.O.)
42.	Reversing lamp and park inhibitor switch - automatic transmission R.P.O.)
43.	Turn signal warning lamp
44.	Instrument voltage regulator
45.	Instrument panel earth
46.	Brake fluid low pressure warning lamp (R.P.O.)
47.	R.H. courtesy switch
48.	L.H. courtesy switch
49.	Side/Head lamp switch
50.	Fuel gauge
51.	Temperature gauge
52.	Instrument illumination lamp
53.	Speedometer
54.	Tachometer

CODE	ITEM
55.	Speedometer illumination lamp
56.	Tachometer illumination lamp
57.	Battery condition indicator
58.	Oil pressure gauge
59.	Generator warning lamp
60.	Oil pressure warning lamp
61.	Main beam warning lamp
62.	Turn signal flasher unit
63.	Fog lamp switch (R.P.O.)
64.	Road lamp switch (R.P.O.)
65.	Interior lamp and panel illumination switch
66.	Windscreen wiper switch
67.	Heater switch
68.	Windscreen wiper switch - 2 speed (R.P.O.)
69.	Radio (R.P.O.)
70.	Radio aerial (R.P.O.)
71.	Accessory connector
72.	Ignition switch
73.	Rear wiring loom connector
74.	Emergency flasher unit (R.P.O.)
75.	Emergency flasher indicator lamp (R.P.O.)
76.	Steering column connector
77.	Steering column connector (R.P.O.)
78.	Emergency flasher switch (R.P.O.)
79.	Parking brake warning switch (R.P.O.)
80.	Transmission selector illumination lamp (R.P.O.)
81.	Accessory illumination connector
82.	Cigar lighter (R.P.O.)
83.	Map - reading lamp (R.P.O.)
84.	Clock (R.P.O.)
85.	Horn switch
86.	Direction indicator switch
87.	Column dip switch
88.	Headlamp flasher switch
89.	Interior light
90.	Fuel gauge sender unit
91.	R.P.O. connectors
92.	R.H. turn signal lamp (rear)
93.	L.H. turn signal lamp (rear)
94.	R.H. stop lamp
95.	L.H. stop lamp
96.	R.H. side lamp (rear)
97.	L.H. side lamp (rear)
98.	R.H. reversing lamp
99.	L.H. reversing lamp
100.	Licence plate lamp
101.	Clock
102.	Cigar lighter
103.	Headlamp flasher relay (R.P.O.)
104.	Driving lamps switch (R.P.O.)
105.	Heated rear window combined switch and warning light (R.P.O.)
106.	Heated rear window fuse (R.P.O.)
107.	Heated rear window relay (R.P.O.)
108.	Heated rear window (R.P.O.)

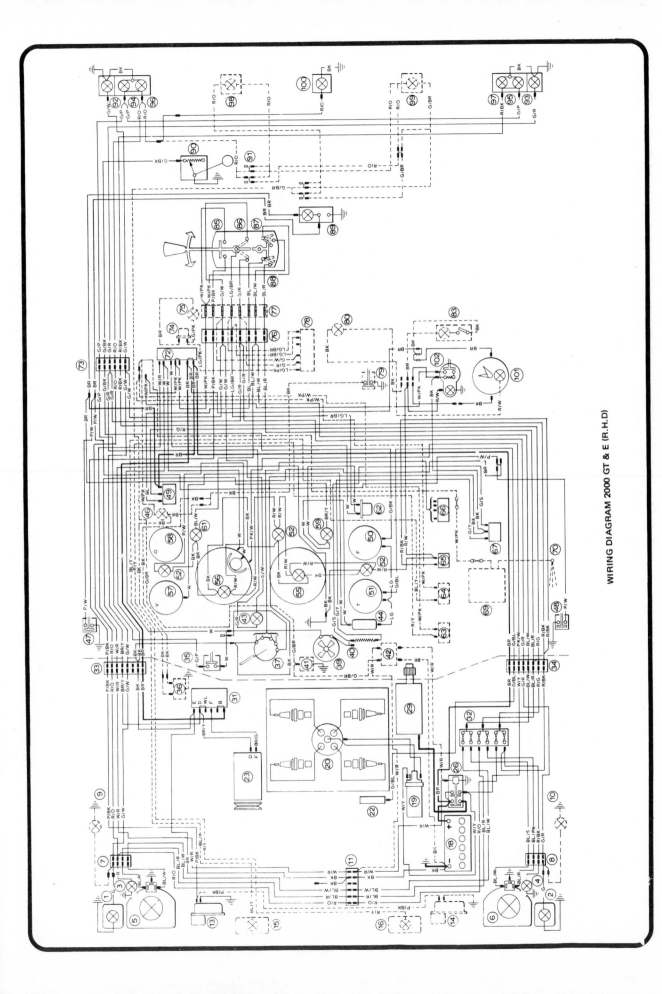

WIRING DIAGRAM 2000 GT & E (R.H.D)

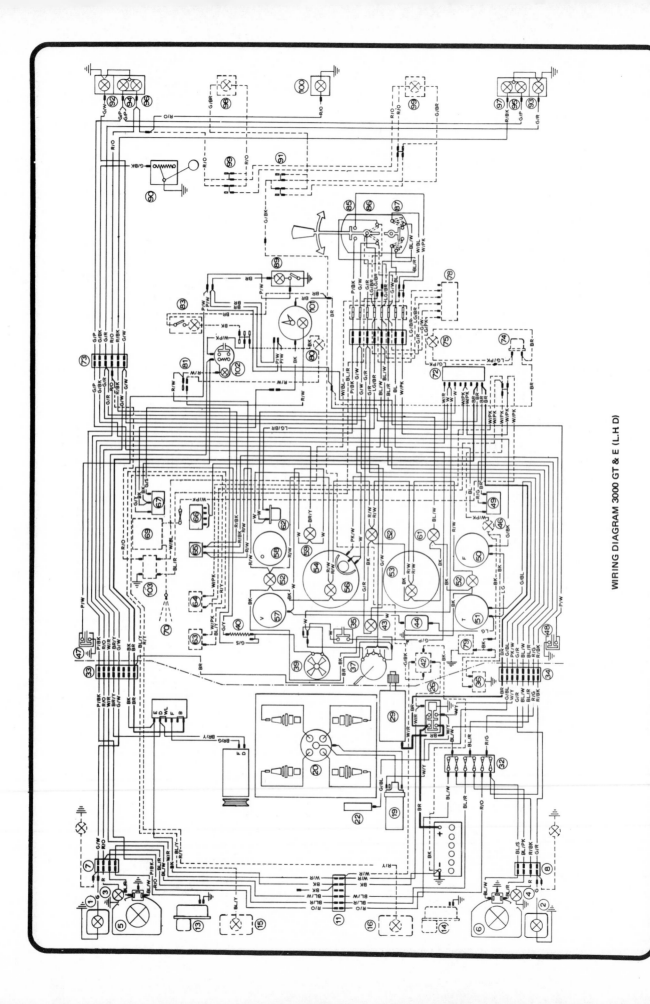

WIRING DIAGRAM 3000 GT & E (L.H D)

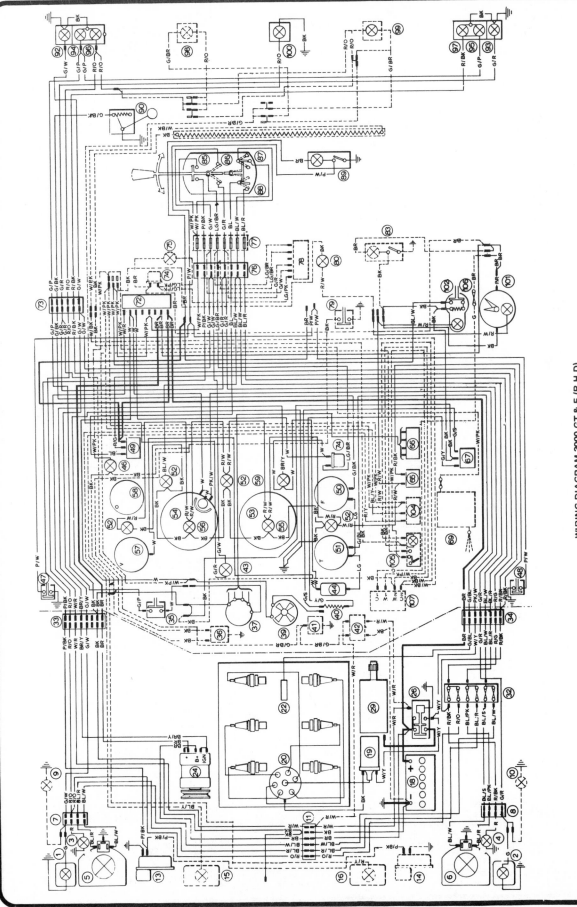

WIRING DIAGRAM 3000 GT & E (R.H.D)

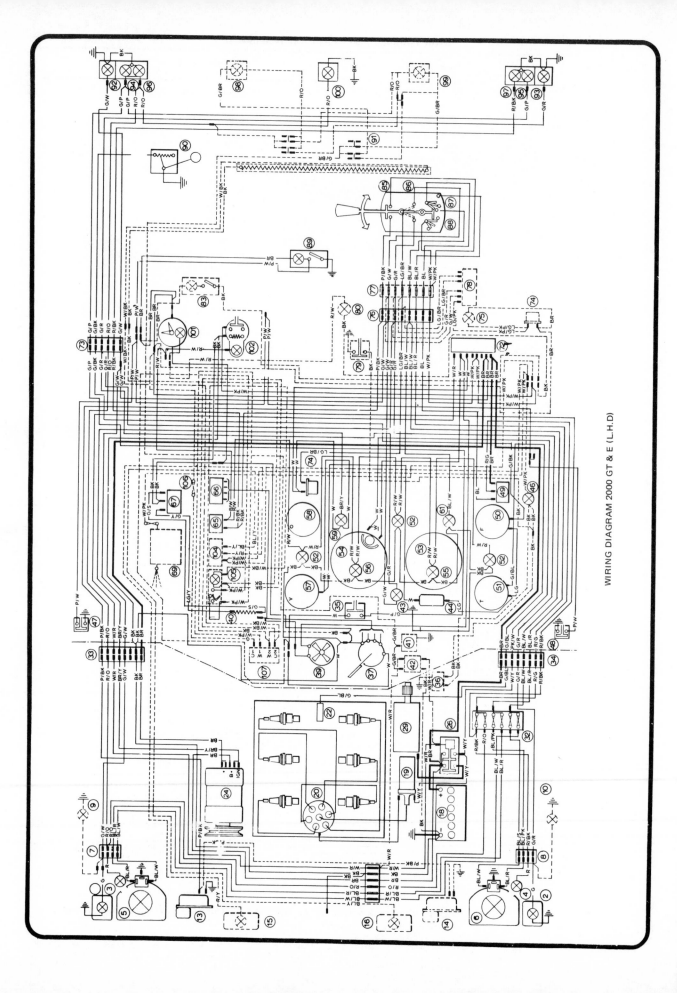

WIRING DIAGRAM 2000 GT & E (L.H.D)

Symptom	Reason/s	Remedy
No electricity at starter motor.	Battery discharged.	Charge battery.
	Battery defective internally.	Fit new battery.
	Battery terminal leads loose or earth lead not securely attached to body.	Check and tighten leads.
	Loose or broken connections in starter motor circuit.	Check all connections and tighten any that are loose.
	Starter motor switch or solenoid faulty.	Test and replace faulty components with new.
Electricity at starter motor: faulty motor.	Starter motor pinion jammed in mesh with flywheel gear ring.	Disengage pinion by turning squared end of armature shaft.
	Starter brushes badly worn, sticking, or brush wires loose.	Examine brushes, replace as necessary, tighten down brush wires.
	Commutator dirty, worn or burnt.	Clean commutator, recut if badly burnt.
	Starter motor armature faulty.	Overhaul starter motor, fit new armature.
	Field coils earthed.	Overhaul starter motor.
Electrical defects.	Battery in discharged condition.	Charge battery.
	Starter brushes badly worn, sticking, or brush wires loose.	Examine brushes, replace as necessary, tighten down brush wires.
	Loose wires in starter motor circuit.	Check wiring and tighten as necessary.
Dirt or oil on drive gear.	Starter motor pinion sticking on the screwed sleeve.	Remove starter motor, clean starter motor drive.
Mechanical damage.	Pinion or flywheel gear teeth broken or worn.	Fit new gear ring to flywheel, and new pinion to starter motor drive.
Lack of attention or mechanical damage.	Pinion or flywheel gear teeth broken or worn.	Fit new gear teeth to flywheel, or new pinion to starter motor drive.
	Starter drive main spring broken.	Dismantle and fit new main spring.
	Starter motor retaining bolts loose.	Tighten starter motor securing bolts. Fit new spring washer if necessary.
Wear or damage.	Battery defective internally.	Remove and fit new battery.
	Electrolyte level too low or electrolyte too weak due to leakage.	Top up electrolyte level to just above plates.
	Plate separators no longer fully effective.	Remove and fit new battery.
	Battery plates severely sulphated.	Remove and fit new battery.
Insufficient current flow to keep battery charged.	Fan belt slipping.	Check belt for wear, replace if necessary and tighten.
	Battery terminal connections loose or corroded.	Check terminals for tightness, and remove all corrosion.
	Dynamo/Alternator not charging properly. *	Remove and overhaul dynamo.
	Short in lighting circuit causing continual battery drain.	Trace and rectify.
	Regulator unit not working correctly.	Check setting, clean, and replace if defective.
Dynamo no charging.	Fan belt loose and slipping, or broken.	Check, replace and tighten as necessary.
	Brushes worn, sticking, broken or dirty.	Examine, clean, or replace brushes as necessary.
	Brush spring weak or broken.	Examine and test. Replace as necessary.
	Commutator dirty, greasy, worn, or burnt.	Clean commutator and undercut segment separators.
	Armature badly worn or armature shaft bent.	Fit new or reconditioned armature.
Dynamo not charging.	Commutator bars shorting.	Undercut segment separations.
	Dynamo bearings badly worn.	Overhaul dynamo, fit new bearings.
	Dynamo field coils burnt, open, or shorted.	Remove and fit rebuilt dynamo.
	Commutator no longer circular.	Recut commutator and undercut segment separators.
	Pole pieces very loose.	Strip and overhaul dynamo. Tighten pole pieces.
Regulator or cut-out fails to work correctly.	Regulator incorrectly set.	Adjust regulator correctly.
	Cut-out incorrectly set.	Adjust cut-out correctly.
	Open circuit in wiring of cut-out and regulator unit.	Remove, examine and renew as necessary.

Symptom	Reason/s	Remedy
Fuel gauge gives no reading.	Fuel tank empty! Electric cable between tank sender unit and gauge earthed or loose. Fuel gauge case not earthed. Fuel gauge supply cable interrupted. Fuel gauge unit broken.	Fill fuel tank. Check cable for earthing and joints for tightness. Ensure case is well earthed. Check and replace cable if necessary. Replace fuel gauge.
Fuel gauge registers full all the time.	Electric cable between tank unit and gauge broken or disconnected.	Check over cable and repair as necessary.
Horn operates all the time.	Horn push either earthed or stuck down. Horn cable to horn push earthed.	Disconnect battery earth. Check and rectify source of trouble. Disconnect battery earth. Check and rectify source of trouble.
Horn fails to operate.	Blown fuse. Cable or cable connection loose, broken or disconnected. Horn has an internal fault.	Check and renew if broken. Ascertain cause. Check all connections for tightness and cables for breaks. Remove and overhaul horn.
Horn emits intermittent or unsatisfactory noise.	Horn incorrectly adjusted.	Adjust horn until best note obtained.
Lights do not come on.	If engine not running, battery discharged. Light bulb filament burnt out or bulbs broken. Wire connections loose, disconnected or broken. Light switch shorting or otherwise faulty.	Push-start car, charge battery. Test bulbs in live bulb holder. Check all connections for tightness and wire cable for breaks. By-pass light switch to ascertain if fault is in switch and fit new switch as appropriate.
Lights come on but fade out.	If engine not running battery discharged.	Push-start car, and charge battery.
Lights give very poor illumination.	Lamp glasses dirty. Reflector tarnished or dirty. Lamps badly out of adjustment. Incorrect bulb with too low wattage fitted. Existing bulbs old and badly discoloured. Electrical wiring too thin not allowing full current to pass.	Clean glasses. Fit new reflectors. Adjust lamps correctly. Remove bulb and replace with correct grade. Renew bulb units. Re-wire lighting system.
Lights work erratically - flashing on and off, especially over bumps.	Battery terminals or earth connection loose. Lights not earthing properly. Contacts in light switch faulty.	Tighten battery terminals and earth connection. Examine and rectify. By-pass light switch to ascertain if fault is in switch and fit new switch as appropriate.
Wiper motor fails to work.	Blown fuse. Wire connections loose, disconnected, or broken. Brushes badly worn. Armature worn or faulty. Field coils faulty.	Check and replace fuse if necessary. Check wiper wiring. Tighten loose connections. Remove and fit new brushes. If electricity at wiper motor remove and overhaul and fit replacement armature. Purchase reconditioned wiper motor.
Wiper motor works very slowly and takes excessive current.	Commutator dirty, greasy or burnt. Drive to wheelboxes too bent or un—lubricated. Wheelbox spindle binding or damaged. Armature bearings dry or unaligned. Armature badly worn or faulty.	Clean commutator thoroughly. Examine drive and straighten out severe curvature. Lubricate. Remove, overhaul, or fit replacement. Replace with new bearings correctly aligned. Remove, overhaul, or fit replacement armature.
Wiper motor works slowly and takes little current.	Brushes badly worn. Commutator dirty, greasy or burnt. Armature badly worn or faulty.	Remove and fit new brushes. Clean commutator thoroughly. Remove and overhaul armature or fit replacement.

Symptom	Reason/s	Remedy
Wiper motor works but wiper blades remain static.	Driving cable rack disengaged or faulty.	Examine and if faulty, replace.
	Wheelbox gear and spindle damaged or worn.	Examine and if faulty, replace.
	Wiper motor gearbox parts badly worn.	Overhaul or fit new gearbox.

* SPECIAL NOTE: Fault finding in Alternators is very difficult. Have the whole unit/circuit checked by a auto electrician. Do not fiddle with it.

Chapter 11 Suspension, dampers and steering

Contents

Specifications

Front Suspension ... ...   Independent MacPherson Strut

Coil Springs (2000 GT)	Standard	Heavy Duty
Identification	Red/Blue	Red/Yellow
Part number	69EB−5310−AA	69EB−5310−BA
Mean load	621 lb (281.9 kg)	621 lb (281.9 kg)
Mean rate	115 lb/in. (20.4 kg/cm)	115 lb/in. (20.4 kg/cm)
Diameter of coils	5.31 in. (134.9 mm)	5.31 in. (134.9 mm)
Wire diameter	445 in. (11.3 mm)	.460 in. (11.7 mm)

Coil Springs (3000 GT)		
Identification	Red	Red/White
Part number	70EB−5310−AB	70EB−5310−BB
Mean load	707 lb (320.7 kg)	707 lb (320.7 kg)
Mean rate	122 lb/in. (21.8 kg/cm)	122 lb/in. (21.8 kg/cm)
Diameter of coils	5.31 in. (134.9 mm)	5.31 in. (134.9 mm)
Wire diameter	.465 in. (11.81 mm)	.472 in. (11.99 mm)

Suspension Units (2000 GT)		
Identification	Green	Yellow
Part number - right hand	69EB−3K033−AA	69EB−3K033−BA
- left hand	69EB−3K034−AA	69EB−3K034−BA

Suspension Units (3000 GT)		
Identification	Violet	Green/White
Part number - right hand	70EB−3K033−AIA	70EB−3K033−BIA
or	70EB−3K033−A2A	70EB−3K033−B2A
- left hand	70EB−3K034−AIA	70EB−3K034−BIA
or	70EB−3K034−A2A	70EB−3K034−B2A

Rear Suspension	Semi elliptical leaf spring
Colour 2000 GT - Standard	Orange/Yellow
- Heavy duty	Green/Red
3000 GT - Standard	White
- Heavy duty...	Blue
Number of leaves	2000 GT Standard 3, all others 4
Spring length between eye centres...	47 in. (114.4 cm)
Width of leaves	2 in. (51 mm)
Length between radius arm bush centres...	9.91 in. (251.7 mm)

Rear shock absorbers	Double acting : hydraulic telescopic
Colour 2000 GT - Standard	Orange
- Heavy duty...	Green
3000 GT - Standard..	Red
- Heavy duty...	Brown/White

Steering Gear Type ... ...   Rack and pinion
     Rack travel lock to lock - 2000 GT   ... ... `‛`...   5.62 in. (14.27 cm)
                          - 3000 GT   5.08 in. (12.9 cm)
     Teeth on pinion   6
     Lubricant capacity.. ... ...   .25 pint (.30 US pint, .15 litre)
     Lubricant type .. ..   Castrol Hypoy 90
     No. turns lock to lock   - 2000 GT... ... ...`,`... ... ...   3.68
                              - 3000 GT... ... ...   3.48
     Pinion bearing pre-load adjustment   ... ...   Selective shims
     Rack damper adjustment   ... ...   Selective shims

Wheels and Tyres
     Wheel size - 2000 GT   - Standard .. ..   4½J x 13
                         - Optional .. ..   5J x 13
             - 3000 GT... ... ...   5J x 13
     Tyre size   - 2000 GT... ... ...   165 x 13 Radial ply
               - 3000 GT... ... ...   185/70 x 13 Radial ply

Tyre Pressures

	Front	Rear
2000 GT - Normal	24 (1.7)	27 (1.9)
Full load...	27 (1.9)	31 (2.2)
3000 GT - Normal	26 (1.8)	26 (1.8)
High speed normal load	28 (2.0)	28 (2.0)
Full load...	28 (2.0)	28 (2.0)
High speed full load	28 (2.0)	33 (2.3)

NOTE: The foregoing tyre pressures are quoted in lb/sq.in. and in brackets kg/sq.cm. The recommended pressures should be taken when the tyre is cold, as a hot tyre normally shows a higher pressure.

Torque Wrench Settings
     Wheel nuts ... ...   50 to 55 lb/ft. (7.0 to 7.7 kg.m)
     Suspension unit upper mounting bolts   ... ...   15 to 18 lb/ft. (2.07 to 2.49 kg.m)
     Track control arm ball stud... ... ...   30 to 35 lb/ft. (4.15 to 4.85 kg.m)
     Torsion bar front clamps   ... ...   15 to 18 lb/ft. (2.07 to 2.49 kg.m)
     Torsion bar to track control arm   ... ...   25 to 30 lb/ft. (3.46 to 4.15 kg.m)
     Track control arm inner bushing   ... ...   22 to 27 lb/ft. (3.04 to 3.73 kg.m)
     Radius arms to axle housing   ... ...   25 to 30 lb/ft. (3.46 to 4.15 kg.m)
     Radius arms to body... ... ...   25 to 30 lb/ft. (3.46 to 4.15 kg.m)
     Shock absorber to axle ... ...   40 to 45 lb/ft. (5.54 to 6.22 kg.m)
     Shock absorber to body ... ...   15 to 20 lb/ft. (2.07 to 2.76 kg.m)
     Rear spring 'U' bolts ... ...   25 to 30 lb/ft. (3.46 to 4.15 kg.m)
     Rear spring front hanger... ... ...   27 to 32 lb/ft. (3.73 to 4.42 kg.m)
     Rear spring rear shackle nuts   8   to 10 lb/ft. (1.11 to 1.38 kg.m)
     Steering arm to suspension unit.. ... ...   30 to 34 lb/ft. (4.2 to 4.7   kg.m)
     Steering gear to crossmember   ... ...   15 to 18 lb/ft. (2.1   to 2.4   kg.m)
     Track rod end to steering arm   ... ...   18 to 22 lb/ft. (2.5   to 3.0   kg.m)
     Flexible coupling to pinion spline ... ...   12 to 15 lb/ft. (1.7   to 2.1   kg.m)
     Universal joint to steering shaft   ... ...   12 to 15 lb/ft. (1.7   to 2.1   kg.m)
     Steering wheel nut.. ... ... us ... ...   20 to 25 lb/ft. (2.8   to 3.4   kg.m)

1. General Description

Each of the independent front suspension Macpherson strut units consists of a vertical strut enclosing a double acting damper surrounded by a coil spring.

The upper end of each strut is secured to the top of the wing valance under the bonnet by rubber mountings.

The wheel spindle carrying the brake assembly and wheel hub is forged integrally with the suspension unit foot.

The steering arms are connected to each unit which are in turn connected to track rods and thence to the rack and pinion steering gear.

The lower end of each suspension unit is located by a track control arm. A stabilising torsion bar is fitted between the outer ends of each track control arm and secured at the front to mountings on the body front member.

A rubber rebound stop is fitted inside each suspension unit thus preventing the spring becoming over-extended and jumping out of its mounting plates. Upward movement of the wheel is limited by the spring becoming fully compressed but this is damped by the addition of a rubber bump stop fitted around the suspension unit piston rod which comes into operation before the spring is fully compressed.

Whenever repairs have been carried out on a suspension unit it is essential to check the wheel alignment as the linkage could be altered which will affect the correct front wheel settings.

Every time the car goes over a bump vertical movement of a front wheel pushes the damper body upwards against the combined resistance of the coil spring and the damper piston.

Hydraulic fluid in the damper is displaced and it is then forced through the compression valve into the space between the inner and outer cylinder. On the downward movement of the suspension, the road spring forces the damper body downward against the pressure of the hydraulic fluid which is forced back again through the rebound valve. In this way the natural oscillations of the spring are damped out and a comfortable ride is obtained.

On the front uprights it is worth noting that there is a shroud inside the coil spring which protects the machined surface of the piston rod from road dirt.

The steering gear is of the rack and pinion type and is located on the front crossmember by two 'U' shaped clamps. The pinion is connected to the steering column by a flexible coupling. Above the flexible coupling the steering column is split by a universal joint that is designed to collapse on impact thus minimising injury to the driver in the event of an accident.

Turning the steering wheel causes the rack to move in a lateral direction and the track rods attached to either end of the rack pass this movement to the steering arms on the suspension/axle units thereby moving the road wheels.

Two adjustments are possible on the steering gear, namely rack damper adjustment and pinion bearing pre-load adjustment, but the steering gear must be removed from the car to carry out these adjustments. Both adjustments are made by varying the thickness of shim-packs.

At the rear the axle is located by two inverted 'U' bolts at each end of the casing to underslung semi-elliptical leaf springs which provide both lateral and longitudinal location. Lateral movement of the rear axle is further controlled by the fitting of radius arms which are angled inwards to the axle casing from their body mounting points.

Double acting telescopic shock absorbers are fitted between the spring plates on the rear axles and reinforced mountings in the boot of the car. These shock absorbers work on the same principle as the front shock absorbers.

In the interests of lessening noise and vibration the springs and dampers are mounted on rubber bushes. A rubber spacer is also incorporated between the axle and the springs.

2. Rear Springs - Routine Maintenance

Every 6,000 miles check the inverted 'U' bolts for tightness and at the same time check the condition of the rubber bushes at either end of each rear spring.

3. Steering Gear - Routine Maintenance

Every 6,000 miles check the steering gear for general wear paying particular attention to the condition of the bellows at either end of the steering gear and the gaiters on the track rod ball joints. If any splits are found it will be necessary to renew the bellows and gaiters.

4. Front Hub Bearings - Maintenance, Removal & Replacement

1. After jacking up the car and removing the front road wheel, disconnect the hydraulic brake pipe at the union on the suspension unit and either plug the open ends of the pipes, or have a jar handy to catch the escaping fluid.
2. Bend back the locking tabs on the two bolts holding the brake calliper to the suspension unit, undo the bolts and remove the calliper.
3. By judicious tapping and levering remove the dust cap from the centre of the hub.
4. Remove the split pin from the nut retainer and undo the larger adjusting nut from the stub axle.
5. Withdraw the thrust washer and the outer tapered bearing.
6. Pull off the complete hub and disc assembly from the stub axle.
7. From the back of the hub assembly carefully prize out the grease seal and remove the inner tapered bearing.
8. Carefully clean out the hub and wash the bearings with petrol making sure that no grease or oil is allowed to get onto the brake disc.
9. Working the grease well into the bearings fully pack the bearing cages and rollers with Castrol LM, NOTE: Leave the hub and grease seal empty to allow for subsequent expansion of the grease.

10 To reassemble the hub assembly first fit the inner bearing and then gently tap the grease seal back into the hub. If the seal was at all damaged during removal a new one must be fitted.
11 Replace the hub and disc assembly on the stub axle and slide on the outer bearing and the thrust washer.
12 Tighten down the centre adjusting nut to a torque of 27 lb/ft. (3.73 kg.m) whilst rotating the hub and disc to ensure free movement then slacken the nut off 90° and fit the nut retainer and new split pin but at this stage do not bend back the split pin.
13 At this stage it is advisable, if a dial gauge is available to check the disc for run-out. The measurement should be taken as near to the edge of the worn, smooth part of the disc as possible and must not exceed .0035 inch (.089 mm). If this figure is found to be excessive check the mating surfaces of the disc and hub for dirt or damage and also check the bearings and cups for excessive wear or damage.
14 If a dial gauge is not available refit the calliper to the suspension unit, using new locking tabs, and tighten the securing bolts to a torque of 45 to 50 lb/ft. (6.22 to 6.94 kg.m).
15 The brake disc run-out can now be checked by means of a feeler gauge or gauges between the casting of the calliper and the disc. Establish a reasonably tight fit with the gauges between the top of the casting and the disc (on the author's car it was found to be .041 inch) and rotate the disc and hub. Any high or low spot will immediately become obvious by the extra tightness of looseness of the fit of the gauges, and the amount of run-out can be checked by adding or subtracting gauges as necessary. It is only fair to point out that this method is not as accurate as when using a dial gauge owing to the rough nature of the calliper casting.
16 Once the disc run-out has been checked and found to be correct, bend the ends of the split pin back and replace the dust cap.
17 Reconnect the brake hydraulic pipe and bleed the brakes as described in Chapter 9, Section 3.

5. Front Hub Bearings - Adjustment

1. To check the conditions of the hub bearings, jack up the front end of the car and grasp the road wheel at two opposite points to check for any rocking movement in the wheel hub. Watch carefully for any movement in the steering gear, which can easily be mistaken for hub movement.
2. If a front wheel hub has excessive movement, this is adjusted by removing the hub cap and then levering off the small dust cap. Remove the split pin through the stub axle and take off the adjusting nut retainer.
3. If a torque wrench is available tighten the centre adjusting nut down to a torque of 27 lb/ft. (3.73 kg.m) and then slacken it off 90° and replace the nut retainer and a new split pin.
4. Assuming a torque wrench is not available however, tighten up the centre nut until a slight drag is felt on rotating the wheel. Then loosen the nut very slowly until the wheel turns freely again and there is just a perceptible end float.
5. Now replace the nut retainer, a new split pin and the dust cap.

6. Front Hub - Removal & Replacement

1. Follow the instructions given in Section 4 of this chapter up to, and including paragraph 7.
2. Bend back the locking tabs and undo the four bolts holding the hub to the brake disc.
3. If a new hub assembly is being fitted it is supplied complete with new bearing cups and bearings. The bearing cups will already be fitted in the hub. It is essential to check that the cups and bearings are of the same manufacture; this can be done by reading the name on the bearings and by looking at the initial letter stamped on the hub. 'T' stands for Timken and 'S' for Skefco.
4. Clean with scrupulous care the mating surfaces of the hub and check for blemishes or damage. Any dirt or blemishes will almost certainly give rise to disc run-out. Using new locking tabs bolt the

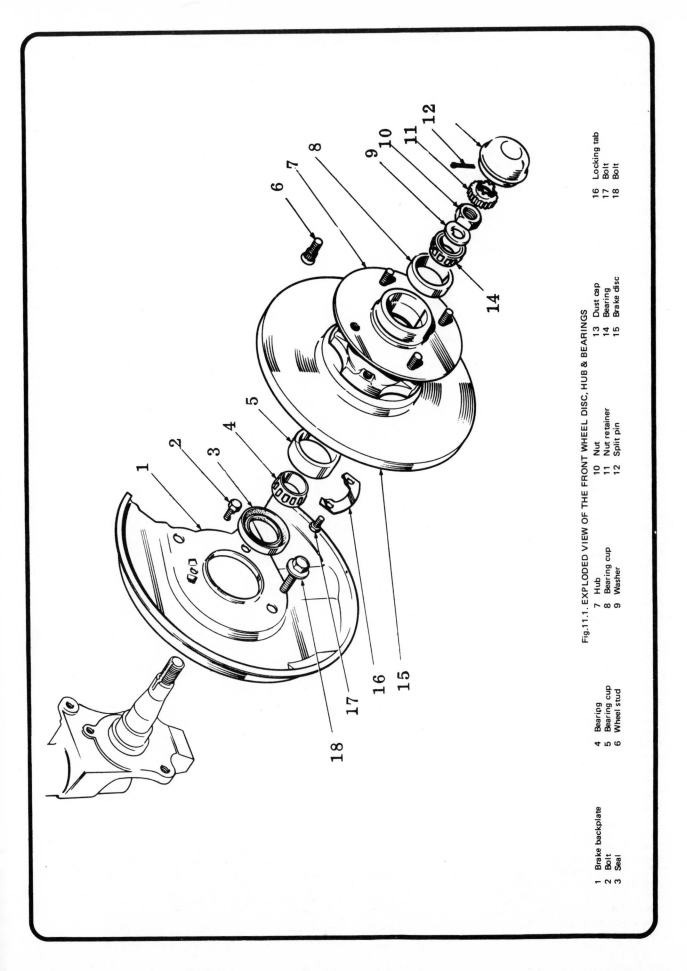

Fig.11.1. EXPLODED VIEW OF THE FRONT WHEEL DISC, HUB & BEARINGS

1 Brake backplate
2 Bolt
3 Seal

4 Bearing
5 Bearing cup
6 Wheel stud

7 Hub
8 Bearing cup
9 Washer

10 Nut
11 Nut retainer
12 Split pin

13 Dust cap
14 Bearing
15 Brake disc

16 Locking tab
17 Bolt
18 Bolt

disc and the hub together and tighten the bolts to a torque of 30 to 34 lb/ft. (4.15 to 4.70 kg.m).

5. To grease and reassemble the hub assembly follow the instructions given in Section 4, paragraphs 9 on.

7. Front Suspension Units - Removal & Replacement

1. It is difficult to work on the front suspension of the Capri without one or two special tools, the most important of which is a set of adjustable spring clips which is Ford tool No.P.5045. This tool, or similar clips are vital and any attempt to dismantle the units without them may result in personal injury.

2. Get someone to sit on the wing of the car and with the spring partially compressed in this way, securely fit the spring clips.

3. Jack up the car and remove the road wheel, then disconnect the brake pipe at the bracket on the suspension leg and plug the pipes or have a jar handy to catch the escaping hydraulic fluid.

4. Disconnect the track rod from the steering arm by pulling out the split pin and undoing the castellated nut, thus leaving the steering arm attached to the suspension unit.

5. Remove the outer end of the track control arm from the base of the suspension unit by pulling out the split pin and undoing the castellated nut.

6. Working under the bonnet undo the three bolts holding the top end of the suspension unit to the side panel and lower the unit complete with the brake calliper away from the car.

7. Replacement is a direct reversal of the removal sequence, but remember to use new split pins on the steering arm to track rod nut and also on the track control arm to suspension unit nut.

8. The top suspension unit mounting bolts should be tightened to a torque of 15 to 18 lb/ft. (2.1 to 2.5 kg.m), the track control arm to suspension unit nut to a torque of 30 to 35 lb/ft. (4.2 to 4.8 kg.m) and the steering arm to track rod nut to a torque of 18 to 22 lb/ft. (2.5 to 3.0 kg.m).

8. Front Coil Spring - Removal & Replacement

1. Get someone to sit on the front wing of the car and with the spring partially compressed in this way securely fit spring clips or if available Fords adjustable spring restrainer tool No.P.5045.

2. Jack up the front of the car, fit stands and remove the road wheel.

3. Working under the bonnet, remove the nut and the angled retainer.

4. Undo and remove the three bolts securing the top of the suspension unit to the side panel.

5. Push the piston rod downwards as far as it will go. It should now be possible to remove the top mounting assembly, the dished washer and the upper spring seat from the top of the spring.

6. The spring can now be lifted off its bottom seat and removed over the piston assembly.

7. If a new spring is being fitted check extremely carefully that it is of the same rating as the spring on the other side of the car. The colour coding of the springs can be found in the specifications at the beginning of this chapter.

8. Before fitting a new spring it must be compressed with the adjustable restrainers and make sure that the clips are placed on the same number of coils, and in the same position as on the spring that has been removed.

9. Place the new spring over the piston and locate it on its bottom seat, then pull the piston upwards and fit the upper spring seat so that it locates correctly on the flats cut on the piston rod.

10 Fit the dished washer to the piston rod ensuring that the convex side faces upwards.

11 Now fit the top mount assembly. With the steering in the straight ahead position fit the angled retainer facing inwards at 90° to the wheel angles and the piston rod nut having previously applied Loctite or similar compound to the thread. Do not fully tighten down the

nut at this stage.

12 If necessary pull the top end of the unit upwards until it is possible to locate correctly the top mount bracket and fit the three retaining bolts from under the bonnet. These nuts must be tightened down to a torque of 15 to 18 lb/ft. (2.1 to 2.5 kg.m).

13 Remove the spring clips, fit the road wheel and lower the car to the ground.

14 Finally, slacken off the piston rod nut, get an assistant to hold the upper spring seat to prevent it turning, and retighten the nut to a torque of 28 to 30 lb/ft. (3.9 to 4.4 kg.m).

9. Torsion Bar - Removal & Replacement

1. Jack up the front of the car, support the car on suitable stands and remove both front road wheels.

2. Working under the car at the front, knock back the locking tabs on the four bolts securing the two front clamps that hold the torsion bar to the frame and then undo the four bolts and remove the clamps and rubber insulators.

3. Remove the split pins from the castellated nuts retaining the torsion bars to the track control arms then undo the nuts and pull off the large washers, carefully noting the way in which they are fitted.

4. Pull the torsion bar forwards out of the two track control arms and remove it from the car.

5. With the torsion bar out of the car remove the sleeve and large washer from each end of the bar again noting the correct fitting positions.

6. Reassembly is a reversal of the above procedure, but new locking tabs must be used on the front clamp bolts and new split pins on the castellated nuts. The nuts on the clamps and the castellated nuts on each end of the torsion bar must not be fully tightened down until the car is resting on its wheels.

7. Once the car is on its wheels the castellated nuts on the ends of the torsion bar should be tightened down to a torque of 25 to 30 lb/ft. (3.46 to 4.15 kg.m) and the new split pins fitted. The four clamp bolts on the front mounting points must be tightened down to a torque of 15 to 18 lb/ft. (2.07 to 2.47 kg.m) and the locking tabs knocked up.

10. Rack & Pinion Steering Gear - Removal & Replacement

1. Before starting this job, set the front wheels in the straight ahead position. Then jack up the front of the car and place blocks under the wheels; lower the car slightly on the jack so that the track rods are in a near horizontal position.

2. Remove the nut and bolt from the clamp at the front of the flexible coupling on the steering column. This clamp holds the coupling to the pinion splines.

3. Working on the front crossmember, knock back the locking tabs on the two nuts on each 'U' clamp, undo the nut and remove the locking tabs and clamps.

4. Remove the split pins and castellated nuts from the ends of each track rod where they join the steering arms. Separate the track rods from the steering arms and lower the steering gear downwards out of the car.

5. Before replacing the steering gear make sure that the wheels have remained in the straight ahead position. Also check the condition of the mounting rubbers round the housing and if they appear worn or damaged renew them.

6. Check that the steering gear is also in the straight ahead position. This can be done by ensuring that the distances between the ends of both track rods and the steering gear housing on both sides are the same.

7. Place the steering gear in its location on the crossmember and at the same time mate up the splines on the pinion with the splines in the clamp on the steering column flexible coupling.

8. Replace the two 'U' clamps using new locking tabs under the

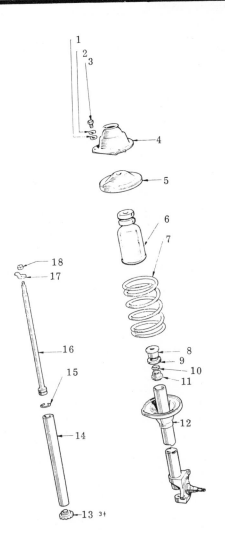

Fig.11.2 EXPLODED VIEW OF THE FRONT SUSPENSION
UNIT

1	Washer	10	Rod gland
2	Spring washer	11	Rod bush and guide
3	Bolt	12	Tube & spindle assembly
4	Upper mounting	13	Compression valve
5	Upper spring seat	14	Cylinder
6	Bump stop	15	Ring
7	Coil spring	16	Piston
8	Piston rod gland cap	17	Cranked retainer
9	Oil seal ring	18	Nut

Fig.11.3. View of the front suspension upper mounting points
showing the cranked retainers correctly fitted pointing inwards 90°

bolts, tighten down the bolts to a torque of 12 to 15 lb/ft. (1.7 to 2.0 kg.m) and bend up the locking tabs.

9. Refit the track rod ends into the steering arms, replace the castellated nuts and tighten them to a torque of 18 to 22 lb/ft. (2.5 to 3.0 kg.m). Use new split pins to retain the nuts.

10 Tighten the clamp bolt on the steering column flexible coupling to a torque of 12 to 15 lb/ft. (1.7 to 2.1 kg.m) having first made sure that the pinion is correctly located in the splines.

11 Jack up the car, remove the blocks from under the wheels and lower the car to the ground. It is advisable at this stage to take your car to your local Ford dealer and have the toe-in checked.

11. Rack & Pinion Steering Gear - Adjustments

1. For the steering gear to function correctly, two adjustments are necessary. These are pinion bearing pre-load and rack damper adjustment.

2. To carry out these adjustments, remove the steering gear from the car as described in the previous section, then mount the steering gear in a soft jawed vice so that the pinion is in a horizontal position and the rack damper cover plate to the top.

3. Remove the rack damper cover plate by undoing the two retaining bolts, then take off the gasket and shims from under the plate. Also remove the small spring and the recessed yoke which bears on the rack.

4. Now remove the pinion bearing pre-load cover plate from the base of the pinion, by undoing the two bolts. Then take off the gasket and shim pack.

5. To set the pinion bearing pre-load correctly, replace the cover plate without the gasket and shims and tighten down the bolts evenly until the cover plate is just touching the pinion bearing.

6. Using feeler gauges, measure the gap between the cover plate and the steering gear casing. To be sure that the cover plate has been evenly tightened, take a reading adjacent to each bolt. These readings should be the same. If they are not, loosen the cover plate and retighten it more evenly.

7. Assemble a shim pack with a gasket on either side of the shims which is .002 inch to .004 inch (.05 to .10 mm) less than the gap previously measured. The thickness of the shim pack includes the two gaskets. Shim thicknesses available are listed below.

2000 G.T.

Part No.	Material	Thickness
3038E-3N597-C	Steel	.010 in. (.254 mm)
3038E-3N597-B	Steel	.005 in. (127 mm)
3038E-3N597-A	Steel	.002 in. (.051 mm)
3038E-3N598-A	Paper	,005 in. (.127 mm)

3000 G.T.

Part No.	Material	Thickness
70EB-3N597-CA	Steel	.010 in. (.254 mm)
70EB-3N597-BA	Steel	.005 in. (.127 mm)
70EB-3N597-AA	Steel	.002 in. (.051 mm)
70EB-3N598-AA	Paper	.005 in. (.127 mm)

8. Remove the cover plate again, fit the assembled shim pack and gasket, with the gasket next to the cover plate, refit the cover plate, refit the cover plate and having applied Loctite or similar sealer on the threads of the bolts, tighten them down with a torque of 6 to 8 lb/ft. (0.9 to 1.1 kg.m).

9. To set the rack damper adjustment, replace the yoke in its location on the rack and make sure it is fully home. Then measure the distance between the bottom of the recess in the yoke and the top of the steering gear casing.

10 Assemble a shim pack with a gasket on either side of the shims which is between .0005 to .0035 inch greater than the dimension measured in the previous paragraph. Shim thicknesses available are as listed below.

Part No.	Material	Thickness
3024E-3K544-C	Steel	.010 in. (.254 mm)
3024E-3K544-B	Steel	.005 in. (.127 mm)
3024E-3K544-A	Steel	.002 in. (.051 mm)
3024E-3581-A	Paper	.005 in. (.127 mm)

11 Refit the spring into its recess in the yoke and fit the shim pack and gaskets. Replace the cover plate having first applied Loctite or similar sealing compound to the bolt threads. Then tighten down the bolts with a torque of 6 to 8 lb/ft. (0.9 to 1.1 kg.m).

12. Rack & Pinion Steering Gear - Dismantling & Reassembly

1. Remove the steering gear from the car as described in Section 10.

2. Unscrew the ball joints and locknuts from the end of each track rod, having previously marked the threads to ensure correct positioning on reassembly. Alternatively the number of turns required to undo the ball joint can be counted and noted.

3. Slacken off the clips securing the rubber bellows to each track rod and the steering gear housing then pull off the bellows. Have a quantity of rag handy to catch the oil which will escape when the bellows are removed.

4. To dismantle the steering gear, it is only necessary to remove the track rod which is furthest away from the pinion on either right or left-hand drive cars.

5. To remove the track rod place the steering gear in a soft jawed vice. Working on the track rod ball joint carefully drill out the pin that locks the ball housing to the locknut. Great care must be taken not to drill too deeply or you will drill into the threads on the rack thus causing irrepairable damage. The hole should be about 3/8th inch deep.

6. Hold the locknut with a spanner, then grip the ball housing with a mole wrench and undo it from the threads on the rack.

7. Take out the spring and ball seat from the recess in the end of the rack and then unscrew the locknut from the threads on the rack. The spring and ball seat must be replaced by new components on reassembly.

8. Carefully prize out the pinion dust seal then withdraw the pinion together with the bearing assembly nearest the flexible coupling. As the bearings utilise bearing tracks and loose balls (14 in each bearing) care must be taken not to lose any of the balls or drop them into the steering gear on reassembly.

9. With the pinion removed, withdraw the complete rack assembly with one track rod still attached from the pinion end of the casing, having first removed the rack damper cover, gasket, shims, springs and yoke as described in Section 11, paragraph 3.

10 Now remove the remaining pinion bearing assembly from the rack casing.

11 It is always advisable to withdraw the rack from the pinion end of the casing. This avoids passing the rack teeth through the bush at the other end of the casing and causing possible damage.

12 Carefully examine all parts for signs of wear or damage. Check the condition of the rack support bush at the opposite end of the casing from the pinion. If this is worn renew it. If the rack or pinion teeth are in any way damaged a completely new steering gear will have to be fitted.

13 Take the pinion oil seal off the top of the casing and replace it with a new seal.

14 To commence reassembly fit the lower pinion bearing and thrust washer into their recess in the casing. The loose balls can be held in place by a small amount of grease.

15 Replace the rack in the casing from the pinion end and position it in the straight ahead position by equalising the amount it protrudes at either end of the casing.

16 Replace the remaining pinion bearing and thrust washer onto the pinion and fit the pinion into the casing so that the larger master spline on the pinion shaft is parallel to the rack and on the right-hand side of the pinion. This applies to both right and left-hand drive cars.

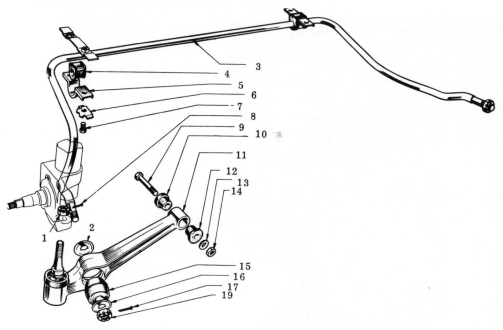

Fig.11.4. EXPLODED VIEW OF THE TORSION BAR & TRACK CONTROL ARM

1	Castellated nut	6	Locking tab	11	Track control arm	16	Dished washer
2	Dished washer	7	Bolt	12	Bush	17	Split pin
3	Torsion bar	8	Split pin	13	Washer	18	Castellated nut
4	Rubber bush	9	Bolt	14	Nut		
5	'U' clamp	10	Bush	15	Bush		

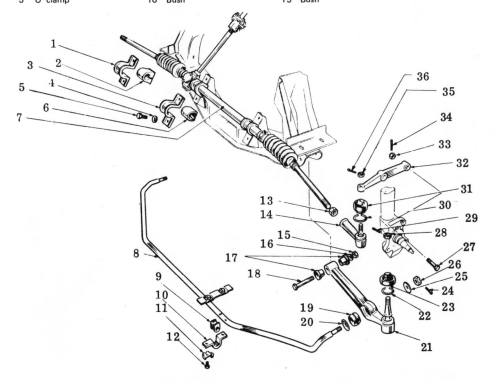

Fig.11.5. EXPLODED VIEW OF THE RACK & PINION & TRACK CONTROL ASSEMBLIES

1	'U' clamp	10	Clamp	19	Bush	28	Castellated nut
2	Rubber bush	11	Locking tab	20	Washer	29	Split pin
3	'U' clamp	12	Bolt	21	Track control arm	30	Ring
4	Washer	13	Locknut	22	Ring	31	Bush
5	Bolt	14	Track rod end	23	Seal	32	Steering arm
6	Bush	15	Nut	24	Split pin	33	Nut
7	Rack housing	16	Washer	25	Washer	34	Split pin
8	Torsion bar	17	Bush	26	Castellated nut	35	Castellated nut
9	Rubber bush	18	Bolt	27	Bolt	36	Split pin

Fig.11.6. View of the steering column universal joint and flexible coupling.

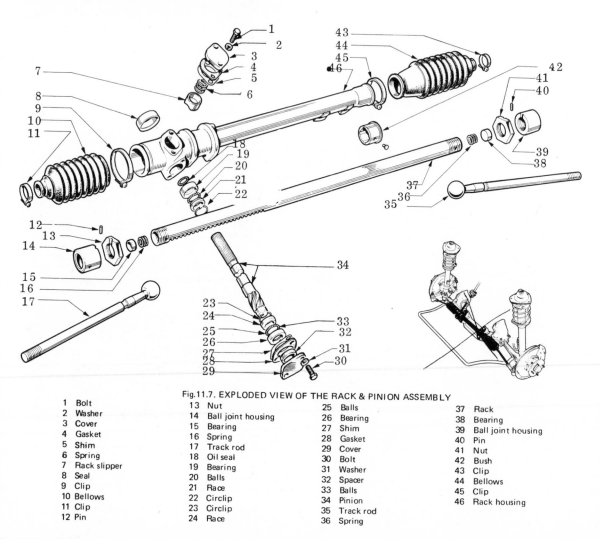

Fig.11.7. EXPLODED VIEW OF THE RACK & PINION ASSEMBLY

1	Bolt	13	Nut	25	Balls	37 Rack
2	Washer	14	Ball joint housing	26	Bearing	38 Bearing
3	Cover	15	Bearing	27	Shim	39 Ball joint housing
4	Gasket	16	Spring	28	Gasket	40 Pin
5	Shim	17	Track rod	29	Cover	41 Nut
6	Spring	18	Oil seal	30	Bolt	42 Bush
7	Rack slipper	19	Bearing	31	Washer	43 Clip
8	Seal	20	Balls	32	Spacer	44 Bellows
9	Clip	21	Race	33	Balls	45 Clip
10	Bellows	22	Circlip	34	Pinion	46 Rack housing
11	Clip	23	Circlip	35	Track rod	
12	Pin	24	Race	36	Spring	

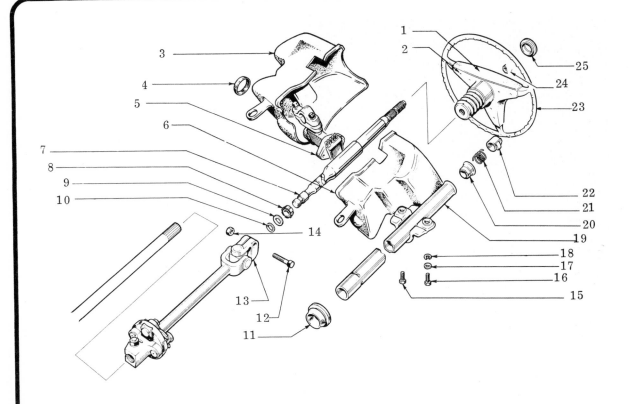

Fig.11.8. EXPLODED VIEW OF THE STEERING COLUMN ASSEMBLY

1 Steering wheel	7 Steering shaft	14 Nut	21 Spring
2 Padding	8 Bearing	15 Bolt	22 Indicator cancellin Cam
3 Shroud	9 Washer	16 Bolt	23 Wheel rim
4 Bezel	10 Seal	17 Washer	24 Steering wheel retaining
5 Ignition switch and	11 Grommet	18 Spring washer	nut
steering lock	12 Bolt	19 Outer column	25 Centre emblem
6 Shroud	13 Universal joint	20 Bearing	

Fig.11.9. View of the left and right-hand screws and bolts to be
removed to release the shroud and steering column

17 Replace the rack damper yoke, springs, shims, gasket and cover plate.

18 To replace the track rod that has been removed, start by fitting a new spring and ball seat to the recess in the end of the rack shaft and replace the locknut onto the threads of the rack.

19 Lubricate the ball, ball seat and ball housing with a small amount of SAE.90 EP oil. Then slide the ball housing over the track and screw the housing onto the rack threads keeping the track rod in the horizontal position until the track rod starts to become stiff to move.

20 Using a normal spring balance hook it round the track rod half an inch from the end and check the effort required to move it from the horizontal position.

21 By adjusting the tightness of the ball housing on the rack threads the effort required to move the track rod must be set at 5 lbs. (2.8 kg.).

22 Tighten the locknut up to the housing and then recheck that the effort required to move the track rod is still correct at 5 lb. (2.8 kg.).

23 On the line where the locknut and ball housing meet, drill a 1/8th inch, (3.18 mm) diameter hole which must be 3/8th inch, (9.52 mm) deep. Even if the two halves of the old hole previously drilled out align a new hole must be drilled.

24 Tap a new retaining pin into the hole and peen the end over to secure it.

25 Replace the rubber bellows and the track rod ends ensuring that they are replaced in exactly the same position from which they were removed.

26 Remove the rack damper cover plate and pour in 0.25 pint (0.3 US pints, 0.15 litre) of SAE.90 EP oil. Then carry out both steering gear adjustments as detailed in the previous section.

27 After replacing the steering gear on the car as described in Section 10, it is strongly recommended that you take the car to your nearest Ford dealer and have the toe-in correctly adjusted.

13. Steering Wheel & Column - Removal & Replacement

1. Place the car with its wheels in the straight ahead position, disconnect the battery by removing the negative earth lead and disconnect the choke cable from the carburetter.

2. Working under the bonnet undo the clamp bolt on the top of the steering column universal joint.

3. Moving inside the car, prize out the centre emblem on the steering wheel, knock back the locking tab on the centre nut and undo the nut. Remove the locking tab and pull the steering wheel off its splines.

4. Undo the two screws securing the steering column shrouds to the column as shown in Fig.11.9. Then remove the two bolts securing the bottom of the shroud and the column to the underside of the fascia. Lift the indicator cancelling cam and its spring off the shaft, noting the position in which they are fitted in relation to the switch.

5. Pull off the multi-pin connectors to the indicator switch and ignition switch, then remove the indicator switch assembly from the top of the column by undoing the two small retaining screws.

6. Withdraw the steering column into the car taking care not to damage the grommet where the column passes through the floor or the car.

7. Replacement is a direct reversal of the above procedure. Note that the clamp bolt on the universal joint must be tightened to a torque of 12 to 15 lb/ft. (1.7 to 2.1 kg.m) and the steering wheel retaining nut to a torque of 20 to 25 lb/ft. (2.8 to 3.4 kg.m). Before replacing this nut ensure that the indicators cancel correctly.

14. Rear Shock Absorbers - Removal & Replacement

1. Chock the front wheels to prevent the car moving, then jack up the rear of the car and for convenience sake remove the road wheels.

2. Working inside the boot, hold the top of the piston and prevent it turning by holding a small spanner (¼ inch A/F) across the flats provided and then with an open ended spanner remove the locknut and main nut from the piston rod.

3. Lift off the large steel washer and the rubber bush.

4. Working under the car, remove the nut, lock washer and bolt that retain the lower end of the damper to the axle casing.

5. Lower the damper from the car, then remove the further rubber bush and steel washer from the top of the piston rod.

6. Replacement is a reversal of the above procedure.

7. The nut on the bolt securing the lower end of the damper must be tightened down to a torque of 40 to 45 lb/ft. (5.54 to 6.22 kg.m).

8. The main nut on the top mounting must be tightened to a torque of 20 to 25 lb/ft. (2.76 to 3.46 kg.m) but the piston must be prevented from rotating during this operation. Most torque wrenches will not allow the flats on the piston rod to be held to prevent turning so it is better to get an assistant to hold the upper half of the damper from under the car.

15. Rear Springs - Removal & Replacement

1. Chock the front wheels to prevent the car moving, then jack up the rear of the car and support it on suitable stands. To make the springs more accessible remove the road wheels.

2. Then place a trolley jack underneath the differential housing to support the rear axle assembly when the springs are removed. Do not raise the jack under the differential housing so that the springs are flattened, but raise it just enough to take the full weight of the axle with the springs fully extended.

3. Undo the rear shackle nuts and remove the combined shackle bolt and plate assemblies. Then remove the rubber bushes.

4. Undo the nut from the front mounting and take out the bolt running through the mounting.

5. Undo the nuts on the ends of the four 'U' bolts and remove the 'U' bolts together with the attachment plate and rubber spring insulators.

6. Replacement is a direct reversal of the above procedure. The nuts on the 'U' bolts, spring front mounting and rear shackles must be torqued down to the figures given in the specifications at the beginning of this chapter only AFTER the car has been lowered onto its wheels.

16. Radius Arms - Removal & Replacement

1. Chock the front wheels to prevent the car moving, then jack up the rear of the car and support it on suitable stands.

2. Undo the nut and remove the bolt holding the rear end of the radius arm to the axle casing.

3. To take the tension off the radius arm it may be necessary to slightly raise the axle casing with a jack.

4. Repeat this procedure on the front mounting nut and bolt and remove the radius arm from the car.

5. Replacement is a reversal of the above procedure but the nuts should be torqued down to the figures given in the specifications at the beginning of this chapter AFTER the car has been lowered onto its wheels.

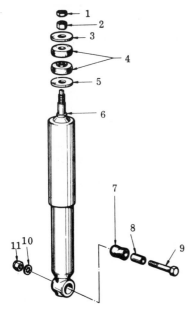

Fig.11.10. EXPLODED VIEW OF THE REAR SHOCK AB— SORBER

1	Locknut	7	Bush
2	Nut	8	Insert
3	Washer	9	Bolt
4	Rubber bushes	10	Shakeproof washer
5	Washer	11	Nut
6	Shock absorber		

Fig.11.11. View of the rear spring 'U' bolts and lower shock absorber mounting

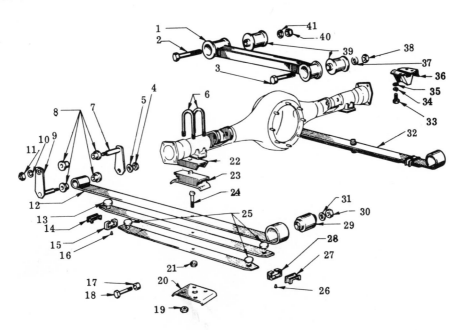

Fig.11.12. EXPLODED VIEW OF THE REAR SPRING & RADIUS ARM ASSEMBLIES

1	Radius arm	12	Spring leaf	23	Insulator	34	Spring washer
2	Bolt	13	Spacer	24	Stud	35	Washer
3	Bolt	14	Clamp insulator	25	Spacers	36	Plate
4	Nut	15	Clamp	26	Pin	37	Washer
5	Washer	16	Pin	27	Clamp insulator	38	Nut
6	'U' bolts	17	Bush	28	Clamp	39	Bush
7	Shackle bar and stud	18	Bolt	29	Bush	40	Bolt
8	Bushes	19	Nut	30	Nut	41	Washer
9	Shackle bar and stud	20	'U' bolts plate	31	Washer		
10	Spring washer	21	Bolt	32	Spring assembly		
11	Nut	22	Plate	33	Bolt		

Before diagnosing faults from the following chart, check that any irregularities are not caused by:—

1. Binding brakes.
2. Incorrect 'mix' of radial and cross-ply tyres.
3. Incorrect tyre pressures.
4. Misalignment of the body frame.

Symptom	Reason/s	Remedy
Steering wheel can be moved considerably before any sign of movement of the wheels is apparent.	Wear in the steering linkage, gear and column coupling.	Check movement in all joints and steering gear and overhaul and renew as required.
Vehicle difficult to steer in a consistent straight line - wandering.	As above. Wheel alignment incorrect (indicated by excessive or uneven tyre wear).	As above. Check wheel alignment.
	Front wheel hub bearings loose or worn.	Adjust or renew as necessary.
	Worn ball joints or suspension arms.	Renew as necessary.
Steering stiff and heavy.	Incorrect wheel alignment (indicated by excessive or uneven tyre wear).	Check wheel alignment.
	Excessive wear or seizure in one or more of the joints in the steering linkage or suspension arm ball joints.	Renew as necessary or grease the suspension unit ball joints.
	Excessive wear in the steering gear unit.	Adjust if possible or renew.
Wheel wobble and vibration.	Road wheels out of balance.	Balance wheels.
	Road wheels buckled.	Check for damage.
	Wheel alignment incorrect.	Check wheel alignment.
	Wear in the steering linkage, suspension arm ball joints or suspension arm pivot bushes.	Check and renew as necessary.
	Broken front spring.	Check and renew as necessary.
Excessive pitching and rolling on corners and during braking.	Defective dampers and/or broken spring.	Check and renew as necessary.

Chapter 12 Bodywork and underframe

Contents

1. General Description

The combined body and underframe is of an all steel welded construction. This makes a very strong and torsionally ridged shell.

The Capri is only available in two door form. The door hinges are welded to the doors and securely bolted to the body. To prevent the doors opening too wide and causing damage check straps are fitted. The driver's door is locked from the outside by means of a key, the other door being locked from the inside.

Toughened safety glass is fitted to all windows; as an additional safety precaution the windscreen glass has a specially toughened 'Zone' in front of the driver. In the event of the windscreen shattering this 'Zone' breaks into much larger pieces than the rest of the screen thus giving the driver much better vision than would otherwise be possible.

The interior of both the 2000 GT and 3000 GT and E are basically the same having a comprehensive range of instruments including separate ammeter or battery voltage state indicator, oil pressure gauge, fuel gauge and water temperature gauge. There is also a separate tachometer.

The Capri uses the Aeroflow type of ventilation system. Air being drawn in through a grille on the scuttle can either be heated or pass straight into the car. Used air passes out through a grille at the base of the rear window.

All models are fitted with bucket type front seats with seat belts as standard. The rear seats are also fitted with anchor points for belts which can be obtained as an optional extra.

2. Maintenance - Bodywork & Underframe

1. The condition of your car's bodywork is of considerable importance as it is on this that the second-hand value of the car will mainly depend. It is very much more difficult to repair neglected bodywork than to renew mechanical assemblies. The hidden portions of the body, such as the wheel arches and the underframe and the engine compartment are equally important, through obviously not requiring such frequent attention as the immediately visible paintwork.

2. Once a year or every 12,000 miles, it is a sound scheme to visit your local main agent and have the underside of the body steam cleaned. This will take about 1½ hours and cost about £4. All traces of dirt and oil will be removed and the underside can then be inspected carefully for rust, damaged hydraulic pipes, frayed electrical wiring and similar maladies. The car should be greased on completion of this job.

3. At the same time the engine compartment should be cleaned in the same manner. If steam cleaning facilities are not available then brush 'Gunk' or a similar cleanser over the whole engine and engine compartment with a stiff paint brush, working it well in where there is an accumulation of oil and dirt. Do not paint the ignition system but protect it with oily rags when the Gunk is washed off. As the Gunk is washed away it will take with it all traces of oil and dirt, leaving the engine looking clean and bright.

4. The wheel arches should be given particular attention as undersealing can easily come away here and stones and dirt thrown up from the road wheels can soon cause the paint to chip and flake, and so allow rust to set in. If rust is found, clean down to the bare metal with wet and dry paper, paint on an anti-corrosive coating such as Kurust, or if preferred, red lead, and renew the paintwork and undercoating.

5. The bodywork should be washed once a week or when dirty. Thoroughly wet the car to soften the dirt and then wash the car down with a soft sponge and plenty of clean water. If the surplus dirt is not washed off very gently, in time it will wear the paint down as surely as wet and dry paper. It is best to use a hose if this is available. Give the car a final wash down and then dry with a soft chamois leather to prevent the formation of spots.

6. Spots of tar and grease thrown up from the road can be removed with a rag dampened with petrol.

7. Once every six months, or every three months if wished, give the bodywork and chromium trim a thoroughly good wax polish, If a chromium cleaner is used to remove rust on any of the car's plated parts remember that the cleaner also removes part of the chromium so use sparingly.

3. Maintenance - Upholstery & Carpets

1. Remove the carpets and thoroughly vacuum clean the interior of the car every three months or more frequently if necessary.

2. Beat out the carpets and vacuum clean them if they are very

dirty. If the headlining or upholstery is soiled apply an upholstery cleaner with a damp sponge and wipe off with a clean dry cloth.

4. Minor Body Repairs

1. At some time during your ownership of your car it is likely that it will be bumped or scraped in a mild way, causing some slight damage to the body.

2. Major damage must be repaired by your local Ford agent, but there is no reason why you cannot successfully beat out, repair, and respray minor damage yourself. The essential items which the owner should gather together to ensure a really professional job are:—
a) A plastic filler such as Holts 'Cataloy'.
b) Paint whose colour matches exactly that of the bodywork, either in a can for application by a spray gun, or in an aerosol can.
c) Fine cutting paste.
d) Medium and fine grade wet and dry paper.

3. Never use a metal hammer to knock out small dents as the blows tend to scratch and distort the metal. Knock out the dent with a mallet or rawhide hammer and press on the underside of the dented surface a metal dolly or smooth wooden block roughly contoured to the normal shape of the damaged area.

4. After the worst of the damaged area has been knocked out, rub down the dent and surrounding area with medium wet and dry paper and thoroughly clean away all traces of dirt.

5. The plastic filler comprises a paste and a hardener which must be thoroughly mixed together. Mix only a small portion at a time as the paste sets hard within five to fifteen minutes depending on the amount of hardener used.

6. Smooth on the filler with a knife or stiff plastic to the shape of the damaged portion and allow to thoroughly dry — a process which takes about six hours. After the filler has dried it is likely that it will have contracted slightly so spread on a second layer of filler if necessary.

7. Smooth down the filler with fine wet and dry paper wrapped round a suitable block of wood and continue until the whole area is perfectly smooth and it is impossible to feel where the filler joins the rest of the paintwork.

8. Spray on from an aerosol can, or with a spray gun, an anti-rust undercoat, smooth down with wet and dry paper, and then spray on two coats of the final finishing using a circular motion.

9. When thoroughly dry polish the whole area with a fine cutting paste to smooth the resprayed area into the remainder of the wing and to remove the small particles of spray paint which will have settled round the area.

10 This will leave the wing looking perfect with not a trace of the previous unsightly dent.

5. Major Body Repairs

1. Because the body is built on the monocoque principle and is integral with the underframe, major damage must be repaired by competent mechanics with the necessary welding and hydraulic straightening equipment.

2. If the damage has been serious it is vital that the body is checked for correct alignment, as otherwise the handling of the car will suffer and many other faults such as excessive tyre wear and wear in the transmission and steering may occur. Fords produce a special alignment jig and to ensure that all is correct a repaired car should always be checked on this jig.

6. Maintenance - Hinges & Locks

Once every six months or 6,000 miles the door, bonnet and boot hinges should be oiled with a few drops of engine oil from an oil can. The door striker plates can be given a thin smear of grease to reduce wear and ensure free movement.

7. Front Bumper - Removal & Replacement

1. Undo the single retaining bolt on either end of the bumper from inside the front wings.

2. Working at the back of the bumper remove the nuts from the two chrome headed bolts, withdraw the bolts and lift the bumper away.

3. Replacement is a reversal of the above procedure, but before replacing the two bolts from inside the wings ensure that the bumper is correctly located. To make sure this is correct it is advisable not to tighten the centre nuts fully down until the end bolts have been located.

8. Rear Bumper - Removal & Replacement

1. From behind the bumper bar remove the nuts from the four chrome headed bolts, withdraw the bolts and lift the bumper away.

2. Replacement is a direct reversal of the removal procedure, but it is advisable not to fully tighten down the nuts until it is certain that the bumper is perfectly straight and correctly located.

9. Windscreen Glass - Removal & Replacement

1. If you are unfortunate enough to have a windscreen shatter, or should you wish to renew your present windscreen, fitting a replacement is one of the few jobs which the average owner is advised to leave to a professional. For the owner who wishes to attempt the job himself the following instructions are given.

2. Cover the bonnet with a blanket or cloth to prevent accidental damage and remove the windscreen wiper blades and arms as detailed in Chapter 10, Sections 33 and 34.

3. Put on a pair of lightweight shoes and get into one of the front seats. With a piece of soft cloth between the soles of your shoes and the windscreen glass, place both feet in one top corner of the windscreen and push firmly. (See Fig.12.1).

4. When the weatherstrip has freed itself from the body flange in that area repeat the process at frequent intervals along the top edge of the windscreen until, from outside the car the glass and weatherstrip can be removed together.

5. If you are having to replace your windscreen due to a shattered screen, remove all traces of sealing compound and broken glass from the weatherstrip and body flange.

6. Gently prize out the clip which covers the joint of the chromium finisher strip and pull the finisher strip out of the weatherstrip. Then remove the weatherstrip from the glass or if it is still on the car, as in the case of a shattered screen, remove it from the body flange.

7. To fit a new windscreen start by fitting the weatherstrip around the new windscreen glass.

8. Apply a suitable sealer such as Expandite SR—51—B to the weatherstrip to body groove. In this groove then fit a fine but strong piece of cord right the way round the groove allowing an overlap of about six inches at the joint.

9. From outside the car place the windscreen in its correct position making sure that the loose end of the cord is inside the car.

10 With an assistant pressing firmly on the outside of the windscreen get into the car and slowly pull out the cord thus drawing the weatherstrip over the body flange. (See Fig.12.2).

11 Apply a further layer of sealer to the underside of rubber to glass groove from outside the car.

12 Replace the chromium finisher strip into its groove in the weatherstrip and replace the clip which covers its joint.

13 Carefully clean off any surplus sealer from the windscreen glass before it has a chance to harden and then replace the windscreen wiper arms and blades.

Fig 12:2 Method of refitting the windscreen

Fig 12:1 Method of removing the windscreen

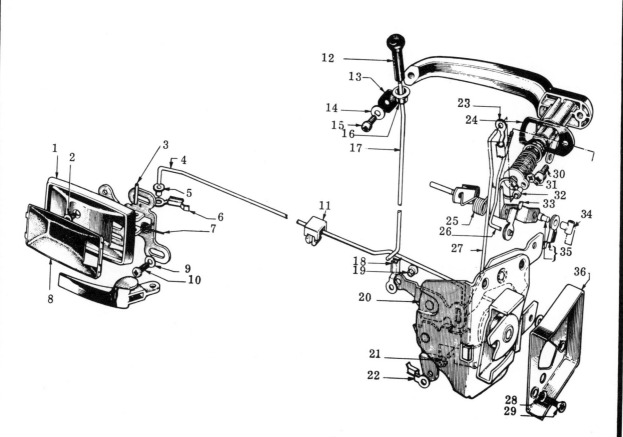

Fig 12:3 EXPLODED VIEW OF THE DOOR CONTROLS

1 Bezel
2 Screw
3 Pivot pin
4 Remote control rod
5 Bush
6 Clip
7 Spring
8 Insert
9 Washer

10 Screw
11 Guide clip
12 Interior lock button
13 Gasket
14 Washer
15 Screw
16 Escutcheon
17 Interior locking rod
18 Clip

19 Bush
20 Door lock assembly
21 Bush
22 Clip
23 Exterior handle
24 Gasket
25 Spring
26 Operating rod
27 Locking rod

28 Washer
29 Screw
30 Screw
31 Lockwasher
32 Bush
33 Clip
34 Stud
35 Bush and clip
36 Cover plate

10. Door Rattles - Tracing & Rectification

1. The most common cause of door rattle is a misaligned, loose, or worn striker plate, however other causes may be:—
a) Loose door or window winder handles.
b) Loose, or misaligned door lock components.
c) Loose or worn remote control mechanism.
2. It is quite possible for door rattles to be the result of a combination of the above faults so a careful examination should be made to determine the exact cause of the rattle.
3. If striker plate wear or misalignment is the cause of the rattle the plate should be renewed or adjusted as necessary. The procedures for these tasks are detailed in Section 11.
4. Should the window winder handle rattle, this can be easily rectified by inserting a rubber washer between the escutcheon and door trim panel.
5. If the rattle is found to be emanating from the door lock it will in all probability mean that the lock is worn and therefore should be replaced with a new unit as described in Section 13.
6. Lastly, if it is worn hinge pins causing the rattle they should be renewed. This is not a D.I.Y. job as a special tool is required for their removal and replacement.

11. Door Striker Plate - Removal, Replacement & Adjustment

1. Striker plate removal and adjustment are not really D.I.Y. tasks as a special tool is required to turn the plate retaining screws. However, if the tool (Churchill No.RIBE M6 special screwdriver) can be hired or loaned from your local Ford dealers, proceed as follows.
2. If it is wished to renew a worn striker plate mark its position on the door pillar with a pencil. This will enable the new plate to be fitted in exactly the same position.
3. To remove the plate, simply undo the four special screws which hold the plate and anti-slip shim in position. Replacement is equally straightforward.
4. To adjust the striker plate slacken the retaining screws until the plate can just be moved, gently close the door, with the outside push button depressed, to the fully closed position. Release the button.
5. Move the door in and out until it is flush with the surrounding bodywork. Then fully depress the button and gently open the door.
6. Check that the striker plate is vertical and tighten down the four special screws. Adjustment is now completed.

12. Door Trim Panel - Removal & Replacement

1. Carefully prize the black plastic trim from its recess in the window winder handle. This will expose the handle retaining screws. Remove the screw, handle and escutcheon.
2. Prize the black plastic trim out of the recess in the escutcheon of the interior lock release handle. Unscrew the screw securing the escutcheon in position. Remove the escutcheon.
3 Unscrew and remove the black plastic knob on the interior door lock. Carefully prize the escutcheon beneath it out of the trim.
4. Remove the two screws securing the lower part of the armrest. Move the armrest towards the top front corner of the door. This will release the retaining lug. Remove the armrest complete.
5. Insert a thin strip of metal with all the sharp edges removed (a six inch steel rule is ideal) between the door and the recessed trim panel. This will release one or two of the panel retaining clips without damaging the trim. The panel can now be gently eased off by hand. Removal is now complete.
6. Replacement is generally a reversal of the removal procedure. NOTE: When replacing the panel ensure that each of the panel retaining clips is firmly located in its hole by sharply striking the panel in the approximate area of each clip with the palm of the hand. This will eliminate the possibility of the trim rattling.

13. Door Lock Assembly - Removal & Replacement

1. Remove the door trim panel as described in Section 12.
2. Temporarily replace the window winder handle and wind the window up. Remove the polythene sheet covering the interior of the door by cutting through the adhesive around its periphery with a sharp blade.
3. Disconnect the remote control rod by freeing it from the clip at the remote handle end.
4. Disconnect the push button rod, exterior operating rod and locking rod from the lock by releasing their clips.
5. Unscrew and remove the two screws securing the window channel.
6. Remove the three screws securing the lock to the door, the lock can now be withdrawn. Remove the four rod connecting clips from the lock. Removal is now complete.
7. Replacement: Replace the four rod connecting clips on the lock.
8. Reposition the lock assembly in the door recess and secure it with the three screws. Replace the two window channel retaining screws.
9. Reconnect all operating rods, and check the operation of the lock.
10 Replace the polythene sheet over the door apertures, a suitable adhesive is Bostik No.3, followed by the door trim panel and fitments.

14. Door Lock Interior Remote Control Handle - Removal & Replacement

1. Remove the door trim panel as described in Section 12, followed by the polythene sheet covering the door apertures.
2. Disconnect the spring clip securing the remote control operating rod to the lock mechanism.
3. Remove the three screws securing the remote control assembly to the door inner panel. Push out the anti-rattle clip around the remote control operating rod and remove the remote control assembly through the door access hole. (See Fig.12.4). Removal is now complete.
4. Replacement is a straightforward reversal of the removal procedure.

15. Door Glasses - Removal & Replacement

1. First remove the door trim panel and window regulator assembly as described in Sections 12 and 19 respectively.
2. The window glass can now be rotated through 90° and removed through the top of the door (see Fig.12.5).
3. Replacement is a straightforward reversal of the removal procedure.

16. Door Outer Belt Weatherstrip - Removal & Replacement

1. Wind the window down to its fullest extent. Carefully prize the weatherstrip out of the groove in the door outer bright metal finish moulding.
2. Replacement: Correctly position the weatherstrip over its groove. With the thumbs, carefully press the strip fully into the groove.
3. Wind the window up and check that the weatherstrip is correctly fitted.

17. Bonnet - Removal & Replacement

1. Open the bonnet lid and prop it in the open position with its stay.
2. Using a suitable sharp implement, scribe a line around the exterior of the hinges in the bonnet. (See Fig.12.6). Unscrew and remove the two nuts and washers on each side, followed by the bolt plates. With the help of an assistant the bonnet can now be lifted off, after releasing the stay.

Fig 12:4 Removing the remote control handle from the door frame

Fig 12:5 Removing the door window glass

Fig 12:6 Scribing around the bonnet hinge positions

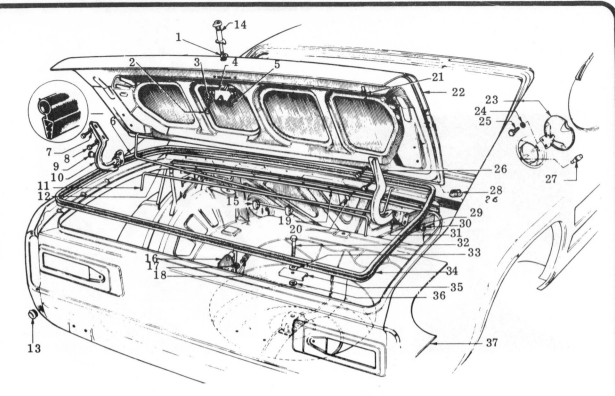

Fig 12:7 EXPLODED VIEW OF THE LUGGAGE COMPARTMENT FITTINGS

1 Washer	11 Bar	21 Rivet	31 Bolt
2 Bolt	12 Reinforcement	22 Door assembly	32 Bolt
3 Washer	13 Plug	23 Bumper	33 Washer
4 Lock	14 Lock assembly	24 Lockwasher	34 Weatherstrip
5 Washer	15 Clip	25 Screw	35 Clamp
6 Weatherstrip	16 Lock	26 Hinge	36 Washer
7 Washer	17 Washer	27 Bumper	37 Mat
8 Bolt and washer	18 Bolt	28 Plug	
9 Bush	19 Anti-rattle	29 Washer	
10 Hinge	20 Rivet	30 Nut	

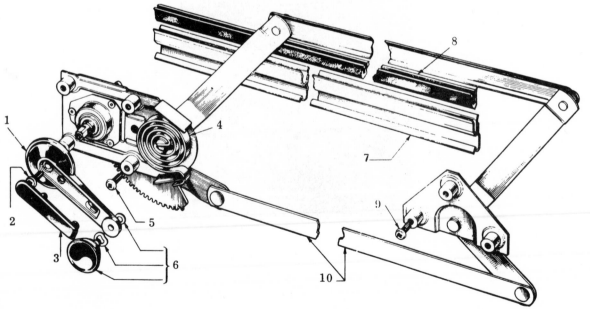

Fig 12:8 EXPLODED VIEW OF THE WINDOW CONTROLS

1 Escutcheon	4 Spring	7 Channel	10 Regulator assembly
2 Retaining screw	5 Screw	8 Sealing strip	
3 Insert	6 Handle assembly	9 Screw	

Fig 12:9 Removing the window regulator assembly from the aperture in the base of the door

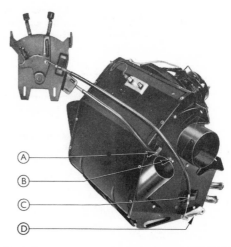

Fig 12:10 Figure shows heater control component positions

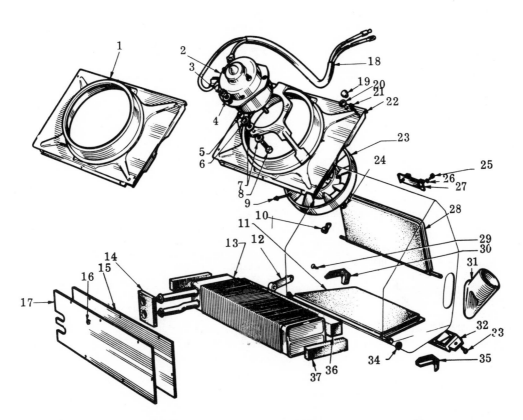

Fig 12:11 EXPLODED VIEW OF THE HEATER AND VENTILATOR UNITS

1 Mounting plate	11 Valve and seal assembly	20 Grommet
2 Motor	12 Lever	21 Rivet
3 Nut	13 Radiator	22 Heater motor mounting
4 Washer	14 Front seal	plate assembly
5 Sleeve	15 Front cover	23 Fan
6 Grommet	16 Screw	24 Ring
7 Washer	17 Front cover	25 Screw
8 Screw	18 Heater motor wiring	26 Washer
9 Rivet	assembly	27 Resistor
10 Lever	19 Plug	28 Valve assembly

29 Screw
30 Deflector
31 Windscreen defroster outlet
32 Deflector
33 Screw
34 Clip spire
35 Deflector
36 Rear seal
37 Side seal

3. Replacement is a reversal of the removal procedure. However, before finally tightening the nuts which secure the bonnet ensure that the hinges are correctly aligned with the scribed lines. This will ensure correct bonnet/body alignment.

18. Boot Lid - Removal & Replacement

1. Open the boot lid to its fullest extent. Using a suitable implement scribe a line around the exterior of the hinges.
2. Remove the two bolts and washers on each side securing the boot lid to its hinges. With assistance the boot lid can now be lifted off.
3. Replacement is a reversal of the removal procedure, however, before fully tightening the boot lid securing bolts ensure that the hinges are aligned with the scribed marks in the lid. This will ensure correct boot lid/body alignment.

19. Window Regulator - Removal & Replacement

1. Remove the door trim panel as described in Section 12. Carefully peel off the polythene sheet over the door apertures.
2. Temporarily replace the window regulator handle and wind the window down. Remove the seven screws securing the regulator assembly to the door.
3. Carefully draw the regulator assembly towards the rear of the door, this will disengage it from the rubber in the base of the window glass.
4. Push the window glass up and support it in the raised position with a wedge. The regulator assembly can now be withdrawn through the access hole in the door. (See Fig.12.9).

20. Heater Assembly - Removal & Replacement

1. Remove the earth terminal connection from the battery. Remove the radiator cap, open the cooling system drain taps and allow all of the coolant to drain. NOTE: If the coolant contains anti-freeze, drain it into a suitable container, this will allow the coolant to be re-used.
2. Next remove the seven cross-head screws securing the under-dash cowl panel, followed by the four parcel shelf securing trim clips, two each side. Remove the two screws on the passenger side, and one of the driver's side, and withdraw the parcel shelf.
3. Slacken the two wire clips and disconnect the two heater pipes from their unions on the bulkhead. This is done from inside the engine compartment.
4. Still in the engine compartment, remove the two screws holding the heater pipe plate and sealing gasket to the bulkhead. Detach the plate and gasket from the bulkhead.
5. Remove the ashtray and pull off the heater control knobs. Detach the heater control quadrant from the dashboard, by removing its two securing screws. Withdraw the control quadrant from beneath the dashboard.
6. Remove the temperature control and direction control outer cable clips from the quadrant plate and detach the two inner cables from the control levers.
7. Note the wiring positions and detach the wires from the heater blower motor.

8. Working under the fascia pull the air supply pipe from the face level vent. Remove the belt rail finishing strip by unscrewing the three securing screws. The face level vent assembly can then be removed after undoing its three securing screws.
9. If it is a G.T. model being worked on it will now be necessary to remove the centre console.
10 Finally remove the four retaining bolts and withdraw the heater assembly.
11 Replacement is generally a reversal of the removal procedure. Note: when the heater assembly is reinstalled it will probably be necessary to adjust the heater control cables as detailed in Section 23.

21. Heater Motor - Removal & Replacement

1. Remove the heater assembly as described in Section 20 and also the heater radiator as detailed in Section 22.
2. Withdraw the blower motor fan, after releasing its retaining spring clip: Note the wiring positions and disconnect the two wires from their terminals on the motor.
3. Lastly unscrew and remove the three screws securing the motor to the mounting plate and remove the motor.
4. Replacement is a reversal of the removal procedure.

22. Heater Radiator - Removal & Replacement

1. Remove the heater assembly from the car as described in Section 20.
2. Remove the two circlips securing the ends of the control flap pivots.
3. Unscrew and remove the sixteen screws holding the right-hand heater side panel in position. Remove the panel.
4. The radiator can now be carefully drawn out of the heater body.
5. Replacement is a reversal of the removal procedure. However, note that after the radiator has been replaced in the body, the foam packing should be positioned before replacing the side panel.

23. Heater Control Cables - Adjustment

1. Control cable adjustment should be carried out whenever the control cables have been disconnected from the heater, or if the heater cannot be 'shut off'. (Note: all bracketed letters refer to Fig.12.10).
2. Move the two heater control levers to the 'OFF' and 'HOT' positions.
3. Release the spring clip (C) securing the direction control cable, outer cable to the heater.
4. Position the heater distribution valve firmly in the 'OFF' position by raising the end of the lever (D) to the end of its travel.
5. Any slack in the direction control cable should now be taken up and the cable secured to the heater with a spring clip.
6. Release the temperature control cable, outer cable from its mounting on the heater, by releasing the spring clip (A).
7. Raise the mixing valve (B) lever to the end of its travel. This will ensure that it is firmly in the 'HOT' position.
8. Take up any slack in the temperature control cable and re-secure it to the heater body with a spring clip.
9. Finally check the heater controls for correct operation.